SCHAUM'S OUTLINE OF

CHINESE GRAMMAR

•

CLAUDIA ROSS, Ph.D.

Professor of Chinese
Department of Modern Languages and Literature
College of the Holy Cross, Worcester, Massachusetts

•

SCHAUM'S OUTLINE SERIES

McGRAW-HILL

New York   Chicago   San Francisco
Lisbon   London   Madrid   Mexico City   Milan
New Delhi   San Juan   Seoul   Singapore
Sydney   Toronto

The *McGraw·Hill* Companies

Claudia Ross is coordinator of the Chinese language program at the College of the Holy Cross in Worcester, MA, and has 20 years' experience teaching Chinese as a second language. She received her Ph.D. in linguistics from the University of Michigan.

Schaum's Outline of
CHINESE GRAMMAR

5 6 7 8 9 0 CUS/CUS 0 9 8 7 6

ISBN 0-07-137764-6

Acknowledgments

I wish to thank the following people for their assistance in the development of this book: Jing-heng Ma, Hsiu-ling Lin, Weina Zhao, Yu-tzu Zhang, Jocelyn Ross, Adam Ross, Grace Chen, and the reviewers and editors of the Schaum's series. All errors are, of course my own.

Contents

Conventions Used in This Book

Presentation of Examples

Examples are presented in traditional characters, simplified characters, and pinyin romanization.

> 這本書很有意思。
> 这本书很有意思。
> zhè běn shū hěn yǒu yìsi.
> *This book is very interesting.*

When no character in an example has a simplified form, a single line of characters is presented.

> 我弟弟很高。
> wǒ dìdi hěn gāo.
> *My younger brother is very tall.*

In pinyin examples, capitalization is used only for proper names.

> 我很喜歡吃中國飯。
> 我很喜欢吃中国饭。
> wǒ hěn xǐhuan chī Zhōngguó fàn.
> *I like to eat Chinese food very much.*

Ungrammatical Forms

Ungrammatical examples are occasionally presented to indicate improper usage. All ungrammatical forms are preceded by ⊗. Ungrammatical forms are always presented along with grammatical forms.

> 我的朋友　　　　　⊗朋友的我
> wǒ de péngyou　　　péngyou de wǒ
> *my friend*

Conventions used in tone marking
<u>neutral tone</u>

This book follows the conventions of Beijing Mandarin in the use of neutral tone:
- The classifier 個/个 ge is presented in neutral tone.
- The second syllable of most nouns occurs in neutral tone: (e.g. 妹妹 mèimei 朋友 péngyou)
- The infixes 不 bù and 得 dé in resultative verb compounds are presented as bu and de (e.g. 看得見 kàndejiàn *able to see*, 買不到 mǎibudào *unable to buy*).

tone sandhi

In spoken Mandarin, certain _tone sandhi_ (tone change) rules apply.
- Third tone change: Third tone is spoken as second tone when it occurs before another third tone (e.g. nǐ hǎo becomes ní hǎo, wǒ xǐhuan becomes wó xǐhuan).

In this book, third tone change is represented in the tone spelling only if the change occurs within a single word. It is not indicated if the change occurs across word boundaries. In this way, the two syllable words 可以 and 水果 are written in pinyin as kéyǐ and shuíguǒ (not as kěyǐ and shuǐguǒ) but the two word phrase 很好 is written in pinyin as hěn hǎo, not hén hǎo.

- Special tone changes:
不 bù becomes bú when it occurs before a fourth toned syllable (e.g. bù huì becomes bú huì, bù duì becomes bú duì.

In this book, fourth tone change is represented in the tone spelling within and across word boundaries.

- The numbers 一 yī one, 七 qī seven, and 八 bā eight sometimes change to second tone before a fourth toned syllable (e.g. 一个 yíge, yíkuài).

In this book these numbers are always represented in first tone.

Conventions for writing de
的 de
    - the marker of noun modification:

圖書館的書
图书馆的书
túshūguǎn de shū
the library's books.

地 de
    - the marker of pre-verbal modification of activity verbs:
偷偷地看
tōutou de kàn
secretly take a look

得 de
    - the marker of post-verbal modification of activity verbs:
跑得快
pǎo de kuài
run fast

- the potential infix in resultative verb compounds:

吃得完

chīdewán

able to finish eating

- the marker of extent modification of adjectival stative verbs:

他累得站不起來。

他累得站不起来。

tā lèi de zhànbuqǐlai.

He is so tired that he can't stand up.

Conventions for writing *zuò*

做 zuò as the verb meaning *to do* or *to assume the role of*:

做菜   做事

zuò cài   zuò shì

to cook   *to work*

作 zuò as a constituent in noun compounds:

作業

作业

zuòyè

homework

Numbers

COUNTING

Numbers 1-99

When numbers are used for counting, they occur without any additional words:

一	yī	*1*
二	èr	*2*
三	sān	*3*
四	sì	*4*
五	wǔ	*5*
六	liù	*6*
七	qī	*7*
八	bā	*8*
九	jiǔ	*9*
十	shí	*10*
○	líng	*0* OR 零 líng *0*

The numbers 11–99 are built upon 1-10 as follows:

十一	shíyī	*11*	三十	sānshí	*30*
十二	shí'èr	*12*	三十五	sānshíwǔ	*35*
十三	shísān	*13*	四十	sìshí	*40*
十四	shísì	*14*	四十五	sìshíwǔ	*45*
十五	shíwǔ	*15*	五十	wǔshí	*50*
十六	shíliù	*16*	五十五	wǔshíwǔ	*55*
十七	shíqī	*17*	六十	liùshí	*60*
十八	shíbā	*18*	六十五	liùshíwǔ	*65*
十九	shíjiǔ	*19*	七十	qīshí	*70*
二十	èrshí	20	七十五	qīshíwǔ	*75*
二十一	èrshíyī	21	八十	bāshí	*80*
二十二	èrshí'èr	22	八十五	bāshíwǔ	*85*
二十三	èrshísān	23	九十	jiǔshí	*90*
二十四	èrshísì	24	九十五	jiǔshíwǔ	*95*
二十五	èrshíwǔ	25	九十九	jiǔshíjiǔ	*99*

1

二 èr and 兩/两 liǎng

- When counting numbers without a following classifier, the number "2" is always

  二 èr :

  一 yī, 二 èr, 三 sān ...
  (For more on classifiers, see Chapter 2: Nouns, Noun Phrases, and Noun

  Modification.)

- When the number "2" is part of the number 12, 22, 32, 42, 52, 62, 72, 82, or 92, it

  is always 二 èr:

  十二 shí'èr、二十二 èrshí'èr、三十二 sānshí'èr ...

- In all other cases, when the number "2" occurs before a classifier, it is 兩/两

  liǎng. (See Chapter 2: Nouns, Noun Phrases, and Noun Modification.)

兩本書	兩個人
两本书	两个人
liǎng běn shū	liǎng ge rén
two books	*two people*

1. Complete the chart by converting the Chinese numbers to Arabic numerals and the Arabic numerals to Chinese numbers:

	Arabic Numeral	Chinese Number			Arabic Numeral	Chinese Number
1.	14	yi shi si 一十四		8.	22	二十二 èr shí èr
2.	23	二十三 èr shí sān		9.	92	九十二 jiu shi er
3.	28	二十八 ershi ba		10.	18	十八 shí bā
4.	56	五十六 wǔ shí liù		11.	77	七十七 qi shi qi
5.	39	san shi jiu 三十九		12.	88	八十八 bā shí bā
6.	74	七十四 qī shí sì		13.	26	二十六 ershi liu
7.	67	六十七 liu shi qi		14.	51	四十一 sì shí yī

Numbers 100-10,000

百	bǎi	*100*
千	qiān	*1,000*
萬/万	wàn	*10,000*

Numbers through 9,999 are constructed as they are in English:

	thousands	hundreds	tens	ones
667	六百	六百 liù bǎi	六十 liù shí	七 qī
2,894	兩千 liǎng qiān	八百 bā bǎi	九十 jiǔ shí	四 sì
9,999	九千 jiǔ qiān	九百 jiǔ bǎi	九十 jiǔ shí	九 jiǔ

In Mandarin, the numbers 10,000 and higher are counted in terms of the number of 萬/万 wàn *ten thousands*, followed by the number of thousands, the number of hundreds, the number of tens, and the number of ones. The number *24,000* is read 兩萬四千/两万四千 liǎng wàn sì qiān *two ten thousands (and) four thousands.* Numbers between 10,000 and 1,000,000 are illustrated here.

	1-900 ten-thousands	thousands	hundreds	tens	ones
89, 667	八萬/万 bā wàn	九千 jiǔ qiān	六百 liù bǎi	六十 liù shí	七 qī
273,561	二十七萬/万 èrshíqī wàn	三千 sān qiān	五百 wǔ bǎi	六十 liù shí	一 yī
892,894	八十九萬/万 bāshíjiǔ wàn	兩千 liǎng qiān	八百 bā bǎi	九十 jiǔ shí	四 sì
2,735,610	兩百七十三萬/万 liǎng bǎi qīshísān wàn	五千 wǔ qiān	六百 liù bǎi	一十 yī shí	
8,979,999	八百九十七萬/万 bā bǎi jiǔshíqī wàn	九千 jiǔ qiān	九百 jiǔ bǎi	九十 jiǔ shí	九 jiǔ

1 Million, 10 Million, 100 Million

1,000,000	百萬/万 bǎi wàn	*(one hundred ten-thousands)*	*one million*
10,000,000	千萬/万 qiān wàn	*(one thousand ten-thousands)*	*ten million*
100,000,000	億/亿 yì	**(or)** 萬萬/万万 wànwàn	*one hundred million*

Note: When the number "2" occurs before 百 bǎi *hundred*, 千 qiān *thousand*, or 萬/万 wàn *ten thousand* it may be either 二 èr or 兩/两 liǎng.

200: 二百 èr bǎi, 兩百/两百 liǎng bǎi

A note on reading ○/零 líng:

An empty hundreds place or tens place may be read as ○/零 líng. Compare the following two numbers:

3,053   三千零五十三
        sān qiān líng wǔshísān

70,182   七萬一百八十二
         七万一百八十二
         qī wàn yī bǎi bāshí èr

When reading a number with a series of zeroes, the word ○/零 líng is only included once:

2,001   兩千○一
       两千○一
       liǎng qiān líng yī

2. Complete the chart by converting the Chinese numbers to Arabic numerals and the Arabic numerals to Chinese numbers:

	Arabic Numeral	Chinese Number	
1.	6,700,000	六百七十万 ○ liubai qishi wan ling?	
2.	51,622	五萬一千六百二十二 五万一千六百二十二 wǔ wàn yī qiān liù bǎi èr shí èr	5 ten thousand 1 thousand 6 22

3.	9,202,002	
4.		三百八十四萬兩千一百 五十六 三百八十四万两千一百 五十六 sān bǎi bā shí sì wàn liǎng qiān yī bǎi wǔ shí liù
5.	74,000	
6.		四十九萬一百三十 四十九万一百三十 sì shí jiǔ wàn yī bǎi sān shí
7.	2,000,000	
8.		兩百五十五萬六千九百零二 两百五十五万六千九百零二 liǎng bǎi wǔ shí wǔ wàn liù qiān jiǔ bǎi líng èr
9.	438,059	
10.		九十九萬三千兩百五十一 九十九万三千两百五十一 jiǔ shí jiǔ wàn sān qiān liǎng bǎi wǔ shí yī

ESTIMATES AND APPROXIMATIONS

<u>差不多</u> chàbuduō *almost*

差不多 chàbuduō +*Number* + *classifier* indicates that a value is near but less than the specified number. 差不多 chàbuduō is always followed by a Number + Classifier. (See Chapter 2: Nouns, Noun Phrases, and Noun Modification, and Chapter 4: Adverbs.)

他差不多八十歲。
他差不多八十岁。
tā chàbuduō bāshí suì.
He is almost 80 years old.

今天特別熱。差不多四十度。
今天特别热。差不多四十度。
jīntiān tèbié rè. chàbuduō sìshí dù.
Today it is particularly hot. It is almost forty degrees.

左右 zuǒyòu *about/more or less*

Number + classiifier 左右 zuǒyòu indicates that a value is a little more or a little less than the specified number. 左右 zuǒyòu is always preceded by a Number + Classifier.

他八十歲左右。
他八十岁左右。
tā bāshí suì zuǒyòu.
He is about 80 years old.

今天四十度左右。
jīntiān sìshí dù zuǒyòu.
Today it is about forty degrees.

以上 yǐshàng *above,* 以下 yǐxià *below*

Number 以上 yǐshàng indicates that a value is equal to or greater than the specified number. *Number* 以下 yǐxià indicates that a value is equal to or less than the specified number. 以上 yǐshàng and 以下 yǐxià may directly follow a number alone, or a noun phrase that includes a number.

五十以上
wǔshí yǐshàng
fifty or more

五十以下
wǔshí yǐxià
fifty or less

三十塊錢以上
三十块钱以上
sānshí kuài qián yǐshàng
thirty dollars or more

三十快錢以下
三十快钱以下
sānshí kuài qián yǐxià
thirty dollars or less

多 duō

Number 多 duō indicates that a value is greater than the specified number. If the number is part of a noun phrase, 多 duō precedes the classifier.

五十多
wǔshí duō
more than fifty

三十多塊錢
三十多块钱
sānshí duō kuài qián
more than thirty dollars

3. Complete the chart to express the following expressions in Chinese and English.

1.	75 people more or less	
2.		一千以上 yī qiān yǐshàng
3.	almost 100 people	
4.		三百塊錢左右 三百块钱左右 sān bǎi kuài qián zuǒyòu
5.	75 or more people	
6.		差不多三百塊錢。 差不多三百块钱。 chàbuduō sān bǎi kuài qián.
7.	40 or fewer	

8.		一百多塊錢 一百多块钱 yī bǎi duō kuài qián
9.	more than 75	
10.		三百以下 sān bǎi yǐxià

ORDINALIZATION

Ordinalization refers to sequencing or ordering: *first, second, third*, etc.

1	一 yī	2	二 èr	3	三 sān	4	四 sì	5	五 wǔ
1st	第一 dì yī	2nd	第二 dì èr	3rd	第三 dì sān	4th	第四 dì sì	5th	第五 dì wǔ

4. Rewrite the Chinese ordinal numbers into English and the English ordinal numbers into Chinese:

1. 3rd

2. 8th

3. 10th

4. 2nd

5. 99th

6. 第五 dì wǔ

7. 第二十 dì èr shí

8. 第九 dì jiǔ

9. 第一 dì yī

10. 第四 dì sì

READING NUMBERS

In certain contexts, numbers are read as individual digits. These include numbers which are part of phone numbers, addresses, licenses, passports, and other documents used for identification. The reading of phone numbers is illustrated here. Decimal fractions described below in this chapter are also read as individual digits.

Note: In standard Mandarin as spoken in Beijing and other parts of China, the number '1' is pronounced yāo.

| 6810-2232 | liù bā yī líng   - èr èr sān èr |
| | liù bā yāo líng - èr èr sān èr |

| 3551-8867 | sān wǔ wǔ yī   - bā bā liù qī |
| | sān wǔ wǔ yāo - bā bā liù qī |

5. Read the following phone numbers. Provide your responses in pinyin.

1.   6839-1234

2.   5334-2387

3.   8833-1111

4.   119 (fire-emergency in China)

5.   114 (information in China)

6.   13521056666 (cell phone number)

FRACTIONS AND PERCENTAGES

Fractions and Percentages Expressed as 'Parts of the Whole'

Fractions and percentages are expressed as a 'parts of the whole' as follows:

A 分 之 **B**

A fēn zhī **B**

B *parts of* A *parts*

五 分 之 一

wǔ fēn zhī yī

one part of five -- one fifth

Notice that in Chinese, the 'whole' is always the first number in the expression.

If the 'whole' is expressed in terms of the number 100, then a <u>percentage</u> of the whole is expressed as '*parts of one hundred.*'

百分之四十 bǎi fēn zhī sì shí	*40 parts of 100 ... 40%*
百 分 之 十 bǎi fēn zhī shí	*10 parts of 100 ... 10%*
百分之五十 bǎi fēn zhī wǔshí	*50 parts of 100 ... 50%*

百分之九十九 bǎi fēn zhī jiǔshí jiǔ	*99 parts of 100 ... 99%*
百分之一 bǎi fēn zhī yī	*1 part of 100 ... 1%*

If the 'whole' is a expressed as a number smaller than 100, then a <u>fraction</u> of the whole is expressed as '*parts of the whole.*'

四分之一 sì fēn zhī yī	*1 part of 4 ... 1/4*
三分之二 sān fēn zhī èr	*2 parts of 3 ... 2/3*
八分之五 bā fēn zhī wǔ	*5 parts of 8 ... 5/8*
十分之一 shí fēn zhī yī	*1 part of 10 ... 1/10*

6. Complete the chart to express the following fractions and percentages in Chinese and in Arabic numerals.

1.	百分之六十 bǎi fēn zhī liùshí	
2.		*18%*
3.	百分之八十九 bǎi fēn zhī bāshí jiǔ	
4.		*66%*
5.	百分之三十二 bǎi fēn zhī sānshí èr	
6.		*35%*
7.	四分之三 sì fēn zhī sān	
8.		*11/12*
9.	十分之九 shí fēn zhī jiǔ	
10.		*4/7*

11.	二分之一 èr fēn zhī yī	
12.		*5/6*

Questioning Percentages and Fractions

The question words 多少 duōshao and 幾/几 jǐ are used to ask about the value of a percent or fraction. In the response, a number replaces the question word. (See Chapter 8: Questions and Question Words.)

<u>Percentages</u>

Q: 百分之多少 ？   A: 百分之七十
bǎi fēn zhī duōshao?   bǎi fēn zhī qīshí
what percent?   *70%*

Q: 百分之多少 ？   A: 百分之二十四
bǎi fēn zhī duōshao?   bǎi fēn zhī èrshí sì
what percent?   *24%*

<u>Fractions</u>

A 分之幾 ？
A 分之几 ？
A fēn zhī jǐ?

Q: 五分之幾 ？   A: 五分之二
  五分之几 ？   五分之二
  wǔ fēn zhī jǐ?   wǔ fēn zhī 二
  How many fifths?   *two-fifths (2/5)*

Q: 九分之幾 ？   A: 九分之五
  九分之几 ？   九分之五
  jiǔ fēn zhī jǐ?   jiǔ fēn zhī wǔ
  How many ninths?   *five-ninths (5/9)*

7. Answer the following questions in Chinese based on the number in parentheses.

1. 百分之多少 ？ *(91%)*
   bǎi fēn zhī duōshao?

2. 百分之多少 ？ *(26%)*
   bǎi fēn zhī duōshao?

3. 百分之多少？ *(49%)*
   bǎi fēn zhī duōshao?

4. 八分之幾？ *(7/8)*
   八分之几？
   bā fēn zhī jǐ?

5. 十一分之幾？ *(10/11)*
   十一分之几？
   shíyī fēn zhī jǐ

6. 五分之幾？ *(4/5)*
   五分之几？
   wǔ fēn zhī jǐ?

Decimal Fractions

Decimal fractions are expressed by 點/点 diǎn followed by the decimal number.

The decimal number is read as a series of individual digits.

Notes: If a number begins with a decimal point, the number may optionally be read as ○點 / ○点 líng diǎn. In decimal fractions, the number '2' is always read as 二 èr.

.5	(○) 點五
	(○) 点五
	(líng) diǎn wǔ
.75	(○) 點七五
	(○) 点七五
	(líng) diǎn qī wǔ
.758	(○) 點七五八
	(○) 点七五八
	(líng) diǎn qī wǔ bā
.7508	(○) 點七五○八
	(○) 点七五○八
	(líng) diǎn qī wǔ líng bā
1.8	一點八／一点八
	yī diǎn bā
34.69	三十四點六九
	三十四点六九
	sānshí sì diǎn liù jiǔ

8. Complete the chart to express these decimal fractions in Chinese and in Arabic numerals.

#	Arabic	Chinese
1.		○點○五/○点○五 líng diǎn líng wǔ
2.	2.3	
3.		一點一○○三/一点一○○三 yī diǎn yī líng líng sān
4.	.666	
5.		○點八六/○点八六 líng diǎn bā liù
6.	9.7	
7.		○點八○六/○点八○六 líng diǎn bā líng liù
8.	1.05	
9.		二十二點二二/二十二点二二 èrshí èr diǎn èr èr
10.	8.4	

Discounts: Percentage Off Total Price

Discounts are expressed as the percentage of the original price at which goods are offered as follows:

Number + 折 zhé

Note: Typically, Arabic numerals rather than Chinese numbers are used with 折 zhé to express discounted price.

九折 (9 折) jiǔ zhé		10 % off
八折 (8 折) bā zhé		20% off
二點五折 (2.5 折) èr diǎn wǔ zhé		75% off
五折 (5 折) wǔ zhé		50% off

三到四折　　(3-4 折) sān dào sì zhé *or* 三折到四折 (3-4 折) sān zhé dào sì zhé	60-70% off
二折　　　(2 折) èr zhé	80% off

The verb used to express discounts is 打 dǎ. The following examples express the percentage and the discounted selling price of an item whose original price was $100.

Note: The question word 幾/几 jǐ is used to ask the percentage of the discount.

Original Price	Percentage of Discount? 打幾折/打几折？ dǎ jǐ zhé?	Discount	Discounted Selling Price
$100	打九折 dǎ jiǔ zhé	10%	$90
$100	打八折 dǎ bā zhé	20%	$80
$100	打二點五折 dǎ èr diǎn wǔ zhé	75%	$25
$100	打五折 dǎ wǔ zhé	50%	$50
$100	打二折 dǎ èr zhé	80%	$20

9. Express these discounts in Chinese using 折 zhé.

1.		40% off
2.		25% off
3.		60% off
4.		65 % off
5.		90% off

10. Compute the discounted price for each of the following items.

	Original Price	Discount	Discounted Selling Price
1.	shoes: $100	8 折	
2.	sweater: $60	9 折	
3.	jacket: $150	4 折	
4.	gloves: $20	2.5 折	
5.	socks: $ 8	5 折	

CHAPTER 2

Nouns, Noun Phrases, and Noun Modification

NOUNS

Mandarin has three kinds of nouns: common nouns, pronouns, and proper nouns.

Common Nouns
Common nouns may be concrete or abstract

書/书 shū *book*, 車/车 chē *car*, 意思 yìsi *meaning*, etc.

Pronouns

Singular
我 wǒ *1st person (I/me)*
你 nǐ *2nd person (you)*
您 nín *2nd person polite form (you)*
他/她/它 tā *3rd person (he, she, it/him, her, it)*
自己 zìjǐ *reflexive pronoun (self)*

Plural
我們/我们 wǒmen *1st person (we, us)*
咱們/咱们 zánmen *1st person inclusive (includes speaker and addressees)(we, us)*
你們/你们 nǐmen *2nd person (you)*
他們/他们，她們/她们，它們/它们 tāmen *3rd person (they, them)*

Proper Nouns
中國/中国 Zhōngguo *China*
美國/美国 Měiguo *America*
孫中山/孙中山 Sūn Zhōngshān *Sun Yatsen*

Features of Mandarin Nouns

- Number: Common nouns are typically neutral with respect to number and have no separate singular and plural forms. Common nouns referring to people may be suffixed with the plural suffix 們/们 men (孩子們/孩子们 háizimen *children*, 學生們/学生们 xuéshengmen *students*), though the use of the plural suffix is relatively uncommon.[*] Pronouns have distinct singular and plural forms.

---

[*] In this form, nouns cannot be further modified by a number + classifier phrase. In addition, they are definite in reference.

- Gender: Common nouns are neutral with respect to gender and Mandarin does not distinguish 'masculine,' 'feminine,' and 'neuter' nouns. Pronouns are neutral in their spoken form. As illustrated above, gender is distinguished in the third person in the contemporary *written* language: 他 tā *he, him* / 她 tā *she, her* / 它 tā *it.*

- Grammatical case: In Mandarin, there are no separate forms of nouns associated with their use as subject (nominative case), possessive (genitive case), object (accusative case), etc. There is no distinction among pronouns equivalent to English 'I/my/me,' etc.

Special Uses of Pronouns

咱們/咱们 zánmen and 我們/我们 wǒmen

Mandarin spoken in and around Beijing makes a distinction between *inclusive we* and *exclusive we*.

Inclusive we includes the speaker and the addressee and is expressed with the word 咱們/咱们 zánmen:

咱們走吧！
咱们走吧！
zánmen zǒu ba!
Let's go!

咱們都是中國人。
咱们都是中国人。
zánmen dōu shì Zhōngguo rén.
We are all Chinese.

Exclusive we includes the speaker and not necessarily the addressee and is expressed with the word 我們/我们 wǒmen:

我們想跟你談談。
我们想跟你谈谈。
wǒmen xiǎng gēn nǐ tántán.
We want to speak with you.

我們都喜歡學中文。
我们都喜欢学中文。
wǒmen dōu xǐhuan xué Zhōngwén.
We all like to study Chinese.

Even in Beijing, 我們/我们 wǒmen may be used for both senses of *we*.

自己 zìjǐ *self*

Mandarin has a single reflexive pronoun, 自己 zìjǐ *self*, which is unmarked for person or gender. 自己 zìjǐ has the following uses.

It occurs as an object to mark identity of reference with the subject:

你在外國一定得照顧自己。
你在外国一定得照顾自己。
nǐ zài wàiguó yīdìng děi zhàogù zìjǐ.
When you are in a foreign country you must take care of yourself.

我不喜歡自己。
我不喜欢自己。
wǒ bù xǐhuan zìjǐ.
I don't like myself.

It can follow a personal pronoun for emphasis, especially for contrastive emphasis. (See section on modification of pronouns below for additional examples using 自己 zìjǐ.)

我希望他們結婚，可是我自己不想結婚。
我希望他们结婚，可是我自己不想结婚。
wǒ xīwàng tāmen jiéhūn, kěshì wǒ zìjǐ bù xiǎng jiéhūn.
I hope they will get married, but I myself don't plan to get married.

這是我自己的事。
这是我自己的事。
zhè shì wǒ zìjǐ de shì.
This is my affair.

1. Complete the following sentences according to the English translations by adding the appropriate pronoun or pronouns.

    1. ____ 是大學生。
       ____ 是大学生。
       ____ shì dàxuéshēng.
       They are college students.

    2. ____ 也是大學生。
       ____ 也是大学生。
       ____ yě shì dàxuéshēng.
       We are also college students.

3. ____ 認識 ____ 嗎？

____ 认识 ____ 吗？

____ rènshi ____ ma?

Do you know them?

4. ____ 念中文嗎？

____ 念中文吗？

____ niàn Zhōngwén ma?

Do you study Chinese?

5. ____ 妹妹、姐姐都念中文。____ 不念中文。

____ 妹妹、姐姐都念中文。____ 不念中文。

____ mèimei, jiějie dōu niàn Zhōngwén. ____ bú niàn Zhōngwén.

My younger sister and older sister both study Chinese. I myself don't study Chinese.

6. ____ 去唱卡拉 OK 吧！

____ qù chàng kǎlāOK ba!

Let's go sing karaoke!

7. ____ 是我校幾個最聰明的女生。

____ 是我校几个最聪明的女生。

____ shì wǒ xiào jǐ ge zuì cōngming de nǚshēng.

They are a few of the brightest women students in our school.

8. ____ 今天晚上有事，不能跟 ____ 吃飯。

____ 今天晚上有事，不能跟 ____ 吃饭。

____ jīntiān wǎnshang yǒu shì, bù néng gēn ____ chī fàn.

I'm busy tonight. I can't eat with you.

9. ____ 是哪位？ *(you polite)*

____ shì něi wèi?

Who are you?

10. ____ 還只是孩子，必須有別人管____。

____ 还只是孩子，必须有别人管____。

____ hái zhǐ shì háizi, bìxū yǒu biéren guǎn ____.

You are still only a child. You have to have other people taking care of you.

NOUN PHRASES

A noun phrase (NP) is a noun and any modifiers of the noun. NPs serve as the topic of a sentence, the subject of a sentence, the direct or indirect object of a verb, or the object of a preposition.

Topic

這個學校，女孩子比男孩子多一點。

这个学校，女孩子比男孩子多一点。

zhè ge xuéxiào, nǚ háizi bǐ nán háizi duō yīdiǎn.

(In) this school, there are somewhat more girls than boys.

Subject

那個大學很有名。

那个大学很有名。

nà ge dàxué hěn yǒu míng.

That college is very famous.

Direct Object of a verb

我昨天晚上看了一個電影。

我昨天晚上看了一个电影。

wǒ zuótiān wǎnshang kàn le yī ge diànyǐng.

I saw a movie last night.

Indirect object of a verb

我不想給你找麻煩。

我不想给你找麻烦。

wǒ bù xiǎng gěi nǐ zhǎo máfan.

I don't want to give you trouble.

Object of a preposition

我每個週末都跟朋友一起玩。

我每个周末都跟朋友一起玩。

wǒ měi ge zhōumò dōu gēn péngyou yīqǐ wán.

I have fun with my friends every weekend.

Note: Verb phrases (VPs) may also be used like NPs. In this case, the VPs are considered 'nominalized.'

吃飯跟睡覺是人類最基本的需求。

吃饭跟睡觉是人类最基本的需求。

<u>chī fàn</u> gēn <u>shuì jiào</u> shì rénlèi zuì jī běn de xūqiú.

<u>Eating</u> and <u>sleeping</u> are human beings' basic needs.

Identity of Reference

There are two ways to indicate identity of reference between NPs in Mandarin: omission and pronominalization.

Omission

When NPs with identical reference occur in the same grammatical role (subject or object) in a series of sentences, all instances of the NP after the first one are often omitted.[*]

NPs with identical reference are both subjects:

我弟弟是大學生，明年就畢業了。
我弟弟是大学生，明年就毕业了。
wǒ dìdi shì dàxuéshēng, míngnián jiù bìyè le.
My younger brother is a college student. Next year he graduates.

Q:那本書怎麼樣？   A: 很有意思。
那本书怎么样？
nà běn shū zěnmeyàng?   hěn yǒu yìsi.
How is that book?   *(It is) very interesting.*

NPs with identical reference are both objects:

Q: 你認識王明嗎？   A: 認識。
你认识王明吗？   认识。
nǐ rènshi Wáng Míng ma?   rènshi.
Do you know Wang Ming?   *I know (him).*

When a NP refers to an inanimate object, a second reference in subject or object position is always omitted.

Q: 你吃過日本菜嗎？   A: 沒吃過。
你吃过日本菜吗？   没吃过。
nǐ chīguo Rìběn cài ma?   méi chīguo.
Have you eaten Japanese food before?   *I've never eaten (it) before.*

Pronominalization

When NPs with identical reference occur in different grammatical roles in a series of sentences, the second occurrence is typically represented with a pronoun.

王明很和氣。我想你一定會喜歡他。
王明很和气。我想你一定会喜欢他。
Wáng Míng hěn héqi. wǒ xiǎng nǐ yīdìng huì xǐhuan tā.
Wang Ming is very friendly. I think you will certainly like him.

---

[*] Omission of an NP marks it as the topic of the passage.

2. Complete the sentences with a pronoun or omission. For some sentences, either choice is possible.

1. 這個東西叫煎餅。你吃過了 ____ 沒有？(它/φ)

    这个东西叫煎饼。你吃过了 ____ 没有？(它/φ)

    zhè ge dōngxi jiào jiānbing. nǐ chīguo le ___ méi yǒu?(tā/φ)

    This is called a fried pancake. Have you eaten one before?

2. 他人很好。人人都尊敬 ___。(他/φ)

    他人很好。人人都尊敬 ___。(他/φ)

    tā rén hěn hǎo. rénrén dōu zūnjìng ___. (tā/φ)

    He is a really good person. Everyone respects him.

3. 中國高中生特別努力，___ 下課以後就回家學習。(他們/φ)

    中国高中生特别努力，___ 下课以后就回家学习。(他们/φ)

    Zhōngguó gāozhōngshēng tèbié nǔlì, ___ xià kè yǐhòu jiù huíjiā xuéxí. (tāmen/φ)

    Chinese high school students are especially hard working. After they get out of class they go home and study.

4. Q:請問，你是誰？ A: 我是你的表哥，你不認識 ___ 嗎？(我/φ)

       请问，你是谁？   我是你的表哥，你不认识 ___ 吗？(我/φ)

    Q: qǐngwèn, nǐ shì shéi? A: wǒ shì nǐde biǎogē nǐ bú rènshi ___ ma? (wǒ/φ)

    Q: *Excuse me. Who are you? A: I am your cousin. Don't you recognize me?*

5. 她還沒看過那個電影。她今天晚上要跟你去看___。(它/φ)

    她还没看过那个电影。她今天晚上要跟你去看___。(它/φ)

    tā hái méi kànguo nà ge diànyǐng. tā jīntiān wǎnshang yào gēn nǐ qù kàn ___. (tā/φ)

    She still hasn't seen that movie. She wants to see it with you tonight.

NOUN MODIFICATION

Noun modification is the description of a noun by another word or phrase. The noun which is being described is the 'head noun' and the description is the 'noun modifier.' *In the Mandarin noun phrase, the modifier always precedes the head noun.*

There are two types of noun modifiers in Mandarin, those that involve numbers and specifiers (這/这 zhè *this* or 那 nà *that*), and those that involve any other kind of phrase. Both types of noun modification structures are described below.

Modification Involving Numbers and Specifiers

Modification Involving Numbers: the Number+Classifier phrase

Common nouns may be described in terms of quantity: *one book, two books, several books,* etc. In Mandarin, numbers may not directly precede a noun. Numbers precede classifiers, and the number+classifier phrase precedes the noun.

一本書
一本书
yī běn shū
one book

三個人
三个人
sān ge rén
three people

Quantifiers, words which indicate an indefinite quantity, may also modify the noun. The following quantifiers must be followed by a classifier.

幾本書
几本书
jǐ běn shū
several books

每個人
每个人
měi ge rén
every person

The phrase 一些 yī xiē *several/a few* may also serve as a quantifier phrase.

一些書
一些书
yīxiē shū
several books

Some classifiers indicate a specific meaning (for example, the shape of a noun, or some information about the quantity of a noun) and are always used with a particular noun in a particular context.

一條河
一条河
yī tiáo hé
one (long thin) river

一塊肉
一块肉
yī kuài ròu
one lump of meat

一張紙
一张纸
yī zhāng zhǐ
one sheet of paper

Some classifiers provide information about the container of a noun, or its size or weight.

一斤苹果
yī jīn píngguǒ
*one pound of apples**

一杯茶
yī bēi chá
one cup of tea

When the noun does not have a specialized classifier, the classifier 個/个 ge is used.

這個問題不太大。我想我們一定可以解決。
这个问题不太大。我想我们一定可以解决。
zhè ge wèntí bú tài dà. wǒ xiǎng wǒmen yīdìng kéyǐ jiějué.
This problem isn't too big. I think we can certainly solve it.

我每個週末都回家。
我每个周末都回家。
wǒ měi ge zhōumò dōu huí jiā.
I go home every weekend.

---

* One 斤 jīn is .5 kilograms, slightly more than a pound.

3. Match each number + classifier with the appropriate noun.

1. 一條/一条 yī tiáo *long thin shape*   a. 車/车 chē *car*
2. 兩張/两张 liǎng zhāng *flat surface*   b. 人 rén *person*
3. 三張/三张 sān zhāng *flat surface*   c. 筆/笔 bǐ *pen*
4. 四輛/四辆 sì liàng *vehicle*   d. 桌子 zhuōzi *table*
5. 五個/五个 wǔ ge *general classifier*   e. 書/书 shū *book*
6. 六枝 liù zhī *long narrow things*   f. 飯/饭 fàn *rice*
7. 七把 qī bǎ *things which can be   g. 汽水 qìshuǐ *soda (pop)*
   grasped with the hand*   h. 紙/纸 zhǐ *paper*
8. 八本 bā běn *volume*   i. 河 hé *river*
9. 九瓶 jiǔ píng *bottle*   j. 椅子 yǐzi *chair*
10. 十碗 shí wǎn *bowl*

4. Rewrite these noun phrases in Mandarin.

1. 12 pencils   6. 7 rivers
2. 5 cups of tea   7. 8 books
3. 22 people   8. 2 chairs
4. 3 bowls of rice   9. 4 sheets of paper
5. 2 cars   10. 5 bottles of soda

Omission of the Head Noun

When the identity of the noun is clear from the context, the number + classifier

phrase can occur without a following noun.

Q:你要買幾枝筆?   A: 兩枝。
　你要买几枝笔?   兩枝。
　nǐ yào mǎi jǐ zhī bǐ?   liǎng zhī
　How many pens do you want to buy?   *Two.*

Classifiers Which Always Occur without a Head Noun

Some classifiers have nominal meaning and do not have an associated noun.

These include the following words:

年　nián　　*year*
天　tiān　　*day*
位　wèi　　*person (polite classifier for people)*

我在日本住了一年。
wǒ zài Rìběn zhù le yī nián.
I lived in Japan for a year.

她一天没吃飯。

她一天没吃饭。

tā yī tiān méi chī fàn.
She didn't eat for a whole day.

哪位是誰？

哪位是谁？

nǎ wèi shì shéi?
Who is that person?

Using the Word 半 bàn *half* with Classifiers

- 半 bàn is used in the expression 'a number and a half.' It follows the classifier:

  一個半月/一个半月 yī ge bàn yuè *1 ½ months*, 五年半 wǔ nián bàn *5 ½*

  years

- When indicating half of a noun, 半 bàn precedes the classifier:

  半個月/半个月 bàn ge yuè *half a month*, 半年 bàn nián *half a year*

5. Rewrite these number phrases in Mandarin, being careful to put the word 半 bàn in the

right place.

1. 2 1/2 days	6. 9 1/2 years
2. 4 1/2 hours	7. 12 1/2 minutes
3. 1/2 bowl of rice	8. 1/2 a book
4. 1 1/2 pounds of rice	9. 5 1/2 bottles of soda
5. 3 1/2 months	10. 1/2 a year

Specifiers

The most common specifiers are 那 nà (alternatively pronounced nèi) *that/those*

and 這/这 zhè (alternatively pronounced zhèi) *this/these.*

Like numbers, specifiers cannot immediately precede a noun. They are followed

by a number + classifier phrase, or by a classifier.

這三本書

这三本书

zhè sān běn shū
these three books

這本書
这本书
zhè běn shū
this book

那三本書
那三本书
nà sān běn shū
those three books

那本書
那本书
nà běn shū
that book

Specifiers may also be used to refer to a physical, concrete object. In this usage, they can occur without a following classifier.

那是什麼？
那是什么？
nà shì shénme?
What's that?

那是毛筆。
那是毛笔。
nà shì máobǐ.
That's a Chinese writing brush.

Specifiers with Literary Usage

本 běn and 某 mǒu may be used as specifiers in formal, literary contexts.

本 běn refers to a specific NP which is associated with the speaker. Its meaning incorporates 'our' and 'this.'

本校成立於一八四五年。
本校成立于一八四五年。
běn xiào chénglì yú yī bā sì wǔ nián.
This school of ours was established in 1845.

羊肉串兒是本店的特產。
羊肉串儿是本店的特产。
yángròu chuàr shì běn diàn de tèchǎn.
Lamb kebabs are the specialty of our store.

某 mǒu refers to an entity whose identity is not revealed by the speaker.

這些是某人的東西。

这些是某人的东西。

zhè xiē shì mǒurén de dōngxi.

These are somebody's things. (These things belong to someone.)

你說的張某是誰？是張明嗎？

你说的张某是谁？是张明吗？

nǐ shuō de Zhāng mǒu shì shéi? shì Zhāng Míng ma?

Who is this Zhang so-and-so that you are talking about? Is it Zhang Ming?

6. Rewrite these NPs in Mandarin:

   1. four pencils
   2. three friends
   3. 17 books
   4. that cup of tea
   5. these 10 years

7. Rewrite these NPs in English:

   1. 二十五張紙/二十五张纸 èrshíwǔ zhāng zhǐ
   2. 那六把椅子 nà liù bǎ yǐzi
   3. 十二個月/十二个月 shí'èr ge yuè
   4. 這五天/这五天 zhè wǔ tiān
   5. 那兩個人/那两个人 nà liǎng ge rén

Time and Money

Calendar Time

The Days of the Week

星期一 xīngqī yī	禮拜一/礼拜一 lǐbài yī	*Monday*
星期二 xīngqī èr	禮拜二/礼拜二 lǐbài èr	*Tuesday*
星期三 xīngqī sān	禮拜三/礼拜三 lǐbài sān	*Wednesday*
星期四 xīngqī sì	禮拜四/礼拜四 lǐbài sì	*Thursday*
星期五 xīngqī wǔ	禮拜五/礼拜五 lǐbài wǔ	*Friday*

星期六	禮拜六/礼拜六	*Saturday*
xīngqī liù	lǐbài liù	
星期天	禮拜天/礼拜天	*Sunday*
xīngqī tiān	lǐbài tiān	
星期日	禮拜日/礼拜日	
xīngqī rì	lǐbài rì	

Years

Years are presented as a series of single digits followed by 年 nián *year*.

1997: 一九九七年 yī jiǔ jiǔ qī nián

1492: 一四九二年 yī sì jiǔ èr nián

1911: 一九一一年 yī jiǔ yī yī nián

The Months of the Year

一月	yīyuè	*January*	七月	qīyuè	*July*
二月	èryuè	*February*	八月	bāyuè	*August*
三月	sānyuè	*March*	九月	jiǔyuè	*September*
四月	sìyuè	*April*	十月	shíyuè	*October*
五月	wǔyuè	*May*	十一月	shíyīyuè	*November*
六月	liùyuè	*June*	十二月	shí'èryuè	*December*

Note: The *names* of the months of the year do not include a classifier. However, when months are counted, a classifier occurs: 一個月/一个月 yī ge yuè *one month*, 兩個月 / 两个月 liǎng ge yuè *two months*, etc.

Dates of the Month

Dates of the month are indicated with a number plus the classifier 號/号 hào (spoken/informal form) or 日 rì (literary/formal form): 三號/三号 sān hào or 三日 sān rì *the third (day of the month)*.

Reciting Dates

Dates are always presented from the <u>largest to the smallest unit</u>:

	Year	Month	Date of the month
August 22, 2001	二零零一年 èr líng líng yī nián	八月 bāyuè	二十二號/号(日) èrshí èr hào (rì)
May 3, 1995	一九九五年 yī jiǔ jiǔ wǔ nián	五月 wǔyuè	三號/号(日) sān hào (rì)
December 31		十二月 shí'èr yuè	三十一號/号(日) sānshí yī hào (rì)

8. Write the Chinese dates in English and the English dates in Chinese.

1. January 1, 1980

2. 一九六九年七月二十日
    yī jiǔ liù jiǔ nián qī yuè èr shí rì

3. July 4, 1776

4. 一九九九年十二月三十一日
    yī jiǔ jiǔ jiǔ nián shí'èr yuè sānshíyī rì

5. October 5, 2002

6. 二零零三年十一月二十五號
    二零零三年十一月二十五号
    èr líng líng sān nián shíyī yuè èrshíwǔ hào

7. February 14, 1997

8. 一九四五年五月八號
    一九四五年五月八号
    yī jiǔ sì wǔ nián wǔyuè bāhào

9. August 16, 1970

10. 一八六三年十一月十九日
     yī bā liù sān nián shíyī yuè shí jiǔ rì

<u>Clock Time</u>

The units of time in Mandarin are 鐘頭/钟头 zhōngtóu or 小時/小时 xiǎoshí
hour, 分 fēn *minute, and* 秒 miǎo *second.*[*]

---

[*] Different regions of China have different preferences for 鐘頭/钟头 zhōngtóu and 小時/小时 xiǎoshí.
鐘頭/钟头 zhōngtóu is used in Beijing and northern China. 小時/小时 xiǎoshí is used in Taiwan.

三個鐘頭/三个钟头   三個小時/三个小时
sān ge zhōngtóu   sān ge xiǎoshí
3 hours   *3 hours*

十二分(鐘/钟)
shí èr fēn (zhōng)
12 minutes

二十秒
èrshí miǎo
20 seconds

When reciting time, time on the hour (o'clock time) is expressed using the expression 點/点 diǎn *dot*. Clock time phrases may end with the noun 鐘/钟 zhōng, *clock*, but the use of 鐘/钟 zhōng is not common in standard Mandarin as spoken in and around Beijing.

兩/两 點/点(鐘/钟)
liǎng diǎn (zhōng)
2 o'clock

六點/点 (鐘/钟)
liù diǎn (zhōng)
6 o'clock

十二點/点 (鐘/钟)
shí'èr diǎn (zhōng)
12 o'clock

Note: When reading or reciting time, *2 o'clock* is read as 兩點/两点 liǎng diǎn.

When time includes minutes, it can be recited as follows:

▪ **minutes past the hour** (with optional 過/过 guò):

( ) 點過 ( ) 分
( ) 点过 ( ) 分
( ) diǎn guò ( ) fēn

七點過十分
七点过十分
qī diǎn guò shí fēn
10 minutes past 7 (7:10)

兩點過二十分
两点过二十分
liǎng diǎn guò èrshí fēn
20 minutes past 2 (2:20)

過/过 guò can be omitted from the phrase, as can the classifier 分 fēn.

十點二十
十点二十
shí diǎn èrshí
10:20

六點十五
六点十五
liù diǎn shíwǔ
6:15

兩點四十五
两点四十五
liǎng diǎn sìshíwǔ
2:45

- 差 chà + **minutes to the hour**

差 chà + *minutes* can occur before the hour or after the hour. 差 chà and 分 fēn cannot be omitted from the expression.

差 chà + *minutes* **before the hour:**

差 ( ) 分 ( ) 點
差 ( ) 分 ( ) 点
chà ( ) fēn ( ) diǎn

差五分九點
差五分九点
chà wǔ fēn jiǔ diǎn
5 minutes to 9 (8:55)

差十分八點
差十分八点
chà shí fēn bā diǎn
10 minutes to 8 (7:50)

差 chà + *minutes* occurring after the hour:

( ) 點 差 ( ) 分
( ) 点 差 ( ) 分
( ) diǎn chà ( ) fēn

九點差五分
九点差五分
jiǔ diǎn chà wǔ fēn
5 minutes to 9 (8:55)

八點差十分
八点差十分
bā diǎn chà shí fēn
10 minutes to 8 (7:50)

Expressions used with clock time

半 bàn *half*

半個鐘頭/半个钟头	bàn ge zhōngtóu	*half an hour*
半個小時/半個小时	bàn ge xiǎoshí	

一個半鐘頭/一个半钟头	yī ge bàn zhōngtóu	*1 1/2 hours*
一個半小時/一个半小时	yī ge bàn xiǎoshí	
四點半/四点半	sì diǎn bàn	*half past 4 (4:30)*

刻 kè *the quarter hour*

一刻鐘/一刻钟	yī kè zhōng	*15 minutes*
三點/点一刻	sān diǎn yīkè	*a quarter past three (3:15)*
四點/点三刻	sì diǎn sān kè	*45 minutes after 4 (4:45)*
五點/点差一刻	wǔ diǎn chà yīkè	*a quarter to five (4:45)*

Note: There is no expression 二刻 èr kè. 30 minutes is expressed as 半 bàn or as 三十 分 sānshí fēn.

9. Complete the chart by converting the times to Arabic numerals or Mandarin. Use 過/过 guò or 差 chà in the Mandarin times where indicated.

1.	2:15 (過/过 guò)	
2.		十一點差五分 十一点差五分 shíyī diǎn chà wǔ fēn
3.	3:45 (差 chà)	
4.		五點過十七分 五点过十七分 wǔ diǎn guò shíqī fēn
5.	7:50 (差 chà)	
6.		十二點半 十二点半 shí'èr diǎn bàn
7.	8:20 (過/过 guò)	
8.		六點差兩分 六点差两分 liù diǎn chà liǎng fēn
9.	4:10	
10.		差一分九點 差一分九点 chà yī fēn jiǔ diǎn

Money

Money is indicated as a series of number + classifier phrases followed by the noun 錢/钱 qián *money*. The units of money in informal spoken Mandarin are 塊/块 kuài *dollar*, 毛 máo *dime (one-tenth of 塊/块 kuài)* and 分 fēn *penny*[*] *(one-tenth of a 毛 máo)*. In formal, written Mandarin the word for dollar is 元 yuán and the word for dime is 角 jiǎo.[†] When 元 yuán and 角 jiǎo are used, the noun 錢/钱 qián does not occur in the phrase. As illustrated below, 元 yuán and 角 jiǎo are generally when the monetary expression can be expressed exclusively in either 元 yuán or 角 jiǎo.

Monetary values of less than one dollar are expressed as follows.

	毛 máo	分 fēn
75 cents	七毛 qī máo	五分 wǔ fēn
12 cents	一毛 yī máo	二分 èr fēn
36 cents	三毛 sān máo	六分 liù fēn

	角 jiǎo
$ .30	三角 sān jiǎo

Monetary values of a dollar or more are expressed as follows:

	塊/块 kuài	毛 máo	分 fēn	錢/钱 qián
$17.35	十七塊/块 shí qī kuài	三毛 sān máo	五分 wǔ fēn	錢/钱 qián
$ 6.22	六塊/块 liù kuài	二毛 èr máo	二分 èr fēn	錢/钱 qián

---

[*] 分 fēn as a unit of money is rapidly disappearing in China.

[†] 元 yuán and 角 jiǎo are the words printed on Chinese currency.

	元 yuán
$17	十七元 shí qī yuán

The noun 錢/钱 qián is optional in a money phrase. If it is omitted, the classifier 毛 máo or 分 fēn *penny* may be omitted if it is the last classifier in the number phrase.

	塊/块 kuài	毛 máo	分 fēn
$17.35	十七塊/块 shí qī kuài	三毛 sān máo	五 wǔ
$23.81	二十三塊/块 èrshísān kuài	八毛 bā máo	一 yī
$48.90	四十八塊/块 sìshí bā kuài	九 jiǔ	
$ 6.20	六塊/块 liù kuài	二 èr	

10. Complete the chart so that all prices are presented in English and Chinese.

	Price in English	Price in Mandarin
1.	$ 18.25	
2.		四十九塊八毛四分錢 四十九块八毛四分钱 sìshíjiǔ kuài bā máo sì fēn qián
3.	$519.31	
4.		兩百三十五塊四 两百三十五块四 liǎng bǎi sānshí wǔ kuài sì
5.	$117.62	
6.		七百二十六元 qī bǎi èrshí liù yuán

Noun Modifiers That End with 的 de

Common nouns may be modified by pronouns, nouns, NPs, verbs, VPs, subject + verb sequences, and clauses.

- The modifier is typically followed by 的 de

- The modifying phrase (*modifier* + 的) always precedes the head noun regardless of the properties of the modifier.

When the modifier is a pronoun, noun, or an adjectival stative verb, the order of the modifier and the head in Mandarin is the same as in the English translation.

Modifier is

*Pronoun**	我 我 wǒ *1st person singular*	我的書 我的书 wǒ de shū *my book*
	你 nǐ *2nd person singular*	你的地址 nǐ de dìzhǐ *your address*
	自己 zìjǐ *reflexive pronoun*	自己的事 zìjǐ de shì *one's own affairs*
Noun	朋友 péngyou *friend*	朋友的書 朋友的书 péngyou de shū *friend's book*
NP	我的朋友 wǒ de péngyou *my friend*	我的朋友的書 我的朋友的书 wǒ de péngyou de shū *my friend's book*
Adjectival Stative Verb	好 hǎo *good*	好的書 好的书 hǎo de shū *a good book*

---

* There is no separate set of possessive pronouns in Mandarin.

Modifiers involving other kinds of verbs or a clause also precede the head noun. Notice, however, that their English equivalents follow the noun, typically in the form of a relative clause. There is no Mandarin equivalent for relative pronouns (*who*, *whom*, *which*) or the complementizer (*that*) which introduces the modifier in English relative clauses. (See Chapter 3: Verbs and Verb Phrases.)

Modifier is

Verb	吃 chī *eat*	吃的人 chī de rén *the people who are eating*
PP +Verb or Verb Phrase	跟我來 跟我来 gēn wǒ lái *come with me*	跟我來的那個人 跟我来的那个人 gēn wǒ lái de nà ge rén *the person who comes with me*
Verb + *Object*	賣花 卖花 mài huā *sell flowers*	賣花的那個人 卖花的那个人 mài huā de nà ge rén *the person who sells flowers*
Subject + *Verb*	我吃 wǒ chī *I eat*	我吃的東西 我吃的东西 wǒ chī de dōngxi *things that I eat*
clause[*]	工資高 gōngzī gāo *wages are high*	工資高的職業 工资高的职业 gōngzī gāo de zhíyè *an occupation in which wages are high*

In formal, written texts, when the modifier includes an activity verb, 所 suǒ can occur before the verb.

李老師所寫的書都很好。
李老师所写的书都很好。
Lǐ lǎoshī suǒ xiě de shū dōu hěn hǎo.
The books that teacher Li wrote are very good.

Pronouns and proper nouns are more restricted than common nouns in their choice of modifiers. Pronouns can be modified by a very limited number of stative verbs:

---

[*] When the modifier is a clause, the verb of the clause is typically a stative verb.

可憐的我/可怜的我
kělián de wǒ
poor me

美麗的她/美丽的她
měilì de tā
beautiful her

聰明的你/聪明的你
cōngming de nǐ
smart you/clever you

Proper nouns can also be modified by a limited number of stative verbs:

偉大的中國/伟大的中国
wěidà de Zhōngguó
great China

壯觀的大峽谷/壮观的大峡谷
zhuàngguān de Dà Xiágǔ
magnificent Grand Canyon

The reflexive pronoun 自己 zìjǐ can be modified by a personal pronoun. 的 de never occurs between a personal pronoun and 自己 zìjǐ. (See section on *Special Uses of Pronouns* above for additional examples using 自己 zìjǐ.)

别人要他來，可是他自己不願意來。
别人要他来，可是他自己不愿意来。
biéren yào tā lái, kěshì tā zìjǐ bú yuànyi lái.
Other people want him to come but he himself is not willing to come.

很多人有愛好，可是我自己沒有愛好。
很多人有爱好，可是我自己没有爱好。
hěn duō rén yǒu àihào, kěshì wǒ zìjǐ méi yǒu àihào.
Lots of people have a hobby, but I don't have a hobby.

The Order of Modifying Phrases

A noun may be modified by any number of modifying phrases. Each modifying phrase occurs in succession, and the last one is followed by the head noun itself:

那個高高瘦瘦的人
那个高高瘦瘦的人
nà ge gāo gāo shòu shòu de rén
that very tall, very thin person

Modifiers which involve specifiers and numbers generally occur at the beginning of the NP, though they may occur closer to the head noun to contrast one NP with another:

高高瘦瘦的那個人
高高瘦瘦的那个人
gāo gāo shòu shòu de nà ge rén
that very tall very thin person (in contrast to some other person)

Modifiers which describe inherent, permanent characteristics of a noun tend to occur closest to the head noun.

那個穿大衣的白頭髮的老人
那个穿大衣的白头发的老人
nà ge chuān dàyī de bái tóufa de lǎo rén
that old white haired man who is wearing an overcoat

11. Put the Mandarin phrases in the proper order to correspond to the English translations.

1. 書的我中文
   书的我中文
   shū de wǒ Zhōngwén
   my Chinese book

2. 中國書出的
   中国书出的
   Zhōngguó shū chū de
   a book published in China

3. 水果很甜的
   shuíguǒ hěn tián de
   very sweet fruit

4. 朋友男的你姐姐
   péngyou nán de nǐ jiějie
   your older sister's boyfriend

5. 事的我喜歡做
   事的我喜欢做
   shì de wǒ xǐhuan zuò
   things I like to do

6. 國家的多人口
   国家的多人口
   guójiā de duō rénkǒu
   a country with a large population

7. 車製造的在美國
   车制造的在美国
   chē zhìzào de zài Měiguó
   a car manufactured in America

8. 那個女孩子說話的跟你
   那个女孩子说话的跟你
   nà ge nǚ háizi shuō huà de gēn nǐ
   that girl who is speaking with you

9. 一個大學某城市的麻州
   一个大学某城市的麻州
   yī ge dàxué mǒu chéngshì de Mázhōu
   a college in a certain city in Massachusetts

10. 中文考試的很難
    中文考试的很难
    Zhōngwén kǎoshì de hěn nán
    a very difficult Chinese exam

12. Translate the following noun phrases into English.

1. 那部很有意思的電影
   那部很有意思的电影
   nà bù hěn yǒu yìsi de diànyǐng

2. 這副日本製造的很貴的耳環 (製造/制造 zhìzào *manufacture,*
   这副日本制造的很贵的耳环   耳環/耳环 ěrhuán *earrings*)
   zhè fù Rìběn zhìzào de hěn guì de ěrhuán

3. 我的兩個哥哥
   我的两个哥哥
   wǒ de liǎng ge gēge

4. 一些關於中國的書 (關於/关于 guānyú *regarding*)
   一些关于中国的书
   yīxiē guānyú Zhōngguó de shū

5. 這個很複雜的中國字 (複雜/复杂 fùzá *complicated*)
   这个很复杂的中国字
   zhè ge hěn fùzá de Zhōngguó zì

6. 很貴的手錶 (手錶/手表 shóubiǎo *wrist watch*)
   很贵的手表
   hěn guì de shóubiǎo

7. 我念的那本書
   我念的那本书
   wǒ niàn de nà běn shū

8. 昨天考試的學生
   昨天考试的学生
   zuótiān kǎoshì de xuésheng

9. 紅顏色的筆
   红颜色的笔
   hóng yánsè de bǐ

10. 學中文的學生
    学中文的学生
    xué Zhōngwén de xuésheng

NP Modification without 的 de

Modifiers which are numerals or specifiers must end in a classifier. Modifiers which belong to other categories usually end in 的, but in some cases, 的 may be absent. Here are some common conditions in which 的 is absent.

- The modifier and the head noun form a compound word or a name for a thing:

白宮	Báigōng	*the White House*
西瓜	xīguā	*watermelon*
大門/大门	dàmén	*front door/main gate*
萬里長城/万里长城	Wànlǐ Chángchéng	*the Great Wall*

If 的 is inserted between the modifier and the head, the phrase is unacceptable
or the meaning of the phrase changes:

⊗白的宮	bái de gōng	*a white palace*
⊗西的瓜	xī de guā	*a western melon*
大的門/大的门	dà de mén	*a big door*
萬里的長城 万里的长城	wànlǐ de chángchéng	*a ten thousand mile wall*

- The modifier and the head noun describe a specific entity with consistent
  reference:

  美國總統/美国总统
  Měiguó zóngtǒng
  The American President

  我媽媽/我妈妈
  wǒ māma
  my mom

  Note: For this kind of phrase, 的 de may occur between the modifier and the head
  with no change in meaning.

- The modifier is a one-syllable stative verb commonly associated with the noun.
  Notice that the meaning may shift when 的 de is included.

好朋友	好的朋友
hǎo péngyou	hǎo de péngyou
good friend (refers to a specific friend)	*a good friend (a type of friend)*
白顏色 白颜色	白的顏色 白的颜色
bái yánsè	bái de yánsè
white	*whitish color*

When a stative verb is preceded by an intensifer, 的 de must occur between the

modifier and the noun:

很好的朋友	⊗很好朋友
hěn hǎo de péngyou	hěn hǎo péngyou
very good friend	

太舊的衣服   ⊗太舊衣服
太旧的衣服   太旧衣服
tài jiù de yīfu   tài jiù yīfu
clothing that is too old

Omission of the Head Noun in 的 de Modification Structures

The head noun may be omitted when its identity is clear from context. Typically, the identity of a noun is clear if it has been mentioned in the preceding discourse:

Q: 橘子怎麼樣?   A: 大的很甜。小的有一點酸。
橘子怎么样?   大的很甜。小的有一点酸。
júzi zěnme yàng?   dà de hěn tián. xiǎo de yǒu yīdiǎn suān.
How are the tangerines?   *The big ones are very sweet.*
                             The small ones are a little sour.

The head noun may also be omitted when the modifier + 的 refers to an entity with the properties of the modifier:

掃地的
扫地的
sǎodì de
something which sweeps the floor = a broom
or
one who sweeps the floor = a floor sweeper

算命的
suàn mìng de
one who figures out someone's life = a fortune teller

要飯的
要饭的
yàofàn de
one who begs for food = begger

送信的
sòng xìn de
one who delivers letters = letter carrier

送報的
送报的
sòng bào de
one who delivers newspapers = newspaper delivery person

教書的
教书的
jiào shū de
one who teaches = teacher

13. Name the entity referred to in each of the following phrases.

1. 做飯的/做饭的 zuò fàn de

2. 看病的 kàn bìng de

3. 開車的/开车的 kāi chē de

4. 有錢的/有钱的 yǒu qián de

5. 沒錢的/没钱的 méi qián de

6. 坐飛機的/坐飞机的 zuò fēijī de

7. 剃頭的/剃头的 tì tóu de

8. 賣東西的/卖东西的 mài dōngxi de

9. 做衣服的 zuò yīfu de

10. 念書的/念书的 niàn shū de

CHAPTER 3

Verbs and Verb Phrases

PROPERTIES OF MANDARIN VERBS

All Mandarin verbs have the following properties:

Full Predicate Status

Mandarin verbs can serve as the predicate in a complete sentence without an intervening helping verb such as the verb 'to be' in English.

> 我<u>喜歡</u>他。
> 我<u>喜欢</u>他。
> wǒ <u>xǐhuan</u> tā.
> *I <u>like</u> him.*

> 那個東西太<u>貴</u>。
> 那个东西太<u>贵</u>。
> nà ge dōngxi tài <u>guì</u>.
> *That thing is too <u>expensive</u>.*

Negation

Mandarin verbs can be directly preceded by negation. The words that are used for negation in Mandarin are 不 bù and 没 méi.

> 妹妹<u>不高</u>。
> mèimei bù <u>gāo</u>.
> *Younger sister is not <u>tall</u>.*

> 我昨天没<u>吃</u>晚飯。
> 我昨天没<u>吃</u>晚饭。
> wǒ zuótiān méi <u>chī</u> wǎnfàn.
> *Yesterday, I didn't <u>eat</u> dinner.*

Verb-NEG-Verb Questions

Mandarin verbs can be used as the repeated word in Verb-NEG-Verb questions (See Chapter 8: Questions and Question Words.) Note that Mandarin verbs are not always translated by verbs in English. This will be discussed in more detail below.

你<u>喜歡</u>不<u>喜歡</u>他？

你<u>喜欢</u>不<u>喜欢</u>他？

nǐ <u>xǐhuan</u> bù <u>xǐhuan</u> tā?
Do you <u>like</u> him?

電影票<u>貴</u>不<u>貴</u>？

电影票<u>贵</u>不<u>贵</u>？

diànyǐng piào <u>guì</u> bú <u>guì</u>?
Are movie tickets <u>expensive</u>?

你<u>會</u>不<u>會</u>说英文？

你<u>会</u>不<u>会</u>说英文？

nǐ <u>huì</u> bú <u>huì</u> shuō Yīngwén?
<u>*Can* you speak English?</u>

他<u>是</u>不<u>是</u>日本人？

tā <u>shì</u> bú <u>shì</u> Rìběn rén?
<u>*Is* he Japanese?</u>

你<u>該</u>不<u>該</u>給小費？

你<u>该</u>不<u>该</u>给小费？

nǐ <u>gāi</u> bù <u>gāi</u> gěi xiǎofèi?
<u>*Should* you give a tip?</u>

留學以前，<u>應該</u>不<u>應該</u>身體檢查？

留学以前，<u>应该</u>不<u>应该</u>身体检查？

liúxué yǐqián, <u>yīnggāi</u> bù <u>yīnggāi</u> shēntǐ jiǎnchá?
Before studying abroad, <u>should</u> you have a physical exam?

Inflection

Mandarin verbs are not inflected. A single verb form is used regardless of the tense, aspect, or modality of the sentence, and regardless of the number or gender of the subject.[*]

他/她/他們<u>吃</u>了水果。

他/她/他们<u>吃</u>了水果。

tā/tā/tāmen <u>chī</u> le shuíguǒ.
He/she/they <u>ate</u> fruit.

---

[*] In inflected languages, verbal inflection also serves to identify the inflected word as a verb and to prevent it from being used in any other category.

他想吃水果。

tā xiǎng chī shuíguǒ.

He wants to eat fruit.

水果讓孩子給吃完了。

水果让孩子给吃完了。

shuíguǒ ràng háizi gěi chīwán le.

The fruit was eaten up by the children.

Based on their meanings and grammatical properties, Mandarin verbs can be grouped into one of three types of verb categories: *Stative Verbs*, *Activity Verbs*, and *Achievement Verbs*. Each of these types of verbs has certain properties which are not shared by the other verb types. Activity verbs and achievement verbs have some properties in common because they both describe *actions*, that is, things that *happen* (e.g. eating, speaking, sitting down, selling, breaking, etc.) Stative verbs do not describe actions and do not share many properties with the other two verb types.

Grammatical Category Shifts

A very important feature of Mandarin is that a word may belong to more than one category depending on the way it is used in a sentence.[*] For example, the word 病 bìng may function as a verb or a noun.

他有病。

tā yǒu bìng.

He has an illness. (noun)

他病了。

tā bìng le.

He has become ill. (verb)

The word 給/给 gěi may function as either a preposition or a verb. (See Chapter 5: Prepositions and Prepositional Phrases.)

他昨天給他的女朋友買了花兒。

他昨天给他的女朋友买了花儿。

tā zuótiān gěi tā de nǚ péngyou mǎi le huār.

Yesterday he bought flowers for his girlfriend. (preposition)

---

[*] This is primarily due to the absence of inflection in Mandarin.

你在中國不必<u>給</u>小費。

你在中国不必<u>给</u>小费。

nǐ zài Zhōngguó búbì gěi xiǎofèi.

In China, you don't have to give tips. (verb)

Many verbs belong to more than one verb category. The meaning of a verb is slightly different depending upon the category in which it is used. For example, the verb 穿 chuān may behave in some contexts like a stative verb, and in others like an achievement verb. As a stative verb it refers to a state and means *to be wearing*. As an achievement verb it refers to an action and means *to put on*. One of the most challenging tasks in learning Chinese is to become familiar with the different ways in which a single word may be used.

Keep in mind that each verb category is identified by a group of properties. If a verb has one of the properties associated with a verb category, it will have all of the properties that characterize that category of verbs. A list of some common verbs which function in two or more categories is provided at the end of this chapter.

STATIVE VERBS

Stative verbs are words which describe states of being. Some stative verbs can be translated as adjectives in English. These are referred to here as *adjectival stative verbs*. Other stative verbs are translated as English verbs. These are referred to here as *non-adjectival stative verbs*. Examples of adjectival and non-adjectival stative verbs include the following.

<u>*adjectival stative verbs*</u>

好	hǎo	*good*
貴/贵	guì	*expensive*
快	kuài	*fast*
着急	zháojí	*anxious*
高興/高兴	gāoxìng	*happy*
舒服	shūfu	*comfortable*
緊張/紧张	jǐnzhāng	*nervous*
大	dà	*big*
白	bái	*white (and other color words)*
甜	tián	*sweet*
簡單/简单	jiǎndān	*simple*

non-adjectival stative verbs

喜歡/喜欢	xǐhuan	*like*
像	xiàng	*resemble*
願意/愿意	yuànyì	*willing*
怕	pà	*fear*
愛/爱	ài	*love*
尊敬	zūnjìng	*respect*
想念	xiǎngniàn	*miss, long for*
懂	dǒng	*understand*

In addition, the linking verbs 是 shì and 姓 xìng, the words which indicate ability and possibilty 會/会 huì, 能 néng, and 可以 kéyǐ, and the obligation words 應該/应该 yīnggāi, 該/该 gāi and 應當/应当 yīngdāng, are stative verbs. They will be discussed in more detail at the end of this section.

Many textbooks and grammars label adjectival stative verbs as 'adjectives.' While these words have the descriptive meaning associated with adjectives, they differ from adjectives in a language like English in one very important way:

> **Adjectival stative verbs are not preceded by a 'helping verb' such as the verb 'to be' in English.**[*]

Compare these correct and incorrect uses of adjectival stative verbs.

Correct	**Incorrect**
她很高。	☹她是(很)高。
tā hěn gāo.	tā shì (hěn) gāo.
She is tall.	
電影票貴。	☹電影票是(很)貴。
电影票贵。	电影票是(很)贵。
diànyǐng piào guì.	diànyǐng piào shì (hěn) guì.
Movie tickets are expensive.	

---

[*] The verb 是 shì may precede a stative verb, but only for contrastive emphasis. When 是 shì occurs before a stative verb, it functions to emphasize the predicate and to contrast it with some belief or expectation held by the speaker or listener.

> 她是很高！
> tā shì hěn gāo!
> *She is tall! (... and until I saw her I didn't believe you when you said she was.)*

Properties of All Stative Verbs

All stative verbs have the following properties:

Negation

The word which negates stative verbs is 不 bù. 没 méi (or 没有 méi yǒu) is not used to negate stative verbs, with one exception. The verb 有 yǒu may only be negated by 没 méi.

她不高。	☹她没高。
tā bù gāo.	tā méi gāo.
She is not tall.	
電影票不貴。	☹電影票没貴。
电影票不贵。	电影票没贵。
diànyǐng piào bú guì.	diànyǐng piào méi guì.
Movie tickets are not expensive.	
公共汽車不快。	☹公共汽車没快。
公共汽车不快。	公共汽车没快。
gōnggòng qìchē bú kuài.	gōnggòng qìchē méi kuài.
Buses are not fast.	
我不喜歡他。	☹我没喜歡他。
我不喜欢他。	我没喜欢他。
wǒ bù xǐhuan tā.	wǒ méi xǐhuan tā.
I don't like him.	
他不願意坐飛機。	☹他没願意坐飛機。
他不愿意坐飞机。	他没愿意坐飞机。
tā bú yuànyì zuò fēijī.	tā méi yuànyì zuò fēijī.
He is not willing to travel by plane.	
他不是大學生。	☹他没是大學生。
他不是大学生。	他没是大学生。
tā bú shì dàxuésheng.	tā méi shì dàxuésheng.
He is not a college student.	
他不會開車。	☹他没會開車。
他不会开车。	他没会开车。
tā bú huì kāi chē.	tā méi huì kāi chē.
He isn't able to drive a car.	

⊗他不有女朋友。   他没有女朋友。
tā bù yǒu nǚ péngyou.   tā méi yǒu nǚ péngyou.
                          He doesn't have a girlfriend.

Aspectual Suffixes

Stative verbs cannot be suffixed with the aspectual suffixes V-了 le or 過/过 guo. The reason for this is that they are not compatible with the meanings contributed by these suffixes. (For a detailed presentation of the meanings associated with these suffixes, see Chapter 6: The Suffixes 了 le, 着 zhe, and 過/过 guo.) As the last example below shows, a stative verb can be followed by 了 le, but only if it is the last word in the sentence. In this case, 了 le must be interpreted as sentence final 了 le in which it contributes the meaning of change of state or new situation. 了 le after a stative verb never contributes the meaning of completion or conclusion associated with V-了 le .

我喜歡他。	⊗我喜歡了他。	⊗我喜歡過他。
我喜欢他。	我喜欢了他。	我喜欢过他。
wǒ xǐhuan tā.	wǒ xǐhuanle tā.	wǒ xǐhuanguo tā.
I like him.		
他是大學生。	⊗他是了大學生。	⊗他是過大學生。
他是大学生。	他是了大学生。	他是过大学生。
tā shì dàxuésheng.	tā shìle dàxuésheng.	tā shìguo dàxuésheng.
He is a college student.		
他會開車。	⊗他會了開車。	⊗他會過開車。
他会开车。	他会了开车。	他会过开车。
tā huì kāi chē.	tā huìle kāi chē.	tā huìguo kāi chē.
He is able to drive a car.		
他很着急。	他很着急了。	⊗他着急過。
tā hěn zhāojí.	tā hěn zhāojíle.	tā zhāojíguo.
He is very anxious.	*He has become anxious.*	
	This sentence cannot have the meaning associated with the use of V-了 le. It cannot mean: *'He was very anxious.'*	

Some stative verbs can be suffixed with the durational aspect marker 着 zhe. 着 zhe emphasizes the general continuation of the state and not the specific length of the duration. Stative verbs which can be suffixed with 着 zhe may often also be used as achievement verbs. See the last section of this chapter for additional examples of this kind of verb.

桌子上放着很多東西。
桌子上放着很多东西。
zhuōzi shàng fàngzhe hěn duō dōngxi.
There are a lot of things sitting on the table.

她戴着很貴的耳環。
她戴着很贵的耳环。
tā dàizhe hěn guì de ěrhuán.
She's wearing very expensive earrings.

Duration and Frequency Complementation

Unlike activity verbs, stative verbs cannot be used with durational complements that quantify duration. For example, one cannot say in Chinese: *I liked him for a year*. Unlike activity verbs and achievement verbs, stative verbs cannot be used with frequency complements that indicate the number of times a situation occurs.

Modification by Intensifiers

Intensifiers are words which express the degree of a state. They are compatible with all words whose meanings can be qualified in terms of degree.[*] Almost all stative verbs can be modified by intensifiers. The small number of exceptions which cannot be modified by intensifiers include the the linking verbs 是 shì and 姓 xìng, the words of possibility and ability, 能 néng and 可以 kéyǐ, and the obligation words 應該/应该 yīnggāi, 該/该 gāi, and 應當/应当 yīngdāng. Note that the word 會/会 huì can be modified by intensifiers.

---

[*] Linguists sometimes refer to words which can be qualified in terms of degree as 'scalar predicates.'

Intensifiers

太	tài	*too*
最	zuì	*the most*
非常	fēicháng	*extremely (colloquial)*
極其/极其	jíqí	*extremely (formal)*
特別	tèbié	*especially*
尤其	yóuqí	*especially*
真	zhēn	*really*
很	hěn	*very*
挺	tǐng	*very, rather*
更	gèng	*even more*
比較/比较	bǐjiào	*relatively (colloquial)*
相當/相当	xiāngdāng	*rather (formal)*
(有)一點/(有)一点	(yǒu) yīdiǎn	*a little*

Intensifier + Stative Verb

太高	tài gāo	*very tall/too tall*
最高	zuì gāo	*the tallest*
非常高	fēicháng gāo	*extremely tall*
極其高/极其高	jíqí gāo	*extremely tall (literary)*
特別高	tèbié gāo	*especially tall*
尤其高	yóuqí gāo	*especially tall*
真高	zhēn gāo	*really tall*
很高	hěn gāo	*very tall*
挺高	tǐng gāo	*very tall*
更高	gèng gāo	*even taller*
比較高/比较高	bǐjiào gāo	*relatively tall*
相當高/相当高	xiāngdāng gāo	*rather tall*
(有)一點高/(有)一点高	yǒu yīdiǎn gāo	*a little tall*

A Note on Stative Verbs, Syllable Length, and Intensifiers

If the stative verb is one syllable in length, it must be preceded by a modifier. In negated sentences, the modifier is 不 bù. In affirmative sentences, the default modifier is the intensifier 很 hěn. Without 很 hěn, the sentence is grammatical but not natural sounding.

你的弟弟很高。   ？你的弟弟高。
nǐ de dìdi hěn gāo.   nǐ de dìdi gāo.
Your younger brother is (very) tall.   *Your younger brother is tall.*

你的弟弟不高。
nǐ de dìdi bù gāo.
Your younger brother is not tall.

Modification Involving Progressive Change

The following structures involving the word 越 yuè indicate a change in a situation over time.

- 越来越/越来越 SV   yuè lái yuè SV   *more and more SV*

- 越 V_1 越 SV   yuè V_1 yuè SV   *the more V_1 the more SV*

All stative verbs which can be modified by intensifiers may occur in these patterns in the position indicated. Only stative verbs are acceptable. Activity verbs and achievement verbs cannot be used in these structures.

越來越/越来越 SV   yuè lái yuè SV   *more and more SV*

弟弟越來越高。
弟弟越来越高。
dìdi yuè lái yuè gāo.
Younger brother is taller and taller. (more and more tall)

礦泉水越來越貴。
矿泉水越来越贵。
kuàngquán shuǐ yuè lái yuè guì.
Spring water is more and more expensive.

她越來越喜歡那個男的。
她越来越喜欢那个男的。
tā yuè lái yuè xǐhuan nà ge nán de.
She likes that guy more and more.

漢字，越寫越好看。
汉字，越写越好看。
Hàn zì, yuè xiě yuè hǎokàn.
Chinese characters, the more you write (them), the nicer looking they get.

越 V₁ 越 SV   yuè V₁ yuè SV   *the more* V₁ *the more SV*

In this pattern, the first verb (V₁) can be either a stative verb or an activity verb, but the second verb (labeled as SV) must be stative.

弟弟越跑越快。

dìdi yuè pǎo yuè kuài.

The more younger brother runs, the faster he gets.

越快越好。

yuè kuài yuè hǎo.

The faster the better.

中國飯，我越吃越喜歡。

中国饭，我越吃越喜欢。

Zhōngguó fàn, wǒ yuè chī yuè xǐhuan.

Chinese food, the more I eat it, the more I like it.

1. Describe 張明 Zhāng Míng in complete sentences using the following stative verbs.

張明 Zhāng Míng is: 張明 Zhāng Míng is not:

1. 高 gāo *tall*   6. 矮 ǎi *short*

2. 胖 pàng *fat*   7. 瘦 shòu *thin*

3. 聰明/聪明 cōngming *smart*   8. 笨 bèn *stupid*

4. 用功 yònggōng *hardworking*   9. 懶 lǎn *lazy*

5. 謙虛/谦虚 qiānxū *modest*   10. 可靠 kěkào *reliable*

2. The main verb in each of the following sentences is a stative verb. Rewrite each sentence in the negative form.

1. 她是學生。
   她是学生。
   tā shì xuésheng.
   She is a student.

2. 我喜歡做飯。
   我喜欢做饭。
   wǒ xǐhuan zuò fàn.
   I like to cook.

CHAP. 3]   VERBS AND VERB PHRASES   57

3. 公共汽車票很貴。

   公共汽车票很贵。

   gōnggòng qìchē piào hěn guì.
   Bus tickets are very expensive.

4. 我要買那本書。

   我要买那本书。

   wǒ yào mǎi nà běn shū.
   I want to buy that book.

5. 那個人很好看。

   那个人很好看。

   nà ge rén hěn hǎo kàn.
   That person is very good looking.

6. 我想跟你說話。

   我想跟你说话。

   wǒ xiǎng gēn nǐ shuō huà.
   I want to speak with you.

7. 這是一個很大的問題。

   这是一个很大的问题。

   zhè shì yī ge hěn dà de wèntí.
   This is a big problem.

8. 你在這兒可以抽煙。

   你在这儿可以抽烟。

   nǐ zài zhèr kéyǐ chōu yān.
   You can smoke here.

9. 我會說日語。

   我会说日语。

   wǒ huì shuō Rìyǔ.
   I can speak Japanese.

10. 那張畫兒很漂亮。

    那张画儿很漂亮。

    nà zhāng huàr hěn piàoliang.
    That picture is very pretty.

3. The main verb in each of the following sentences is 有 yǒu. Rewrite each sentence in the negative form.

    1. 他有一個弟弟。

      他有一个弟弟。

      tā yǒu yī ge dìdi.
      He has a younger brother.

    2. 桌子上有書。

      桌子上有书。

      zhuōzi shàng yǒu shū.
      There are books on the table.

    3. 他們有問題。

      他们有问题。

      tāmen yǒu wèntí.
      They have a problem/question.

    4. 屋子裏有人。

      屋子里有人。

      wūzi lǐ yǒu rén.
      There are people in the room.

    5. 他很有錢。

      他很有钱。

      tā hěn yǒu qián.
      He has a lot of money. (negative: He doesn't have money.)

4. Select the right intensifier from the list above to complete each sentence according to its English translation.

    1. 我有一隻狗。這隻狗 ___ 好。

      我有一只狗。这只狗 ___ 好。

      wǒ yǒu yīzhī gǒu. zhè zhī gǒu ___ hǎo.
      I have a dog. This dog is very good.

    2. 他 ___ 喜歡我。

      他 ___ 喜欢我。

      tā ___ xǐhuan wǒ.
      He likes me a lot.

    3. 我也 ___ 喜歡他。

      我也 ___ 喜欢他。

      wǒ yě ___ xǐhuan tā.
      I also like him extremely much.

4. 他 ＿＿ 喜歡在公園裏跑。

   他 ＿＿ 喜欢在公园里跑。

   tā ＿＿ xǐhuan zài gōngyuán lǐ pǎo.
   He likes best to run in the park.

5. 他跑得＿＿快。

   他跑得＿＿快。

   tā pǎode ＿＿ kuài.
   He runs extremely fast. (use a colloquial intensifier)

6. 他 ＿＿ 喜歡吃牛肉。

   他 ＿＿ 喜欢吃牛肉。

   tā ＿＿ xǐhuan chī niúròu.
   He especially likes to eat beef.

7. 我想他吃得 ＿＿ 多。他 ＿＿ 胖。

   我想他吃得 ＿＿ 多。他 ＿＿ 胖。

   wǒ xiǎng tā chīde ＿＿ duō. tā ＿＿ pàng.
   I think he eats too much. He is a little fat.

8. 说實在，養一隻狗＿＿麻煩。

   说实在，养一只狗＿＿麻烦。

   shuō shízài, yǎng yīzhī gǒu ＿＿ máfan.
   Truthfully speaking, raising a dog is relatively bothersome/time-consuming.

9. 並且，要花＿＿多錢。

   并且，要花 ＿＿多钱。

   bìngqiě, yào huā ＿＿ duō qián.
   Also, you have to spend a lot of money.

10. 可是＿＿有意思。

    kěshì ＿＿ yǒu yìsī.
    But it is really interesting.

5. Write Mandarin sentences using the 越來越/越来越 yuè lái yuè + Stative Verb
pattern with each of the following pairs of phrases.

   1. 他的朋友 ... 多

      tā de péngyou ... duō
      His friends ... more

   2. 他的問題 ... 少

      他的问题 ... 少

      wèntí... shǎo
      His problems ... fewer

3. 你的故事 ... 複雜

你的故事 ... 复杂

nǐ de gùshì ... fùzá

your story ... complex

4. 書 ... 貴

书 ... 贵

shū ... guì

books ... expensive

5. 汽車 ... 快

汽车 ... 快

qìchē ... kuài

cars ... fast

6. Use the pattern 越 V 越 SV yuè V yuè SV with each of the following pairs of phrases to write Mandarin sentences that match the English meanings.

1. *The more you do it the better it gets.*
   做 ... 好 zuò ... hǎo *do ... well/good*

2. *The more you read the faster you get.*
   念 ... 快 niàn ... kuài *read ... fast*

3. *The more you sleep the more tired you get.*
   睡 ... 累 shuì ... lèi *sleep ... tired*

4. *The more you eat the fatter you get.*
   吃 ... 胖 chī ... pàng *eat ... fat*

5. *The more you practice the more accurate you get.*
   練習/练习 ... 準/准 liànxí ... zhǔn *practice ... accurate*

7. Translate these sentences into English.

1. 他跑得越来越快。

   他跑得越来越快。

   tā pǎo dé yuè lái yuè kuài.

2. 我越来越累。(累 lèi *tired*)

   我越来越累。

   wǒ yuè lái yuè lèi.

3. 你越来越年輕！(年輕/年轻 niánqīng *young*)

   你越来越年轻！

   nǐ yuè lái yuè niánqīng!

4. 他的發音越來越標準。(發音/发音 fāyīn *pronunciation*,
   他的发音越来越标准。 標準/标准 biāozhǔn *accurate*)
   tā de fāyīn yuè lái yuè biāozhǔn.

5. 他長得越來越高。(長/长 高 zhǎng gāo *grow tall*)
   他长得越来越高。
   tā zhǎng dé yuè lái yuè gāo.

6. 中國綠茶越來越貴。(綠茶/绿茶 lǜ chá *green tea*),
   中国绿茶越来越贵。
   Zhōngguó lǜ chá yuè lái yuè guì.

7. 數學越來越難。(數學/数学 shùxué *math*,
   数学越来越难。   難/难 nán *difficult*)
   shùxué yuè lái yuè nán.

8. 這件事情越來越複雜。(事情 shìqing *situation*,
   这件事情越来越复杂。 複雜/复杂 fùzá *complicated*)
   zhè jiàn shìqing yuè lái yuè fùzá.

9. 她的朋友越來越多。
   她的朋友越来越多。
   tā de péngyou yuè lái yuè duō.

10. 這種音樂越來越流行。(音樂/音乐 yīnyuè *music*,
    这种音乐越来越流行。   流行 liúxíng *popular*)
    zhè zhǒng yīnyuè yuè lái yuè liúxíng.

Modification of Adjectival Stative Verbs

In addition to modification by preceding intensifiers, adjectival stative verbs can also be modified in the following ways.

Modification by Intensifier Suffixes

A small number of intensifiers are verb suffixes. They include 極了/极了 jíle *extremely*, 得不得了 de bùdéliǎo *extremely*, and 得很 de hěn *very*. These intensifier suffixes can only modify adjectival stative verbs.

Intensifier Suffix	Stative Verb +Intensifier	Example Sentence
極了/极了 jíle *extremely*	好極了/好极了 hǎojíle *extremely good*	美國大學學費貴極了。 美国大学学费贵极了。 Měiguó dàxué xuéfèi guìjíle. *The tuition at American universities is extremely expensive.*
得很 dehěn *very*	好得很 hǎodehěn *very good*	美國大學學費貴得很。 美国大学学费贵得很。 Měiguó dàxué xuéfèi guìdehěn. *The tuition at American universities is very expensive.*
得不得了 debùdéliǎo *extremely*	好得不得了 hǎodebùdéliǎo *extremely good*	美國大學學費貴得不得了。 美国大学学费贵得不得了。 Měiguó dàxué xuéfèi guìdebùdéliǎo. *The tuition at American universities is extremely expensive.*

Modification by Repetition

Some one-syllable adjectival stative verbs can serve as noun modifiers when they are repeated. The meaning of this structure is equivalent to *very+stative verb+noun*.

高高的那個人 高高的那个人 gāo gāo de nà ge rén *that very tall person*	很高的那個人 很高的那个人 hěn gāo de nà ge rén *that very tall person*
那個瘦瘦的孩子 那个瘦瘦的孩子 nà ge shòu shòu de háizi *that very thin child*	那個很瘦的孩子 那个很瘦的孩子 nà ge hěn shòu de háizi *that very thin child*

Modification by Extent Phrases: *So Adjectival Stative Verb that …*

Extent phrases introduce the consequence of an adjectival stative verb. They are formed as follows:

Adj. Stative Verb 得 de VP/Clause

那種車貴得沒有人買。
那种车贵得没有人买。
nà zhǒng chē guì de méi yǒu rén mǎi.
That kind of car is so expensive that no one buys it.

她<u>高興得</u>说不出話來。

她<u>高兴得</u>说不出话来。

tā <u>gāoxīng de</u> shuō bu chū huà lái.

She is <u>so happy that</u> she can't speak.

他<u>累得</u>站着睡覺。

他<u>累得</u>站着睡觉。

tā <u>lèi de</u> zhànzhe shuì jiào.

He is <u>so tired that</u> he is sleeping standing up.

8. Select the best extent phrase from the list below to complete each sentence and translate each sentence into English.

1. 今天熱得 _____ 。   (熱/热 rè *hot*)

   今天热得 _____ 。

   jīntiān rè de _____ .

2. 他窮得 _____ 。   (窮 qióng *poor*)

   tā qióng de _____ .

3. 我累得 _____ 。   (累 lèi *tired*)

   wǒ lèi de _____ .

4. 我忙得 _____ 。   (忙 máng *busy*)

   wǒ máng de _____ .

5. 法國酒貴得 _____ 。   (貴/贵 guì *expensive*)

   法国酒贵得 _____ 。

   Fǎguó jiǔ guì de _____ .

6. 他的脚大得 _____ 。   (脚 jiǎo *foot/feet*)

   tā de jiǎo dà de _____ .

7. 這次考試長得 _____ 。   (長/长 cháng *long*)

   这次考试长得 _____ 。

   zhè cì kǎoshì cháng de _____ .

8. 我嚇得 _____ 。   (嚇/吓 xià *frightened*)

   我吓得 _____ 。

   wǒ xià de _____ .

9. 他懶得 _____ 。   (懶/懒 lǎn *lazy*)

   他懒得 _____ 。

   tā lǎn de _____ .

10. 她好得 _____ 。

    tā hǎo de _____ .

Extent Phrases

a. 連大衣都沒有。

   连大衣都没有。

   lián dàyī dōu méi yǒu.

   he doesn't even have an overcoat.

b. 人人都喜歡她。

   人人都喜欢她。

   rén rén dōu xǐhuan tā.

   everyone likes her.

c. 穿不上鞋子。

   chuānbushàng xiézi.

   can't put on shoes.

d. 睡不着了。

   shuìbuzháo le.

   couldn't sleep.

e. 我們都寫不完。

   我们都写不完。

   wǒmen dōu xiěbuwán.

   we all couldn't finish.

f. 做不了功課。

   做不了功课。

   zuòbuliǎo gōngkè.

   unable to do school work

g. 誰也買不起。

   谁也买不起。

   shéi yě mǎibuqǐ.

   no one can afford to buy it.

h. 就哭起來了。

   就哭起来了。

   jiù kūqilai le.

   began to cry.

i. 連飯都不做。

連饭都不做。

lián fàn dōu bú zuò.

doesn't even cook.

j. 忘了吃飯。

忘了吃饭。

wàng le chī fàn.

forgot to eat.

Properties of 是 shì, 姓 xìng and 有 yǒu

是 shì *to be*   NP₁ 是 shì NP₂

The verb 是 shì joins two NPs and expresses a relationship of identity between the NPs.

我是學生。

我是学生。

wǒ shì xuésheng.

I am a student.

我的朋友是日本人。

wǒ de péngyou shì Rìběn rén.

My friend is Japanese.

今天是七月四號。

今天是七月四号。

jīntiān shì qīyuè sìhào.

Today is July 4th.

In affirmative sentences, when NP₂ refers to time, money, or age, 是 shì may be omitted.

今天(是)七月四號。

今天(是)七月四号。

jīntiān (shì) qīyuè sì hào.

Today is July 4th.

那本書(是)二十塊錢。

那本书(是)二十块钱。

nèi běn shū (shì)èrshí kuài qián.

That book is $20.

妹妹(是)幾歲？
妹妹(是)几岁？
mèimei (shì) jǐ suì?
How old is younger sister?

是 shì may never be omitted in negated sentences. The negation of 是 shì is

always 不是 bú shì.

今天不是七月四號。
今天不是七月四号。
jīntiān bú shì qīyuè sìhào.
Today is not July 4ᵗʰ.

那本書不是二十塊錢。
那本书不是二十块钱。
nèi běn shū bú shì èrshí kuài qián.
That book is not $20.

妹妹不是六歲。
妹妹不是六岁。
mèimei bú shì liù suì.
Younger sister is not 6 years old.

姓 xìng   to be surnamed

姓 xìng introduces a surname (family name).

The polite way to inquire about a surname is as follows:

Q: 您貴姓？   A: 我姓高。
　　您貴姓？   　　wǒ xìng Gāo.
　　nín guì xìng?   *My family name is Gao.*
　　What is your family name?

The neutral way to inquire about a surname is as follows:

Q: 你姓什麼？   A: 我姓高。
　　你姓什么？   　　wǒ xìng Gāo.
　　nǐ xìng shénme?   *My family name is Gao.*
　　What is your family name?

Notice that the reply is the same for both forms of the question.*

姓 xìng is always followed by the family name alone. When including a family name plus a given name or title, the word 是 shì is used.

她姓高。她是高老師。
她姓高。她是高老师。
tā xìng Gāo. tā shì Gāo lǎoshī.
Her family name is Gao. She is teacher Gao.

她姓王。他是王美玲。
tā xìng Wáng. tā shì Wáng Měilíng.
Her family name is Wang. She is Wang Meiling.

有 yǒu *to have, to exist*

有 yǒu has two distinct meanings:

- Possessive 有 yǒu *to have*

  我有一本中英字典。
  wǒ yǒu yī běn Zhōng-Yīng zìdiǎn.
  I have a Chinese-English dictionary.

- Existential 有 yǒu *to exist*

  桌子上有一本中英字典。
  zhuōzi shàng yǒu yī běn Zhōng-Yīng zìdiǎn.
  On the table there is a Chinese-English dictionary.

  Existential 有 yǒu does not take a subject.

  Existential 有 yǒu typically occurs in expressions referring to location. (See

Chapter 9: Location, Directional Movement, and Distance.)

9. Fill in the blanks with 是 shì, 姓 xìng, or 有 yǒu.

  1. 我的中文老師 ___ 黄。
     我的中文老师 ___ 黄。
     wǒ de Zhōngwén lǎoshī ___ Huáng.
     My Chinese teacher's family name is Huang.

---

* A rarely used, self-deprecating reply to the polite question is as follows. (敝 bì means *lowly/miserable*.)
敝姓高。
bìxìng Gāo.
My lowly surname is Gao.

2. 她的先生 ___ 陳。

她的先生 ___ 陈。

tā de xiānsheng ___ Chén.

Her husband's family name is Chen.

3. 他們 ___ 兩個孩子，一個兒子一個女兒。

他们 ___ 两个孩子，一个儿子一个女儿。

tāmen ___ liǎng ge háizi, yī ge érzi yī ge nǚ'ér.

They have two children, a son and a daughter.

4. 他們的兒子 ___ 大學生

他们的儿子 ___ 大学生。

tāmen de érzi ___ dàxuéshēng.

Their son is a college student.

5. 他 ___ 二十歲。

他 ___ 二十岁。

tā ___ èrshí suì.

He is 20 years old.

6. 那個大學 ___ 一萬多學生。

那个大学 ___ 一万多学生。

nà ge dàxué ___ yīwàn duō xuésheng.

That college has more than 10,000 students.

7. 黃老師的女兒不 ___ 學生了。

黄老师的女儿不 ___ 学生了。

Huáng lǎoshī de nǚ'ér bù ___ xuésheng le.

Teacher Huang's daughter is not a student anymore.

8. 她 ___ 工程師。

她 ___ 工程师。

tā ___ gōngchéngshī.

She is an engineer.

Properties of Stative Verbs of Ability, Possibility, and Permission

會/会 huì, 能 néng, and 可以 kéyǐ are equivalent in meaning to modal

auxiliary verbs in English. The meanings they convey are as follows.

會/会 huì   *future, probability, ability or skill: 'will,' 'can'*

能   néng   *physical ability, capability: 'can'*

可以 kéyǐ   *permission: 'may,' 'can'*

The English equivalents of these words are not inflected and are therefore not full verbs. As we have seen, in Mandarin, these words have the properties of full verbs. In Mandarin, they are typically followed directly by another verb, though they may occur without a following verb in response to a question or in other contexts in which the following verb is implied.

Q: 你會說英文嗎？   A: 會。
你会说英文吗？   会。
nǐ huì shuō Yīngwén ma?   huì.
Can you speak English?   *Yes.*

Q: 在這兒可以不可以抽煙？   A: 可以。
在这儿可以不可以抽烟？   kéyǐ
zài zhèr kéyǐ bù kéyǐ chōu yān?   *It's okay.*
Is it okay to smoke here?

When used in the V-NEG-V structure, 會/会 huì and 不會/不会 bú huì may be split up. 會/会 huì occurs as the first verb of the VP, before any prepositional phrase or location phrase. 不會/不会 bú huì occurs at the end of the VP, after the object. (See Chapter 8: Questions and Question Words.)

Q: 你會說英文不會？   A: 會。
你会说英文不会？   会。
nǐ huì shuō Yīngwén bú huì?   huì.
Can you speak English?   *Yes.*

10. Select 會/会 huì, 能 néng, or 可以 kéyǐ to complete each sentence. Some sentences may have two correct choices.

1. Q: 我的車壞了。你 ___ 不 ___ 幫我修？
我的车坏了。你 ___ 不 ___ 帮我修？
wǒ de chē huài le. nǐ ___ bu ___ bāng wǒ xiū?
My car is broken. Can you help me fix it?

2. A: 對不起。我不 ___ 。
对不起。我不 ___ 。
duìbuqǐ. wǒ bù ___.
Sorry. I can't.

3. Q: 你 ___ 不 ___ 寫這個字？

你 ___ 不 ___ 写这个字？

nǐ ___ bù ___ xiě zhè ge zì?
Can you write this character?

4. A: ___ 。

___ 。

___ .

I can.

5. 媽，我今天晚上 ___ 不___ 去看電影？

妈，我今天晚上 ___ 不___ 去看电影？

mā, wǒ jīntiān wǎnshang ___ bù ___ qù kàn diànyǐng?
Mom, can I go see a movie tonight?

6. 你 ___ 不 ___ 騎自行車？

你 ___ 不 ___ 骑自行车？

nǐ ___ bù ___ qí zìxíngchē?
Can you ride a bicycle?

7. 那個小孩子 ___ 說話了嗎？

那个小孩子 ___ 说话了吗？

nà ge xiǎo háizi ___ shuō huà le ma?
Can that child speak yet?

8. 高中生___ 不___ 開車？

高中生___ 不___ 开车？

gāozhōngshēng ___ bù ___ kāi chē?
Can high school students drive?

9. 你___ 不___ 把這張桌子搬進去？

你___ 不___ 把这张桌子搬进去？

nǐ ___ bu ___ bǎ zhè zhāng zhuōzi bān jìn qù?
Can you move this table in?

10. 你___ 不___ 跟我們一起去旅遊？

你___ 不___ 跟我们一起去旅游？

nǐ ___ bù ___ gēn wǒmen yīqǐ qù lǚyóu?
Can you go traveling with us?

11. Complete these sentences to match the English translations, adding the parenthesized expressions in the correct location.

   1. 你在圖書館借那本書。(能)

      你在图书馆借那本书。(能)

      nǐ zài túshūguǎn jiè nà běn shū. (néng)

      You can borrow that book at the library.

   2. 你當然借我的車。(可以)

      你当然借我的车。(可以)

      nǐ dāngrán jiè wǒ de chē. (kéyǐ)

      Of course you can borrow my car.

   3. 開車的時候用手機嗎？(可以)

      开车的时候用手机吗？(可以)

      kāi chē de shíhou yòng shǒujī ma? (kéyǐ)

      When you drive a car can you use a cell phone?

   4. 我跟你談話？(可以不可以)

      我跟你谈话？(可以不可以)

      wǒ gēn nǐ tánhuà? (kéyǐ bù kéyǐ)

      Can I speak with you?

   5. 美國人都開車嗎？(會)

      美国人都开车吗？(会)

      Měiguó rén dōu kāichē ma? (huì)

      Can all Americans drive?

   6. 我今天晚上跟你念書？(能不能)

      我今天晚上跟你念书？(能不能)

      wǒ jīntiān wǎnshang gēn nǐ niàn shū? (néng bu néng)

      Can I study with you tonight?

   7. 這個門，你開得開嗎？(能)

      这个门，你开得开吗？(能)

      zhè ge mén, nǐ kāidekāi ma? (néng)

      Can you open this door?

   8. 我只做早飯。(會)

      我只做早饭。(会)

      wǒ zhǐ zuò zǎofàn. (huì)

      I can only cook breakfast.

9. 貓都抓老鼠。(會)

   猫都抓老鼠。(会)

   māo dōu zhuā láoshǔ. (huì)

   All cats can catch mice.

10. 你說外語？(會不會)

    你说外语？(会不会)

    nǐ shuō wàiyǔ? (huì bú huì)

    Can you speak a foreign language?

Properties of Words of Obligation

應該/应该 yīnggāi, 該/该 gāi, and 應當/应当 yīngdāng are three of the words

used to express obligation in Mandarin. They are included in this chapter because they

have the properties of stative verbs, including the ability to occur in Verb-NEG-Verb

questions. The other words of obligation are adverbs. They are presented in more detail

in Chapter 4: Adverbs.

ACTIVITY VERBS

Activity verbs refer to actions that have duration. Examples include:

看	kàn	*to read/to look*
寫/写	xiě	*to write*
説/说	shuō	*to talk*
聽/听	tīng	*to listen*
買/买	mǎi	*to shop*
睡	shuì	*to sleep*
念	niàn	*to study*

Properties of Activity Verbs

Negation

Activity verbs may be negated with 不 bù or 沒 méi. 不 bù is used for non-past

or general time. 沒 méi is used to indicate that the action did not happen in the past.

(See Chapter 6: The Suffixes 了 le, 著 zhe, and 過/过 guo.)

我不吃早飯。

我不吃早饭。

wǒ bù chī zǎofàn.

I don't eat breakfast.

我今天早上没吃早飯。

我今天早上没吃早饭。

wǒ jīntiān zǎoshang méi chī zǎofàn.
Today I didn't eat breakfast.

Aspectual Suffixes

Activity verbs can be suffixed by the aspect markers 了 le, 着 zhe, and 過/过 guo. (See Chapter 6: The Suffixes 了 le, 着 zhe, and 過/过 guo.)

- Perfective aspect marker V-了 le.

  我已經吃了早飯。

  我已经吃了早饭。

  wǒ yǐjing chīle zǎofàn.
  I've already eaten breakfast.

- Durational suffix V-着 zhe.

  他正吃着饭呢。

  tā zhèng chīzhe fàn ne.
  He's eating.

- Experiential aspect marker 過/过 guo.

  我吃過中國飯。

  我吃过中国饭。

  wǒ chīguo Zhōngguó fàn.
  I have eaten Chinese food before.

Duration

Activity verbs describe actions which have duration. As noted above, they can be suffixed by the durational suffix V-着 zhe. The suffix highlights the ongoing activity.

爸爸喝着咖啡看報紙。

爸爸喝着咖啡看报纸。

bàba hēzhe kāfēi kàn bàozhǐ.
Dad drinks coffee while reading the newspaper.

Activity verbs can also be used with other expressions which indicate duration. These include the following:

- 正 zhèng + VP, 正在 zhèngzài + VP. These phrases immediately precede the verb and often occur with the durational suffix V-着 zhe.

他正在洗澡。一會兒給你回電話。

他正在洗澡。一会儿给你回电话。

tā zhèngzài xǐ zǎo. yīhuìr gěi nǐ huí diànhuà.
He's taking a shower right now. He'll call you back soon.
(He's right in the middle of a shower.)

- Durational complements. These expressions follow the verb. When the verb is not followed by an object, the durational complement immediately follows the verb:

Verb + Duration

他睡了一個鐘頭。

他睡了一个钟头。

tā shuì le yī ge zhōngtou.
He slept for an hour.

When the verb is followed by an object and a durational complement, the sentence may take either of the following forms:

Verb + Duration 的 de Object *or*	**Verb + Object Verb + Duration**
他睡了一個鐘頭的覺。	他睡覺睡了一個鐘頭。
他睡了一个钟头的觉。	他睡觉睡了一个钟头。
tā shuì le yī ge zhōngtou de jiào.	tā shuì jiào shuì le yī ge zhōngtou.
He slept for an hour.	*He slept for an hour.*

Frequency

Activity verbs may be suffixed with frequency complements.

When the verb is not followed by an object, the frequency complement simply follows the verb:

Verb + Frequency

那部電影，我已經看了兩次。

那部电影，我已经看了两次。

nà bù diànyǐng, wǒ yǐjing kàn le liǎng cì.
That movie, I've already seen it two times.

When the verb is followed by an object and a frequency complement, the structure is as follows:

Verb + Object   Verb + Frequency

我今天吃餃子已經吃了兩次。

我今天吃饺子已经吃了两次。

wǒ jīntiān chī jiǎozi yǐjing chīle liǎng cì.

Today I've already eaten dumplings twice.

Obligatory Objects

Almost all activity verbs are transitive, taking a direct object NP. Many activity verbs have a default object which automatically occurs with the verb unless the verb has a specific object. These default objects are typically absent in the English translations, but their presence in Mandarin is required. Activity verbs with default objects include the following:

Activity Verb			Activity Verb + Default Object		English Translation
看	kàn	read	看書/看书	kàn shū	read
寫/写	xiě	write	寫字/写字	xiě zì	write
說/说	shuō	talk	說話/说话	shuō huà	talk
吃	chī	eat	吃飯/吃饭	chī fàn	eat
睡	shuì	sleep	睡覺/睡觉	shuì jiào	sleep

Verb + Default Object:

我們吃<u>飯</u>吧！

我们吃<u>饭</u>吧！

wǒmen chī <u>fàn</u> ba!

Let's eat!

Verb + Question Word:

你要吃<u>什麼</u>？

你要吃<u>什么</u>？

nǐ yào chī <u>shénme</u>?

<u>*What*</u> *do you want to eat?*

When there is a more specific object, it replaces the default object:

Verb + Content Object

我們吃<u>餃子</u>吧。

我们吃<u>饺子</u>吧。

wǒmen chī <u>jiǎozi</u> ba.

Let's <u>eat dumplings</u>.

Resultative Endings

Activity verbs refer to open-ended actions. Resultative verb endings can be added to activity verbs to indicate the ending or result of the action, Only activity verbs can be suffixed with resultative verb endings.

看見	kànjiàn	*to perceive*
寫錯/写错	xiěcuò	*to write incorrectly*
説好/说好	shuōhǎo	*to come to an agreement*
聽懂/听懂	tīngdǒng	*to understand (by listening)*
買到/买到	mǎidào	*to buy*
念完	niànwán	*to finish studying*

For more on resultative endings, including exercises involving the resultative structure, see Chapter 7: The Resultative Structure and Potential Suffixes.

12. Rewrite these sentences to include the frequency or duration expression.

1. 我聽了音樂。(一個小時)
   我听了音乐。(一个小时)
   wǒ tīng le yīnyuè. (yī ge xiǎoshí)
   I listened to music for an hour.

2. 我每天看電視。(一個半鐘頭)
   我每天看电视。(一个半钟头)
   wǒ měitiān kàn diànshì. (yī ge bàn zhōngtóu)
   I watch television every day for an hour and a half.

3. 我去年坐了飛機。(三次)
   我去年坐了飞机。(三次)
   wǒ qùnián zuò le fēijī. (sān cì)
   I rode a plane three times last year.

4. 我去過法國。(四次)
   我去过法国。(四次)
   wǒ qùguo Fǎguó. (sì cì)
   I went to France four times.

5. 我每天晚上學中文。(三個小時)
   我每天晚上学中文。(三个小时)
   wǒ měitiān wǎnshang xué Zhōngwén. (sān ge xiǎoshí)
   I study Chinese every night for three hours.

6. 我看了那個電影。(兩次)
   我看了那个电影。(两次)
   wǒ kàn le nà ge diànyǐng. (liǎng cì)
   I saw that movie twice.

7. 我睡覺了。(七個鐘頭)
   我睡觉了。(七个钟头)
   wǒ shuì jiào le. (qī ge zhōngtóu)
   I slept for seven hours.

8. 我吃過中國飯。(幾次)
   我吃过中国饭。(几次)
   wǒ chīguo Zhōngguó fàn. (jǐ cì)
   I ate Chinese food a few times.

9. 我用過筷子。(一次)
   我用过筷子。(一次)
   wǒ yòngguo kuàizi. (yī cì)
   I've used chopsticks once.

10. 我每天寫中國字。(一個小時)
    我每天写中国字。(一个小时)
    wǒ měitiān xiě Zhōngguó zì. (yī ge xiǎoshí)
    I write Chinese characters for an hour every day.

Modification by Manner Adverbials

Activity verbs can be modified by phrases which indicate *the manner in which an activity is performed*. Mandarin uses two patterns to express modification in terms of manner.

Pattern 1: The manner phrase occurs after the verb. This pattern is used to describe the way that the *verb* is performed by the subject.

The marker for this kind of adverbial modification is 得 de.

Verb 得 de Stative Verb

吃得慢　　　　　　　　我妹妹吃得很慢。
chī de màn　　　　　　wǒ mèimei chī de hěn màn.
eat slowly　　　　　　*My little sister eats slowly.*

寫/写得好	你中國字寫得很好。
xiěde hǎo	你中国字写得很好。
write well	nǐ Zhōngguo zì xiěde hěn hǎo.
	You write Chinese characters well.

Note: Negation precedes the stative verb:

説得不準	他的四聲説得不準。
说得不准	他的四声说得不准。
shuō de bù zhǔn	tā de sìshēng shuō de bù zhǔn.
speaks inaccurately	*He speaks his tones inaccurately.*

If the verb is followed by an object and a manner adverbial, <u>verb + object</u> must be stated before <u>verb 得 de stative verb</u>.

Verb + Object Verb 得 de Stative Verb

她吃飯吃得很慢。
她吃饭吃得很慢。
tā chī fàn chī de hěn màn.
She eats slowly.

她寫中文字寫得很好。
她写中文字写得很好。
tā xiě Zhōngwén zì xiě de hěn hǎo.
She writes Chinese characters well.

她説日文説得很標準。
她说日文说得很标准。
tā shuō Rìwén shuō de hěn biāozhǔn.
She speaks Japanese accurately.

她吃飯吃得很慢。
她吃饭吃得很慢。
tā chī fàn chī de hěn màn.
She eats slowly.

Note: When an activity verb is modified by a stative verb in this way, the VP behaves like a stative verb phrase. The verb cannot be suffixed by the aspect markers 了 le or 過/过 guo. 着 zhe is also not acceptable.

⊗她説了日文説得很標準。
她说了日文说得很标准。
tā shuō le Rìwén shuō de hěn biāozhǔn.

⊗她寫過中文字寫得很好。

她写过中文字写得很好。

tā xiěguo Zhōngwén zì xiě de hěn hǎo.

Pattern 2: The manner phrase occurs before the VP. This pattern describes the way that *the entire VP* is performed by the subject.

The marker for this kind of adverbial modification is 地 de.

Stative Verb 地 de VP

他慢慢地把門開開了。

他慢慢地把门开开了。

tā mànmān de bǎ mén kāi kāi le.
He slowly opened the door.

你得好好兒地準備功課。

你得好好儿地准备功课。

nǐ děi hǎohāor de zhǔnbèi gōngkè.
You'd better prepare your lessons well.

Negation precedes the adverbial modifier.

他沒有好好兒地做。

他没有好好儿地做。

tā méi yǒu hǎohāor de zuò.
He didn't do the job well.

13. Complete these sentences with the appropriate Mandarin words to match the English translation. Use the 'Verb + Object Verb 得 de Stative Verb' pattern.

1. 妹妹寫英文 _____ 。(慢)
   妹妹写英文 _____ 。(慢)
   mèimei xiě Yīngwén _____ . (màn)
   Little sister writes English slowly.

2. 中學生吃飯_____ 。(多)
   中学生吃饭_____ 。(多)
   zhōngxuéshēng chī fàn _____ . (duō)
   Middle school students eat a lot.

3. 姐姐說話_____ 。(快)
   姐姐说话_____ 。(kuài)
   jiějie shuō huà _____ . (kuài)
   Older sister speaks quickly.

4. 弟弟吃飯_____ 。(慢)
   弟弟吃饭_____ 。(慢)
   dìdi chī fàn _____ . (màn)
   Little brother eats slowly.

5. 爸爸看書_____ 。(多)
   爸爸看书_____ 。(多)
   bàba kàn shū _____ . (duō)
   Dad reads a lot.

6. 我寫字_____ 。(不好)
   我写字_____ 。(不好)
   wǒ xiě zì _____ . (bù hǎo)
   I write Chinese characters poorly.

7. 媽媽開車_____ 。(好)
   妈妈开车_____ 。(好)
   māma kāi chē _____ . (hǎo)
   Mom drives well.

8. 哥哥喝咖啡_____ 。(少)
   gēge hē kāfēi _____ . (shǎo)
   Older brother drinks little coffee.

9. 姐姐寫字_____ 。(漂亮)
   姐姐写字_____ 。(漂亮)
   jiějie xiě zì _____ . (piàoliang)
   Older sister writes characters beautifully.

10. 弟弟看電視_____ 。(多)
    弟弟看电视_____ 。(多)
    dìdi kàn diànshì _____ . (duō)
    Younger brother watches a lot of television.

14. Put the adverbial phrase in the right place in each sentence to match the English translations.

   1. 他把蛋糕吃完了。(偷偷地)
      tā bǎ dàngāo chīwán le. (tōutou de)
      He secretly ate the cake up.

2. 你得做。(好好兒地)
   你得做。(好好儿地)
   nǐ děi zuò. (hǎohāor de)
   You have to do it well.

3. 走。(慢慢)
   zǒu. (màn màn)
   Don't hurry off. (Go slowly)

4. 寫吧！(快快)
   写吧！(快快)
   xiě ba! (kuài kuài)
   Hurry and write it.

5. 她把門開開了。(慢慢地)
   她把门开开了。(慢慢地)
   tā bǎ mén kāikai le. (mànmān de)
   She slowly opened the door.

6. 她躺在床上看書。(靜靜地)
   她躺在床上看书。(静静地)
   tā tǎng zài chuángshàng kàn shū. (jìng jìng de)
   She quietly lay on the bed reading.

7. 風從南方吹來。(輕輕地)
   风从南方吹来。(轻轻地)
   fēng cóng nánfāng chuī lái. (qīngqīng de)
   The breeze blows softly from the south.

8. 他哭起來了。(不知不覺地)
   他哭起来了。(不知不觉地)
   tā kūqilai le. (bù zhī bù jué de)
   He unconsicously started to cry.

9. 他們跑回家了。(高高興興地)
   他们跑回家了。(高高兴兴地)
   tāmen pǎo huí jiā le. (gāogāo xìngxìng de)
   They ran home happily.

10. 請你把事情再說一邊。(慢慢兒地)
    请你把事情再说一边。(慢慢儿地)
    qǐng nǐ bǎ shìqing zài shuō yībiān. (mànmār de)
    Please explain the situation again slowly.

ACHIEVEMENT VERBS

Achievement verbs are verbs whose actions are instantaneous and have no duration. The actions of many achievement verbs also result in a change of state. They include:

忘	wàng	to forget
死	sǐ	to die
穿	chuān	to put on (clothing) (on the torso or legs)
戴	dài	to put on (clothing) (on the head or arms)
碰	pèng	to bump
破	pò	to break
跳	tiào	to jump
賣/卖	mài	to sell
來/来	lái	to come (to a location identified with the speaker)
去	qù	to go (to a location distinct from the location of the speaker)
站	zhàn	to stand (a change from being seated to standing)
坐	zuò	to sit (a change from standing to seated)
放	fàng	to place down (a change from up to down)
開/开	kāi	to open (a change from closed to open)

Properties of Achievement Verbs

Negation

Like activity verbs, achievement verbs may be negated with 不 bù or 沒 méi. 不 bù is used for non-past or general time. 沒 méi is used to indicate that the action did not happen in the past. (See Chapter 6: The Suffixes 了 le, 着 zhe, and 過/过 guo.)

他不賣自行車。他賣汽車。
他不卖自行车。他卖汽车。
tā bú mài zìxíngchē. tā mài qìchē.
He doesn't sell bicycles. He sells cars.

他沒騎過自行車。
他没骑过自行车。
tā méi qíguo zìxíngchē.
He's never ridden a bicycle before.

Aspectual Suffixes

Achievement verbs may be marked as completed or terminated with the perfective suffix V-了 le.

他昨天忙得忘了吃飯。
他昨天忙得忘了吃饭。
tā zuótiān máng de wàng le chī fàn.
Yesterday he was so busy that he forgot to eat.

他死了。
tā sǐ le.
He died.

她賣了她的車。
她卖了她的车。
tā mài le tā de chē.
She sold her car.

Some achievement verbs describe repeatable actions. Those which do may be suffixed with the experiential suffix V-過/过 guo.

Repeatable Event	**Non-Repeatable Event**
我去過中國。	⊗我忘過你的名字。
我去过中国。	我忘过你的名字。
wǒ qùguo Zhōngguó.	wǒ wàngguo nǐ de míngzi.
I've gone to China before.	*(intended: I forgot your name before)*

Duration

Since achievement verbs do not have duration, they cannot be suffixed with the durational suffix V-着 zhe and they cannot occur with durational complements or with any expressions which mark duration.

Frequency

Achievement verbs may be suffixed with frequency complements. The complement immediately follows the verb.

我坐了一次飛機。
我坐了一次飞机。
wǒ zuò le yī cì fēijī.
I rode on a plane once before.

Properties of the Achievement Verbs 給/给 gěi and 送 sòng

The achievement verbs 給/给 gěi and 送 sòng are distinguished from most verbs in Mandarin because they can take both a direct object and an indirect object. Most Mandarin verbs take no object or a single, direct object. 給/给 gěi and 送 sòng can also occur with a direct object and no indirect object.

Direct Object and Indirect Object

你不必給我任何東西。

你不必给我任何东西。

nǐ búbì gěi wǒ rènhé dōngxi.
You don't have to give me anything.

我們應該送他什麼樣的禮物？

我们应该送他什么样的礼物？

wǒmen yīnggāi sòng tā shénme yàng de lǐwù?
What kind of gift should we present to him?

Direct Object

在中國不必給小費。

在中国不必给小费。

zài Zhōngguó búbì gěi xiǎofèi.
You don't have to give a tip in China.

你不必送禮物。

你不必送礼物。

nǐ búbì sòng lǐwù.
You don't have to give a gift.

15. The main verb in each of the following sentences is an activity verb or an achievement verb. Rewrite each sentence in the negative form. When doing this exercise, consult Chapter 6: The Suffixes 了 le, 着 zhe, and 過/过 guo. Note that V-了 le does not occur in sentences negated with 沒 méi.

1. 我看了那個電影。

   我看了那个电影。

   wǒ kàn le nà ge diànyǐng .
   I saw that movie.

2. 他坐了公共汽車。

   他坐了公共汽车。

   tā zuò le gōnggòng qìchē.
   He traveled by bus.

3. 我們星期六上課。

   我们星期六上课。

   wǒmen xīngqīliù shàng kè.
   We attend class on Saturday(s).

4. 我昨天上了中文課。

   我昨天上了中文课。

   wǒ zuótiān shàng le Zhōngwén kè.
   I attended Chinese class yesterday.

5. 她今天吃了冰淇淋。
   tā jīntiān chī le bīngqilín.
   She ate ice cream today.

6. 我今天戴了手錶。
   我今天戴了手表。
   wǒ jīntiān dài le shóubiǎo.
   I put on a watch today.

7. 他穿了大衣。
   tā chuān le dàyī.
   He wore an overcoat.

8. 他送了禮物。
   他送了礼物。
   tā sòng le lǐwù.
   He presented a gift.

9. 我今天吃了早飯。
   我今天吃了早饭。
   wǒ jīntiān chī le zǎofàn.
   I ate breakfast today.

10. 我們明天考中文。
    我们明天考中文。
    wǒmen míngtiān kǎo Zhōngwén.
    Tomorrow we have a test in Chinese.

MEMBERSHIP IN MORE THAN ONE VERB CATEGORY

Many verbs shift their verb categories based on the overall properties of the sentence in which they occur. When functioning as a member of a particular category, the verb has all of the properties of that category and also the meaning associated with verbs in that category. Notice how the meanings of the following verbs shift slightly depending upon the category to which they belong. Since many achievement verbs describe actions which have resulting states, shifts between the categories of state and achievement are particularly common.

	Stative Verb	Achievement Verb	Activity Verb
坐 zuò	他們在屋子裏坐着。 他们在屋子里坐着。	請坐(下)。 请坐(下)。 qǐng zuò (xià). *Please sit (down).*	他每天上班坐一個多鐘頭的車。 他每天上班坐一个多钟头的车。

	tāmen zài wūzi lǐ zuòzhe. *They are sitting in the room.*		tā měitiān shàng bān zuò yī ge duō zhōngtóu de chē. *Every day he travels by bus more than one hour to get to work.*
開/开 kāi	門開着呢 。 门开着呢。 mén kāizhe ne. *The door is open.*	他把門開開了。 他把门开开了。 tā bǎ mén kāikai le. *He opened the door.*	他每天都開車。 他每天都开车。 tā měitiān dōu kāi chē. *He drives every day.*
放 fàng	桌子上放着很多東西。 桌子上放着很多东西。 zhuōzi shàng fàngzhe hěn duō dōngxi. *There are a lot of things placed (sitting) on the table.*	她把她的皮包放在桌子上了。 tā bǎ tā de píbāo fàng zài zhuōzi shàng le. *She took her handbag and put it on the table.*	
戴 dài	她戴着很貴的耳環。 她戴着很贵的耳环。 tā dàizhe hěn guì de ěrhuán. *She is wearing very expensive earrings.*	他戴上了帽子。 tā dài shàng màozi le. *He put on a hat.*	
掛/挂 guà	牆上掛着他女朋友的照片。 墙上挂着他女朋友的照片。 qiáng shàng guàzhe tā nǚ péngyou de zhàopiàn. *His girlfriend's photo is hanging on the wall.*	他把他女朋友的照片掛在牆上。 他把他女朋友的照片挂在墙上。 tā bǎ tā nǚ péngyou de zhàopiàn guà zài qiáng shàng. *He hung his girlfriend's photo on the wall.*	

穿 chuān	他穿着很厚的大 衣。 tā chuānzhe hěn hòu de dàyī. *He is wearing a very thick overcoat.*	昨天很冷。我穿了 很厚的大衣。 zuótiān hěn lěng. wǒ chuān le hěn hòu de dàyī. *It was very cold yesterday. I put on a very thick overcoat.*	
站 zhàn	怎麼回事？外邊站 着很多人。 怎么回事？外边站 着很多人。 zěnme huí shì? wàibian zhànzhe hěn duō rén. *What's going on? There are a lot of people standing outside.*	老師快來了。站起 來吧！ 老师快来了。站起 来吧！ lǎoshī kuài lái le. zhànqilai ba! *The teacher is almost here. Stand up!*	
有 yǒu	他很有錢。 tā hěn yǒu qián. *He has a lot of money.*	他有了一筆錢。 他有了一笔钱。 tā yǒu le yī bǐ qián. *He has acquired a sum of money.*	

CHAPTER 4

Adverbs

CHARACTERISTICS OF ADVERBS

Adverbs are words that modify the VP. In Mandarin, they have the following characteristics:

Position in the VP

Adverbs occur at the beginning of the VP, before the verb and any prepositional phrase.

我<u>一定</u>去。
wǒ <u>yīdìng</u> qù.
I am <u>definitely</u> going.

他們<u>都</u>會說法語。
他们<u>都</u>会说法语。
tāmen <u>dōu</u> huì shuō Fǎyǔ.
They can <u>all</u> speak French.

他<u>常</u>給女朋友打電話。
他<u>常</u>给女朋友打电话。
tā <u>cháng</u> gěi nǚ péngyou dǎ diànhuà.
He <u>often</u> phones his girlfriend.

Exclusion from V-NEG-V Structure

Adverbs do not participate in Verb-NEG-Verb question formation.

☹你一定不一定去？
nǐ yīdìng bù yīdìng qù?
Are you definitely going?

☹他常不常來？
他常不常来？
tā cháng bù cháng lái?
Does he often come?

Co-occurrence with Other Adverbs

Adverbs may co-occur with adverbs from other meaning groups (presented below). Generally, adverbs which indicate uniqueness such as 就 jiù, 只 zhǐ, 才 cái, and 光 guāng occur closest to the verb.

他可能只會寫一兩個字。
他可能只会写一两个字。
tā kénéng zhǐ huì xiě yī liǎng ge zì。
Perhaps he can only write one or two characters.

你們都必須更認真一些。
你们都必须更认真一些。
nǐmen dōu bìxū gèng rènzhēn yīxiē.
You should all be more conscientious.

你得馬上回家。
你得马上回家。
nǐ děi mǎshàng huí jiā.
You should go home immediately.

Adverbs and Negation

Adverbs usually occur before negation.

我還不懂。
我还不懂。
wǒ hái bù dǒng.
I still don't understand

他今天也許不來。
他今天也许不来。
tā jīntiān yéxǔ bù lái.
Perhaps he won't come today. (He may not come today.)

A small number of adverbs may occur before or after negation. Those which can include 都 dōu and 一定 yīdìng.

我不一定去。
wǒ bù yīdìng qù.
I am not definitely going.

我們不都去。
我们不都去。
wǒmen bù dōu qù.
We are not all going.

我一定不去。

wǒ yīdìng bú qù.

I am definitely not going.

我們都不去。

我们都不去。

wǒmen dōu bú qù.

We are all not going.

As these examples illustrate, the relative position of adverb and negation influences the meaning of the sentence. The changes in meaning will be discussed below in the section on 都 dōu.

COMMON ADVERBS CATEGORIZED BY MEANING

Universality

都	dōu	*all/always (see below for special focus)*
總 (是)	zǒng(shì)	*always*
老	lǎo	*always (colloquial)*
向來	xiànglái	*always (in the past up to the present time)*
從來/从来	cónglái	*never (Note: 從來/从来 must be followed by negation. When 從來/从来 is used, the verb is usually suffixed with the experiential suffix 過/过 guo)*

你老吃豆腐。今天吃別的東西吧！

你老吃豆腐。今天吃别的东西吧！

nǐ lǎo chī dòufu. jīntiān chī biéde dōngxi ba!

You always eat beancurd. Eat something else today!

我從來沒出過國。

我从来没出过国。

wǒ cónglái méi chūguo guó.

I have never been abroad before.

Special Focus

<u>都 dōu *all/always*</u>

The basic function of 都 dōu is to indicate that something is true for an entire noun phrase. The NP to which 都 dōu refers must come before the VP.

- When the subject is plural, the presence of 都 dōu typically indicates that the VP is true for the entire subject:

我們都喜歡看電影。

我们都喜欢看电影。

wǒmen dōu xǐhuan kàn diànyǐng.
We all like to see movies.

- 都 dōu can also be used to indicate that the VP is true for the entire object. In order for 都 dōu to refer to the object, the object must occur before the VP as a 'topic.' (See Chapter 13: Focusing Constructions.)

那些書，我都看過了。	☹我都看過了那些書。
那些书，我都看过了。	我都看过了那些书。
nàxiē shū, wǒ dōu kànguo le.	wǒ dōu kànguo le nàxiē shū.
I've read all of those books before.	
(Those books, I've read them all before.)	

日本、中國、我都去過。	☹我都去過日本、中國。
日本、中国、我都去过。	我都去过日本、中国。
Rìběn, Zhōngguó, wǒ dōu qùguo.	wǒ dōu qùguo Rìběn,
Japan, China, I have been to them both.	Zhōngguó.

都 dōu can be interpreted as referring to the object if the object is implied but not specified.

我都懂。

wǒ dōu dǒng.
I understand completely.

(你的話，) 我都懂。

(你的话，) 我都懂。

(nǐ de huà，) wǒ dōu dǒng.
(What you say,) I understand completely.
I understand everything you say.

- 都 dōu can occur before or after negation. The relative position of 都 dōu and negation influences the meaning of the sentence.

都 dōu before negation indicates that the negated predicate refers to the entire NP:

Not true for the entire subject

我們都不喜歡那個電影。

我们都不喜欢那个电影。

wǒmen dōu bù xǐhuan nà ge diànyǐng.

We all do not like that movie. (None of us like that movie.)

我們都沒吃過日本菜。

我们都没吃过日本菜。

wǒmen dōu méi chīguo Rìběn cài.

We have all not eaten Japanese food. (None of us have eaten Japanese food.)

Not true for the entire object

你的話，我都不懂。

你的话，我都不懂。

nǐ de huà, wǒ dōu bù dǒng.

What you said, I don't understand at all. (I completely do not understand.)

日本、中國、我都沒去過。

日本、中国、我都没去过。

Rìběn, Zhōngguó, wǒ dōu méi qùguo.

Japan, China, I haven't been there.

都 dōu after negation indicates that the negated predicate does not refer to all of

the NP. That is, it conveys the meaning *not all*.

Not all of the subject

我們不都喜歡那個電影。

我们不都喜欢那个电影。

wǒmen bù dōu xǐhuan nà ge diànyǐng.

Not all of us like that movie. (Some of us don't like it.)

Q:今天的晚會，你的同學都來   A: 不都來。
   嗎？   不都来。
   今天的晚会，你的同学都来   bù dōu lái.
   吗？   *They won't all come. (not all)*
   jīntiān de wǎnhuì, nǐ de tóngxué
   dōu lái ma?
   Are all of your classmates coming to
   tonight's party?

Not all of the object

Q: 你懂嗎 ?   A: 我不都懂。

你懂吗 ?   我不都懂。

nǐ dǒng ma?   wǒ bù dōu dǒng.

Do you understand?   *I don't completely understand. (not all)*

Q: 中國菜，你都喜歡嗎 ?   A: 不都喜歡。

中国菜，你都喜欢吗 ?   不都喜欢。

Zhōngguó cài, nǐ dōu   bù dōu xǐhuan.

xǐhuan ma?   *I don't like all of it. (not all)*

Do you like all Chinese food?

- Words that translate 都 dōu in English include *all*, *both*, *always*, etc. Note that Mandarin does not use separate words to distinguish two entities (*both*) from more than two entities (*all*).

- 都 dōu is used with question words to indicate indefinite meaning. (See Chapter 8: Questions and Question Words.)

誰都喜歡吃餃子。

谁都喜欢吃饺子。

shéi dōu xǐhuan chī jiǎozi.

Everyone likes to eat dumplings.

Inclusion and Continuity

也	yě	*also*
還/还	hái	*still*
仍然	réngrán	*still, as before*
一直	yī zhí	*continuously*
向來/向来	xiànglái	*all along/always in the past up to the present*
一向	yī xiàng	*all along/always in the past up to the present (often used with negation)*

弟弟想明天到海邊去玩。妹妹也想去。

弟弟想明天到海边去玩。妹妹也想去。

dìdi xiǎng míngtiān dào hǎibiān qù wán. mèimei yě xiǎng qù.

Younger brother is going to the ocean tomorrow to have fun. Younger sister wants to go too.

我一向不喜歡看電影。

我一向不喜欢看电影。

wǒ yīxiàng bù xǐhuan kàn diànyǐng.
I've never liked to watch movies.

我一直想去中國學習。

我一直想去中国学习。

wǒ yīzhí xiǎng qù Zhōngguó xuéxí.
I've always wanted to go to China to study.

你已經吃了很多。還想吃嗎？

你已经吃了很多。还想吃吗？

nǐ yǐjing chīle hěn duō. hái xiǎng chī ma?
You've already eaten a lot. Do you still want to eat?

她仍然是我的好朋友。

tā réngrán shì wǒ de hǎo péngyou.
She is still my good friend.

Frequency, Repetition and Quantity

再三	zài sān	*repeatedly*
往往	wángwǎng	*often/frequently*
常	cháng	*often*
常常	cháng cháng	*often*
經常/经常	jīngcháng	*regularly/frequently/without fail*
再	zài	*do again in the future*
又	yòu	*do again in the past*
多	duō	*more*
少	shǎo	*less*

老師再三告訴我別忘了學習。

老师再三告诉我别忘了学习。

lǎoshī zài sān gàosu wǒ bié wàng le xuéxí.
The teacher told me again and again not to forget to study.

這個字我往往寫錯。

这个字我往往写错。

zhè ge zì wǒ wángwǎng xiěcuò.
This character I often write incorrectly.

他經常幫助別人。

他经常帮助别人。

tā jīngcháng bāngzhù biéren.
He always helps others.

我今天又忘了怎麼寫。

我今天又忘了怎么写。

wǒ jīntiān yòu wàng le zěnme xiě.
Today I forgot how to write it again.

我最好再寫幾次。

我最好再写几次。

wǒ zuì hǎo zài xiě jǐ cì.
I'd best write it again several times.

他往往遲到。

他往往迟到。

tā wángwǎng chídào.
He's often late.

他常出去不關門。

他常出去不关门。

tā cháng chūqu bù guān mén.
He often goes out without shutting the door.

你得少看電視，多注意功課。

你得少看电视，多注意功课。

nǐ děi shǎo kàn diànshì, duō zhùyì gōngkè.
You should watch less television and pay more attention to your schoolwork.

Obligation

affirmative

應該/应该	yīnggāi	*should*
應當/应当	yīngdāng	*should*
該/该	gāi	*should*
必得	bìděi	*must*
得	děi	*must*
必須/必须	bìxū	*must*
非得	fēiděi	*must*

negative

不應該/不应该	bù yīnggāi	*need not; do not have to*
不應當/不应当	bù yīngdāng	*need not; do not have to*
不該/不该	bù gāi	*need not; do not have to*
不必	búbì	*need not; do not have to*
不用	bú yòng	*need not; do not have to***
甭	béng	*need not; do not have to (colloquial)*
不須/不须	bù xū	*not necessary to*
可不	kě bù	*should not*
可別	kě bié	*should not*
(應)該不/(应)该不	(yīng)gāi bù	*must not*

這件事情很重要。你可別忘了！
这件事情很重要。你可别忘了！
zhè jiàn shìqing hěn zhòngyào. nǐ kě bié wàng le!
This matter is very important. Don't forget it!

你應該按時上課。不應該遲到。
你应该按时上课。不应该迟到。
nǐ yīnggāi ànshí shàng kè. bù yīnggāi chídào.
You should come to class on time. You shouldn't be late.

你不必每天都洗頭髮。
你不必每天都洗头发。
nǐ búbì měitiān dōu xǐ tóufa.
You don't have to wash your hair everyday.

我懂了。你甭再説了。
我懂了。你甭再说了。
wǒ dǒng le. nǐ béng zài shuō le.
I understand. You don't have to say it again.

注冊前必須付學費。
注册前必须付学费。
zhùcè qián bìxū fù xuéfèi.
Before you register you must pay tuition.

**甭 béng is a contraction of 不用 bú yòng.

申請駕駛証，你非得親自去。

申请驾驶证，你非得亲自去。

shēnqǐng jiàshǐ zhèng, nǐ fēiděi qīnzì qù.

When you apply for a driver's license you must go in person.

Note: While included in this group of adverbs, 應該/应该 yīnggāi, 該/该 gāi and 應當/应当 yīngdāng have the properties of stative verbs. (See Chapter 3: Verbs and Verb Phrases.)

Special Focus

非 V 不可 fēi V bù kě *must*

While not an adverb, the expresssion 非 V 不可 fēi V bù kě *must* is also used to indicate affirmative obligation. The literal meaning of 非 V 不可 fēi V bù kě is *it is not possible to not do V.* Note that the verb is incorporated into the expression.

今天晚上的會議很重要。非去不可。

今天晚上的会议很重要。非去不可。

jīntiān wǎnshang de huìyì hěn zhòngyào. fēi qù bù kě.

Tonight's meeting is very important. You must go.

這件事情很重要。 非做不可。

这件事情很重要。 非做不可。

zhè jiàn shìqing hěn zhòngyào. fēi zuò bù kě.

This task is very important. You must do it.

Certainty or Possibility

一定	yīdìng	*certainly*
肯定	kěndìng	*certainly*
畢竟/毕竟	bìjìng	*after all, in the final analysis*
的確/的确	díquè	*in fact, really*
果然	guǒrán	*sure enough*
可能	kěnéng	*possibly*
也許/也许	yéxǔ	*maybe*
或者	huòzhě	*perhaps (colloquial)*
或許/或许	huòxǔ	*perhaps, maybe (literary)*

他説他今天晚上一定來。

他说他今天晚上一定来。

tā shuō tā jīntiān wǎnshang yídìng lái.
He said he is definitely coming tonight.

Q: 你跟我去旅行嗎？   A: 我肯定去。

    你跟我去旅行吗？   我肯定去。

    nǐ gēn wǒ qù lǚxíng ma?   wǒ kěndìng qù.
Q: Are you going to travel with me? A: I am definitely going.

他畢竟是一個小孩子。你不能對他要求太高。

他毕竟是一个小孩子。你不能对他要求太高。

tā bìjìng shì yī ge xiǎo háizi. nǐ bù néng duì tā yāoqiú tài gāo.
He is only a child after all. You should not demand too much of him.

她的確是個好人。

她的确是个好人。

tā díquè shì ge hǎo rén.
She is certainly a good person.

他説他今天給我錢，果然給我錢了。

他说他今天给我钱，果然给我钱了。

tā shuō tā jīntiān gěi wǒ qián, guǒrán gěi wǒ qián le.
He said he would give me money today. Sure enough, he gave me money.

他很忙，可能不會跟我們一起去看電影。

他很忙，可能不会跟我们一起去看电影。

tā hěn máng, kěnéng bú huì gēn wǒmen yīqǐ qù kàn diànyǐng.
He is very busy, (and) perhaps won't be able to go with us to see a movie.

她也許會晚一點。

她也许会晚一点。

tā yéxǔ huì wǎn yīdiǎn.
Perhaps she will be a little late.

快一點吧！或者還來得及吃晚飯。

快一点吧！或者还来得及吃晚饭。

kuài yīdiǎn ba! huòzhě hái láidejí chī wǎnfàn.
Hurry up! Perhaps we will be on time for dinner.

或許我能做此事。[*]

或许我能做此事。

huòxǔ wǒ néng zuò cǐ shì.

Perhaps I will be able to do this.

Uniqueness or Punctuality

就	jiù	*only/precisely (see below for special focus)*
才	cái	*only/merely, only then (see below for special focus)*
光	guāng	*solely/merely*
剛/刚	gāng	*exactly/just*
淨/净	jìng	*completely, merely/barely*
僅/仅	jǐn	*merely/barely*
正(在)	zhèng (zài)	*precisely, right now*

他光説，不願意做。

他光说，不愿意做。

tā guāng shuō, bú yuànyi zuò.

He only talks, he's not willing to do anything.

他剛走了。

他刚走了。

tā gāng zǒu le.

He just left.

他淨讀書，都不出去玩。

他净读书，都不出去玩。

tā jìng dú shū, dōu bù chū qù wán.

He only studies, (and he) never goes out to have fun.

他們正(在)唱着歌呢。

他们正(在)唱着歌呢。

tāmen zhèng(zài) chàngzhe gē ne.

They are singing right now.

___

[*] This example from Far East Chinese-English Dictionary (遠東漢英大詞典/远东汉英大词典 yuǎndōng hànyīng dà cídiǎn), Far East Publishing Company, 1995.

Special Focus

就 jiù - *only, precisely*

- 就 jiù as a marker of uniqueness:

  我就有一塊錢。
  我就有一块钱。
  wǒ jiù yǒu yī kuài qián.
  I only have one dollar.

- 就 jiù as a marker of identification. In this sense it is often used to signal a

location at the end of a series of directions:

  圖書館就在這兒。
  图书馆就在这儿。
  túshūguǎn jiù zài zhèr。
  The library is right here.

As a marker of identification 就 jiù may also signal that a person has been

located:

  白：你找誰？
  你找谁？
  nǐ zhǎo shéi?
  Who are you looking for?

  王：我找白麗娜。
  我找白丽娜。
  wǒ zhǎo Bái Lìnà.
  I am looking for Bai Lina.

  白：我就是。
  我就是。
  wǒ jiù shì.
  That's me.

- 就 jiù as a marker of immediacy: the VP will happen momentarily.

  我就來。
  我就来。
  wǒ jiù lái.
  I'll be right there.

When 就 jiù occurs in sentences indicating narrative sequence, it contributes the meaning of immediacy: the second action happens right after the first one. (For more on sequence sentences, see Chapter 12: Phrase and Clause Connection.)

我吃了飯就走。
我吃了饭就走。
wǒ chīle fàn jiù zǒu.
I'll eat and leave.

才 cái *only/merely, only then*

才 cái reflects a situation viewed from the speaker's perspective. It signals that the situation expressed in the VP is less than what the speaker had expected.

- When 才 cái occurs in a simple sentence, it can often be translated with the English word *only* or *merely*.

  她才五歲。
  她才五岁。
  tā cái wǔ suì.
  She is only 5 years old.

  你才吃了一點。
  你才吃了一点。
  nǐ cái chī le yīdiǎn.
  You've only eaten a little.

- 才 cái may occur before the second VP in a series of two VPs. In this case, it often indicates that the event described by the second VP occurs *only after* the completion of the event described by the first VP. The VPs may have different subjects.

  我們做完了事才能下班。
  我们做完了事才能下班。
  wǒmen zuòwán le shì cái néng xià bān.
  Only after we finish work can we go off duty.
  (literally: After we finish work, only then can we go off duty.)

  等你把作業做完才能看電視。
  等你把作业做完才能看电视。
  děng nǐ bǎ zuòyè zuòwán cái néng kàn diànshì.
  Wait until you finish your homework and only then can you watch television.

你跟我去我才願意去。

你跟我去我才愿意去。

nǐ gēn wǒ qù wǒ cái yuànyi qù.

Only if you go with me am I willing to go.

(literally: If you go with me, only then am I willing to go.)

Approximation

幾乎/几乎	jīhū	*just about/almost*
差一點/差一点	chà yīdiǎn	*almost (usually in negative context)*
差不多	chàbuduō	*almost*
快	kuài	*almost, momentarily, soon*

他的狗幾乎被車壓死了。

他的狗几乎被车压死了。

tā de gǒu jīhū bèi chē yāsǐ le.

His dog was almost crushed to death by a car.

我差一點忘了。

我差一点忘了。

wǒ chà yīdiǎn wàng le.

I almost forgot.

他差不多都懂。

tā chàbuduō dōu dǒng.

He understands almost everything.

現在差不多兩點一刻。

现在差不多两点一刻。

xiànzài chàbuduō liǎng diǎn yī kè.

Now it is almost 2:15.

我們快做完了。

我们快做完了。

wǒmen kuài zuòwán le.

We're almost done.

Note: For expressions used in numerical approximations, see 'Estimates and

Approximations' in Chapter 1: Numbers.

Temporal Reference

Beginnings and Endings

原來/原来	yuánlái	*originally, at first, all along*
本來/本来	běnlái	*originally, at first*
當初/当初	dāngchū	*originally, at first*
起初	qǐchū	*originally, at first (same as 當初/当初)*
最後/最后	zuì hòu	*finally, in the end*
最終/最终	zuì zhōng	*finally, in the end (literary)*
到底	dàodǐ	*after all*

我以爲她是中國人，原來她是日本人。

我以为她是中国人，原来她是日本人。

wǒ yǐwéi tā shì Zhōngguó rén, yuánlái tā shì Rìběn rén.
I thought she was Chinese. All along she was Japanese.

他本來對歷史沒有興趣，現在他很喜歡學歷史了。

他本来对历史没有兴趣，现在他很喜欢学历史了。

tā běnlái duì lìshǐ méi yǒu xìngqù, xiànzài tā hěn xǐhuan xué lìshǐ le.
Originally he wasn't interested in history. Now he likes to study it a lot.

我當初不喜歡學中文，最後喜歡了。

我当初不喜欢学中文，最后喜欢了。

wǒ dāngchū bù xǐhuan xué Zhōngwén, zuì hòu xǐhuan le.
At the beginning I didn't like to study Chinese. In the end I liked it.

他起初有一點緊張，後來他放心了。

他起初有一点紧张，后来他放心了。

tā qǐchū yǒu yīdiǎn jǐnzhāng, hòulái tā fàng xīn le.
At the beginning he was a bit nervous, afterwards he calmed down.

她非常努力，最終達到了目的。

她非常努力，最终达到了目的。

tā fēicháng nǔlì, zuì zhōng dádào le mùdì.
She was extremely hardworking, (and) in the end she achieved her goal.

你到底喜不喜歡他？

你到底喜不喜欢他？

nǐ dàodǐ xǐ bù xǐhuan tā?
After all, do you like him or not?

Other Temporal Reference

忽然	hūrán	*suddenly*
突然	tūrán	*suddenly and unexpectedly*
快	kuài	*soon*
馬上/马上	mǎshàng	*immediately*
剛才/刚才	gāngcái	*just before now*
近來/近来	jìnlái	*recently*
曾經/曾经	céngjīng	*once in the past*
暫時/暂时	zànshí	*temporarily*

我忽然想起來了他的名字。

我忽然想起来了他的名字。

wǒ hūrán xiǎngqilai le tā de míngzi.

I suddenly remembered his name.

他突然死了。

tā tūrán sǐ le.

He suddenly and unexpectedly died.

這件事來得很突然。

这件事来得很突然。

zhè jiàn shì lái de hěn tūrán.

This matter came up very suddenly and unexpectedly.

我們得馬上回家。

我们得马上回家。

wǒmen děi mǎshàng huí jiā.

We have to go home immediately.

我剛才說的話你懂不懂？

我刚才说的话你懂不懂？

wǒ gāngcái shuō de huà nǐ dǒng bù dǒng?

The thing I just told you, do you understand (it) or not?

對不起。我近來沒辦法跟你聯絡。

对不起。我近来没办法跟你联络。

duìbuqǐ. wǒ jìnlái méi bànfǎ gēn nǐ liánluò.

I am sorry. I recently have been unable to get in touch with you.

我曾經告訴過你學中文很有意思。

我曾经告诉过你学中文很有意思。

wǒ céngjīng gàosuguo nǐ xué Zhōngwén hěn yǒu yìsi.

I already told you, studying Chinese is very interesting.

對不起，我們暫時没有電。

对不起，我们暂时没有电。

duìbuqǐ, wǒmen zànshí méi yǒu diàn.

I am sorry. We temporarily do not have electricity.

Speaker Perspective

These adverbs are subjective, conveying the speaker's attitude towards an event. See Chapter 14: Speaker Perspective, for additional structures which convey speaker perspective and for additional exercises using these adverbs.

明明	míngmíng	*clearly*
好像	hǎoxiàng	*seemingly, apparently*
顯得/显得	xiǎndé	*seemingly, apparently*
並/并	bìng	*not at all (must occur with negative)*
居然	jūrán	*unexpectedly*
白	bái	*in vain*
徒然	túrán	*in vain*
簡直/简直	jiǎnzhí	*simply (must occur with negation)*

他明明知道。他爲什麽不説？

他明明知道。他为什么不说？

tā míngmíng zhīdao. tā wéi shénme bù shuō?

He clearly knows. Why doesn't he speak?

他好像不高興的樣子。

他好像不高兴的样子。

tā hǎoxiàng bù gāoxìng de yàngzi.

He is apparently unhappy.

他今天顯得很累的樣子。

他今天显得很累的样子。

tā jīntiān xiǎndé hěn lèi de yàngzi.

He is seemingly tired today.

他並不是我的好朋友。

他并不是我的好朋友。

tā bìng bú shì wǒ de hǎo péngyou.

He is absolutely not my good friend.

他居然請我吃晚飯了。

他居然请我吃晚饭了。

tā jūrán qǐng wǒ chī wǎnfàn le.

He unexpectedly invited me to dinner. (Out of the blue, he invited me to dinner.)

今天沒考試。我白預備了。

今天没考试。我白预备了。

jīntiān méi kǎoshì. wǒ bái yùbèi le.

There was no test today. I wasted my time studying.

商店都已經關門了。我們徒然來了。

商店都已经关门了。我们徒然来了。

shāngdiàn dōu yǐjing guān mén le. wǒmen túrán lái le.

The stores have all already closed. We came in vain.

他說的話我簡直不懂。

他说的话我简直不懂。

tā shuō de huà wǒ jiǎnzhí bù dǒng.

I simply don't understand what he says.

1. Select the best adverb from among the choices to complete each sentence.

    1. 他說他懂。他 ＿＿＿ 不懂。(並，又，向來)
        他说他懂。他 ＿＿＿ 不懂。(并，又，向来)
        tā shuō tā dǒng. tā ＿＿＿ bù dǒng. (bìng, yòu, xiànglái)
        He said he understands. He really doesn't understand.

    2. 我 ＿＿＿ 不吃肉。(肯定，一向，原來)
        wǒ ＿＿＿ bù chī ròu. (kěndìng, yīxiàng, yuánlái)
        I never eat meat.

    3. 我 ＿＿＿ 不會出國。(的確，暫時，畢竟)
        我 ＿＿＿ 不会出国。(的确，暂时，毕竟)
        wǒ ＿＿＿ bú huì chū guó. (díquè, zànshí, bìjìng)
        I temporarily am unable to leave the country.

    4. 我們＿＿＿ 喝茶。今天喝汽水吧。(常，老，從來)
        我们＿＿＿ 喝茶。今天喝汽水吧。(常，老，从来)
        wǒmen ＿＿＿ hē chá. jīntiān hē qìshuǐ ba. (cháng, lǎo, cónglái)
        We always drink tea. Today let's drink soda.

    5. 我 ＿＿＿ 沒喝過汽水。(向來，一直，從來)
        我 ＿＿＿ 没喝过汽水。(向来，一直，从来)
        wǒ ＿＿＿ méi hēguo qìshuǐ. (xiànglái, yīzhí, cónglái)
        I've never drunk soda before.

6. 她 ___ 在那兒工作。(也，仍然，光)

   她 ___ 在那儿工作。(也，仍然，光)

   tā ___ zài nàr gōngzuò. (yě, réngrán, guāng)

   She is still working there.

7. 學生 ___ 不喜歡考試。(一向，一直，還)

   学生 ___ 不喜欢考试。(一向，一直，还)

   xuésheng ___ bù xǐhuan kǎoshì. (yīxiàng, yīzhí, hái)

   Students always don't like to take exams.

8. 我 ___ 吃中國飯。(常，都，再三)

   我 ___ 吃中国饭。(常，都，再三)

   wǒ ___ chī Zhōngguó fàn. (cháng, dōu, zài sān)

   I often eat Chinese food.

9. 我昨天晚上 ___ 吃了中國飯。(一直，也，又)

   我昨天晚上 ___ 吃了中国饭。(一直，也，又)

   wǒ zuótiān wǎnshang ___ chīle Zhōngguó fàn. (yīzhí, yě, yòu)

   Last night I ate it again.

10. 我想學生都___ ___ 吃冰淇淋。

    　　　(應該，不必，必須；都，多，得)

    我想学生都___ ___ 吃冰淇淋。

    　　　(应该，不必，必须；都，多，得)

    wǒ xiǎng xuésheng dōu ___ ___ chī bīngqilín.

    　　　(yīnggāi, búbì, bìxū; dōu, duō, děi)

    I think students should all eat more ice cream.

11. 大學生 ___ ___ 喝啤酒。(必得，可別，應該；少，再，往往)

    大学生 ___ ___ 喝啤酒。(必得，可别，应该；少，再，往往)

    dàxué shēng ___ ___ hē píjiǔ.

    　　　(bìděi, kě bié, yīnggāi; shǎo, zài, wángwǎng)

    College students should drink less beer.

12. 老師說我們 ___ ___ 睡覺。

    　　　(不用，應該，必得；再三，常，多)

    老师说我们 ___ ___ 睡觉。

    　　　(不用，应该，必得；再三，常，多)

    lǎoshī shuō wǒmen ___ ___ shuì jiào.

    　　　(búyòng, yīnggāi, bìděi; zàisān, cháng, duō)

    Teacher says we should sleep more.

13. 大學生 ＿＿ 把太多時間花在電子郵件上。
（不應該，不必，不用）

大学生 ＿＿ 把太多时间花在电子邮件上。
（不应该，不必，不用）

dàxuéshēng ＿＿ bǎ tài duō shíjiān huā zài diànzi yóujiàn shàng.
(bù yīnggāi, búbì, búyòng)

College students shouldn't spend so much time on email.

14. 她 ＿＿＿很年輕。（又，一定，仍然）

她 ＿＿＿很年轻。（又，一定，仍然）

tā ＿＿＿ hěn niánqīng. (yòu, yīdìng, réngrán)

She's still very young.

15. 媽媽 ＿＿＿ 喝咖啡。（老，都，就）

妈妈 ＿＿＿ 喝咖啡。（老，都，就）

māma ＿＿＿ hē kāfēi. (lǎo, dōu, jiù)

Mom always drinks coffee.

16. 學生 ＿＿＿ 做功課。（應當，必須，不必）

学生 ＿＿＿ 做功课。（应当，必须，不必）

xuésheng ＿＿＿ zuò gōngkè. (yīngdāng, bìxū, búbì)

Students must do their schoolwork.

17. 那個飯館的飯 ＿＿＿ 好吃。（一向，畢竟，的確）

那个饭馆的饭 ＿＿＿ 好吃。（一向，毕竟，的确）

nà ge fànguǎn de fàn ＿＿＿ hǎo chī. (yīxiàng, bìjìng, díquè)

The dishes in that restaurant are really good.

18. 現在 ＿＿＿ 九點了。上課吧。（幾乎，就，差不多）

现在 ＿＿＿ 九点了。上课吧。（幾乎，就，差不多）

xiànzài ＿＿＿ jiǔ diǎn le. shàng kè ba. (jīhū, jiù, chàbuduō)

It's almost 9 o'clock. Let's go to class.

19. 你 ＿＿＿ 不喜歡吃這個菜。（也許，從來，居然）

你 ＿＿＿ 不喜欢吃这个菜。（也许，从来，居然）

nǐ ＿＿＿ bù xǐhuan chī zhè ge cài. (yéxǔ, cónglái, jūrán)

Perhaps you won't like this dish.

20. 我 ＿＿＿ 不喜歡。（當然，仍然，果然）

我 ＿＿＿ 不喜欢。（当然，仍然，果然）

wǒ ＿＿＿ bù xǐhuan. (dāngrán, réngrán, guǒrán)

Sure enough, I didn't like it.

21. 老師説我 ___ 會考得很好。(顯得，一直，一定)

老师说我 ___ 会考得很好。(显得，一直，一定)

lǎoshī shuō wǒ ___ huì kǎo de hěn hǎo. (xiǎndé, yīzhí, yīdìng)

Teacher says I can definitely do well on the exams.

22. 那個大學的學生 ___ 很聰明。(的確，肯定，畢竟)

那个大学的学生 ___ 很聪明。(的确，肯定，毕竟)

nà ge dàxué de xuésheng ___ hěn cōngming. (díquè, kěndìng, bìjìng)

The students in that college are in fact really smart.

23. 我們都是朋友。你 ___ 客氣。(甭，非得，不應該)

我们都是朋友。你 ___ 客气。(甭，非得，不应该)

wǒmen dōu shì péngyou. nǐ ___ kèqi. (béng, fēiděi, bù yīnggāi)

We are all friends. You don't have to be so polite.

24. 他 ___ 覺得有一點累。(馬上，快，忽然)

他 ___ 觉得有一点累。(马上，快，忽然)

tā ___ juéde yǒu yīdiǎn lèi.(mǎshàng, kuài, hūrán)

He suddenly felt a little tired.

25. 他 ___ 對京劇有興趣。(曾經，一向，仍然)

他 ___ 对京剧有兴趣。(曾经，一向，仍然)

tā ___ duì jīngjù yǒu xìngqù.(céngjīng, yīxiàng, réngrán)

He's always been interested in Beijing opera.

2. Complete this paragraph by filling in the blanks with the appropriate adverbs.

1. 我弟弟跟他的朋友 ___ 喜歡打籃球。

我弟弟跟他的朋友 ___ 喜欢打篮球。

wǒ dìdi gēn tā de péngyou ___ xǐhuan dǎ lánqiú.

My younger brother and his friends all like to play ball.

2. 每天下了課以後他們 ___ 到公園去打球。

每天下了课以后他们 ___ 到公园去打球。

měitiān xià le kè yǐhòu tāmen ___ dào gōngyuán qù dǎ qiú.

Every day after class they always go to the park to play ball.

3. 到了夏天，他們早上 ___ 到公園去。

到了夏天，他们早上 ___ 到公园去。

dào le xiàtiān, tāmen zǎoshang ___ dào gōngyuán qù.

When it gets to be summer, they go right to the park in the morning.

4. 晚上六七點鐘 ＿＿＿ 在公園裏打球。

   晚上六七点钟 ＿＿＿ 在公园里打球。

   wǎnshang liù qī diǎn zhōng ＿＿＿ zài gōngyuán lǐ dǎ qiú.

   At 6 or 7 o'clock in the evening they are still in the park playing ball.

5. 天黑了他們 ＿＿ 回家。

   天黑了他们 ＿＿ 回家。

   tiān hēi le tāmen ＿＿＿ huí jiā.

   When it gets dark, only then do they go home.

6. 第二天 ＿＿ 來公園打球。

   第二天 ＿＿ 来公园打球。

   dì èr tiān ＿＿＿ lái gōngyuán dǎ qiú.

   The next day they come to the park again to play ball.

7. 天氣不好 ＿＿ 不打。

   天气不好 ＿＿ 不打。

   tiānqì bù hǎo ＿＿＿ bù dǎ.

   Only when the weather is bad do they not play. (When the weather is bad, only then do they not play.)

CHAPTER 5

Prepositions and Prepositional Phrases

COMMONLY USED PREPOSITIONS

The following is a list of the most common Mandarin prepositions. Those that are only used in formal, literary contexts are marked as "Lit."

General Prepositions

跟	gēn	*with, from (receive from a source)*
給/给	gěi	*to/for (transmit to a person or do for the benefit of a person)*
替	tì	*for, on behalf of (a person)*
對/对	duì	*towards (in the direction of a person or location (does not involve movement)*
為/为	wéi	*for, on behalf of*
由	yóu	*by (a person or other initiator of the action), as a result of (Lit.)*
於/于	yú	*in, at on; by (a person or other initiator of the action) (Lit.)*
用	yòng	*with (an object which functions as an instrument)*

Prepositions Referring to Location or Time

到	dào	*to (location or time) (involves movement)*
從/从	cóng	*from (location or time) (involves movement)*
自從/自从	zìcóng	*from (time) (Lit.)*
在	zài	*at (location or time)*
進/进	jìn	*into (a location) (involves movement)*
出	chū	*out of (a location) (involves movement)*
往	wáng	*towards (a location; involves movement)*
朝	cháo	*towards (a person or location) (involves movement) (Lit.)*
向	xiàng	*towards (a person or location) (involves movement)*

PROPERTIES OF PREPOSITIONS AND PREPOSITIONAL PHRASES

- Prepositions must be followed by a NP. The NP that follows the preposition is the *object* of the preposition, and the preposition + object is a prepositional phrase (PP).

你有空嗎？我想跟你談話。

你有空吗？我想跟你谈话。

nǐ yǒu kōng ma? wǒ xiǎng gēn nǐ tán huà.

Do you have free time? I want to speak with/to you.

- In Mandarin, the PP goes before the Verb + Object. Note that in English, the PP goes after the Verb + Object.

他每天跟女朋友聊天。

tā měitiān gēn nǚ péngyou liáo tiān.

He chats with his girlfriend every day.

- Nothing goes between the PP and the following verb. Adverbs, and other modifiers either go before the PP or after the object of the verb:

Correct	**Incorrect**
這本書請你再給我看看。	⊗這本書請你給我再看看。
这本书请你再给我看看。	这本书请你给我再看看。
zhè běn shū qǐng nǐ zài gěi wǒ kàn kàn.	zhè běn shū qǐng nǐ gěi wǒ zài kàn kàn.
This book, please read it to me again.	
(Please read this book to me again.)	
我明天會給他打電話。	⊗我明天給他會打電話。
我明天会给他打电话。	我明天给他会打电话。
wǒ míngtiān huì gěi tā dǎ diànhuà.	wǒ míngtiān gěi tā huì dǎ diànhuà.
I will call him tomorrow.	

THE MEANING OF MANDARIN PREPOSITIONS

Mandarin prepositions are often somewhat different from prepositions in English in the meaning they convey.

One English Preposition, Several Different Mandarin Prepositions

To

- If the preposition indicates movement <u>to</u> a location or time, with the location as the intended destination, the Mandarin preposition is 到 dào.

我到圖書館去了。

我到图书馆去了。

wǒ dào túshūguǎn qù le.

I went to the park.

我每天上午九點到下午三點上課。

我每天上午九点到下午三点上课。

wǒ měitiān shàngwǔ jiǔ diǎn dào xiàwǔ sāndiǎn shàng kè.

I attend class every day from 9 a.m. to 3 p.m.

- If the preposition indicates movement <u>towards</u> a direction or location which is not the final destination, the Mandarin preposition is 往 wǎng, 向 xiàng, or 朝 cháo.

他往北走了。

tā wǎng běi zǒu le.

He went (<u>towards</u> the) north.

他向 山走了。

tā xiàng shān zǒu le.

He went <u>towards</u> the mountains.

- If the preposition indicates a recipient, the Mandarin preposition is 給/给 gěi.

昨天晚上我給媽媽寫信了。

昨天晚上我给妈妈写信了。

zuótiān wǎnshang wǒ gěi māma xiě xìn le.

Last night I wrote a letter <u>to</u> mom. (to: Mom is the recipient)

With

- If the preposition indicates joint participant in some situation described by the verb, the Mandarin preposition is 跟 gēn.

我每天跟朋友吃午飯。

我每天跟朋友吃午饭。

wǒ měitiān gēn péngyou chī wǔfàn.

I eat lunch <u>with</u> friends every day.

- If the preposition indicates an instrument used by the subject to perform the action of the verb, the Mandarin preposition is 用 yòng.

我不會用毛筆寫字。

我不会用毛笔写字。

wǒ bú huì yòng máobǐ xiě zì.

I can't write characters <u>with</u> a Chinese writing brush.

One Mandarin Preposition, Several Different English Prepositions

給/给 gěi

- If the preposition indicates the beneficiary of the action, the English preposition is *for*.

  孩子想給媽媽做晚飯。
  孩子想给妈妈做晚饭。
  háizi xiǎng gěi māma zuò wǎnfàn.
  The children are planning to cook dinner for mom.

- If the preposition indicates the recipient of the object of the verb, the English preposition is *to*.

  弟弟給他女朋友送了花。
  弟弟给他女朋友送了花。
  dìdi gěi tā nǚ péngyou sòng le huā.
  Younger brother sent flowers to his girlfriend.

Preposition with Idiomatic Meaning

- To express *interest in* something, the Mandarin preposition is 對/对 duì in the following expression.

  對 NP 有興趣
  对 NP 有兴趣
  duì NP yǒu xìngqù
  to be interested in NP

  我對科學有興趣。
  我对科学有兴趣。
  wǒ duì kēxué yǒu xìngqu.
  I am interested in science.

Prepositions Associated with Formal, Literary Language

朝 cháo *towards*

朝前走。你可以看到一個學校。
朝前走。你可以看到一个学校。
cháo qián zǒu. nǐ kéyǐ kàndào yī ge xuéxiào.
Go straight ahead. (lit: Go towards the front.) You can see a school.

於/于 yú *in, at, on*

這個學校成立於一八四三年。

这个学校成立于一八四三年。

zhè ge xuéxiào chénglì yú yī bā sì sān nián.
This school was established <u>in</u> 1843.

由 yóu *by*

這件事情由他自己去做吧。

这件事情由他自己去做吧。

zhè jiàn shìqing yóu tā zìjǐ qù zuò ba.
This matter should be taken care of <u>by</u> him.

自從/自从 (date) (以來/以来) zì cóng (date) (yǐ lái) *from (date)*

自從一九九一年以來，中國不斷地發展。

自从一九九一年以来，中国不断地发展。

zìcóng yī jiǔ jiǔ yī nián yǐlái, Zhōngguó búduàn de fāzhǎn.
Since 1991 China has been developing continuously.

PREPOSITIONS AND VERBS

Some words function either as a preposition or as a verb depending upon the context.

		Preposition	Verb
對/对	duì	*to/towards*	*to be correct*
給/给	gěi	*to/for*	*to give*
跟	gēn	*with*	*to follow*
到	dào	*to (a location)*	*to arrive*
進/进	jìn	*into*	*to enter*

The context will always make it clear whether a word is functioning as a preposition or as a verb. If it is a preposition, it will always be followed by an object NP and then by a verb. If it is a verb, it may be followed by an object NP, but the object NP will not be followed by a verb. Compare these:

		as a Preposition	**as a Verb**
對/对	duì	他没對我说話。	不對！
		他没对我说话。	不对！
		tā méi duì wǒ shuō huà.	bú duì!
		He did not speak to me.	*not correct!*

給/给	gěi	我想給媽媽寫信。 我想给妈妈写信。 wǒ xiǎng gěi māma xiě xìn. *I'm planning to write a letter to mom.*	他不願意給我錢。 他不愿意给我钱。 tā bú yuànyi gěi wǒ qián. *He's not willing to give me money.*
跟	gēn	我每個週末跟他吃飯。 我每个周末跟他吃饭。 wǒ měi ge zhōumò gēn tā chī fàn. *I eat with him every weekend.*	弟弟老跟着媽媽。 弟弟老跟着妈妈。 dìdi lǎo gēnzhe māma. *Little brother is always following mom.*
到	dào	你什麼時候到我家來？ 你什么时候到我家来？ nǐ shénme shíhòu dào wǒ jiā lái? *When are you coming to my house?*	你什麼時候到？ 你什么时候到？ nǐ shénme shíhòu dào? *When do you arrive?*
進/进	jìn	他進城去了。 他进城去了。 tā jìn chéng qù le. *He went into the city.*	請進。 请进。 qǐng jìn. *Please enter.*

給/给 gěi as a Verb Suffix

給/给 gěi may serve as a suffix on verbs which involve the movement of a direct object to a recipient:

借給/借给	jiègěi	*loan to*
送給/送给	sònggěi	*send to*
賣給/卖给	màigěi	*sell to*
還給/还给	huángěi	*return to*

In these structures, the recipient follows the verb + 給/给 gěi. The direct object of the verb is typically presented as the object of 把 bǎ:

我把我的車賣給他了。
我把我的车卖给他了。
wǒ bǎ wǒ de chē màigěi tā le.
I sold my car to him.

他把禮物送給老師了。
他把礼物送给老师了。
tā bǎ lǐwù sònggěi lǎoshī le.
He presented a gift to the teacher.

1. Complete these sentences by adding the appropriate preposition to match the English meanings.

1. 我不想 ＿＿＿ 他说話了。

   我不想 ＿＿＿ 他说话了。

   wǒ bù xiǎng ＿＿＿ tā shuō huà le.
   I don't want to speak with him anymore.

2. 我弟弟 ＿＿＿＿＿＿ 科學很有興趣。

   我弟弟 ＿＿＿＿＿＿ 科学很有兴趣。

   wǒ dìdi ＿＿＿＿＿ kēxué hěn yǒu xìngqù.
   My younger brother is very interested in science.

3. 他 ＿＿＿ 媽媽说「我長大了要當科學家。」

   他 ＿＿＿ 妈妈说「我长大了要当科学家。」

   tā ＿＿＿ māma shuō "wǒ zhǎng dà le yào dāng kēxué jiā."
   He said to mom "When I grow up I want to be a scientist."

4. 孩子＿＿＿＿媽媽包餃子。姐姐＿＿＿ 朋友出去買東西。

   孩子＿＿＿＿妈妈包饺子。姐姐＿＿＿ 朋友出去买东西。

   háizi ＿＿＿ māma bāo jiǎozi. jiějie ＿＿＿ péngyou chūqu mǎi dōngxi.
   The children wrap dumplings with mom. Older sister is going out with her friends to buy things.

5. 我 ＿＿＿ 我朋友買了電影票。

   我 ＿＿＿ 我朋友买了电影票。

   wǒ ＿＿＿ wǒ péngyou mǎi le diànyǐng piào.
   I bought a movie ticket for my friend.

6. 父母 ＿＿＿ 客人很客氣。

   父母 ＿＿＿ 客人很客气。

   fùmǔ ＿＿＿ kèren hěn kèqi.
   Father and mother are very polite to guests.

7. 我們 ＿＿＿ 上走吧。

   我们 ＿＿＿ 上走吧。

   wǒmen ＿＿＿ shàng zǒu ba.
   Let's go up.

8. 我的男朋友每天 ＿＿＿ 我寫信。

   我的男朋友每天 ＿＿＿ 我写信。

   wǒ de nán péngyou měitiān ＿＿＿ wǒ xiě xìn.
   My boyfriend writes to me every day.

9. 今天的天氣非常好。我們 ＿＿＿ 公園裏吃飯吧。

今天的天气非常好。我们 ＿＿＿ 公园里吃饭吧。

jīntiān de tiānqì fēicháng hǎo. wǒmen ＿＿＿ gōngyuán lǐ chī fàn ba.

Today's weather is extremely good. Let's eat in the park.

10. Q: 你是 ＿＿＿ 哪兒來的？ A: 我是 ＿＿＿ 波士頓來的。

　　 你是 ＿＿＿ 哪儿来的？　　 我是 ＿＿＿ 波士顿来的。

　　 nǐ shì ＿＿＿ nǎr lái de?　　　 wǒ shì ＿＿＿ Bōshìdùn lái de.

Q: Where are you from?　　　 A: I am from Boston.

11. 王老師 ＿＿＿ 張老師上課了。

王老师 ＿＿＿ 张老师上课了。

Wáng lǎoshī ＿＿＿ Zhāng lǎoshī shàng kè le.

Teacher Wang taught class for Teacher Zhang.

12. 我 ＿＿＿ 地理有興趣。

我 ＿＿＿ 地理有兴趣。

wǒ ＿＿＿ dìlǐ yǒu xìngqù.

I am interested in geography.

13. 我每個週末開 ＿＿＿ 紐約去吃中國飯。

我每个周末开 ＿＿＿ 纽约去吃中国饭。

wǒ měi ge zhōumò kāi ＿＿＿ Niǔyuē qù chī Zhōngguó fàn.

Every weekend I drive to New York to eat Chinese food.

14. 汽車 ＿＿＿ 建國門駛去。

汽车 ＿＿＿ 建国门驶去。

qìchē ＿＿＿ Jiànguó Mén shǐqù.

The car is driving towards Jianguo Gate.

15. 這件事 ＿＿＿您處理。

这件事 ＿＿＿您处理。

zhè jiàn shì ＿＿＿ nín chùlǐ.

This matter should be handled by you.

16. 侍者 ＿＿＿ 客人打開車門。

侍者 ＿＿＿ 客人打开车门。

shìzhě ＿＿＿ kèren dǎkāi chē mén.

The attendant opened the car door for the guests.

CHAPTER 6

The Suffixes 了 le , 着 zhe, and 過/过 guo

了 le

了 le may occur at the end of the sentence (S-了 le) or it may follow the verb (V-了 le). The meaning contributed by 了 le in a sentence depends upon whether it is S-了 le or V-了 le. The properties of these two types of 了 le are as follows.

S-了 le

Sentence-final 了 le (S-了 le) indicates that the sentence provides information that is new in some way.

- The situation is a change from a previous situation.

  你長得很高了！
  你长得很高了！
  nǐ zhǎng de hěn gāo le !
  You have grown tall!/You have become tall!

- The situation is new information for the listener.

  我不吃肉了。
  wǒ bù chī ròu le.
  I don't eat meat now/anymore.

- The situation is about to happen. 快 kuài, here meaning *soon*, or 快要 kuài yào, marking future time, can occur at the beginning of the VP.

  她快(要)畢業了。
  她快(要)毕业了。
  tā kuài (yào) bì yè le.
  She graduates soon.

S-了 occurs before the question marker 嗎/吗 ma and other sentence-final particles.

他的病好了嗎？

他的病好了吗？

tā de bìng hǎo le ma?

Has his illness gotten better?

東西貴了吧。

东西贵了吧。

dōngxi guì le ba.

Things have probably gotten more expensive.

In negated sentences, negation + S-了 can be translated as *not anymore*.

我<u>不</u>愛你<u>了</u>。

我<u>不</u>爱你<u>了</u>。

wǒ <u>bú</u> ài nǐ <u>le</u>.

I don't love you anymore.

1. Translate the following Mandarin sentence into English, capturing the meaning of S-了 in each sentence.

1. 你的孩子高了。

   nǐ de háizi gāo le.

2. 我今天早晨坐了公共汽車了。   (公共汽車/公共汽车

   我今天早晨坐了公共汽车了。   gōnggòng qìchē *public bus*)

   wǒ jīntiān zǎochén zuò le gōnggòng qìchē le.

3. 我不吃早飯了。

   我不吃早饭了。

   wǒ bù chī zǎofàn le.

4. 妹妹說她不喜歡你了。

   妹妹说她不喜欢你了。

   mèimei shuō tā bù xǐhuan nǐ le.

5. 弟弟寫字寫得很快了。

   弟弟写字写得很快了。

   dìdi xiě zì xiě de hěn kuài le.

6. 我這個星期很忙了。

   我这个星期很忙了。

   wǒ zhè ge xīngqī hěn máng le.

7. 我不坐飛機了。   (飛機/飞机 fēijī *a plane*)

   我不坐飞机了。

   wǒ bú zuò fēijī le .

8. 我不想考試了。   (考試/考试 kǎo shì *to take a test*)

   我不想考试了。

   wǒ bù xiǎng kǎo shì le .

9. 今天忽然冷了。   (冷 lěng *cold*)

   jīntiān hūrán lěng le.

10. 我們已經走了很遠了。我累了，不能走了。(累 lèi *tired*)

    我们已经走了很远了。我累了，不能走了。

    wǒmen yǐjing zǒu le hěn yuǎn le. wǒ lèi le, bù néng zǒu le.

V-了 le

V-了 le in Independent Sentences

The verb suffix 了 le (V-了 le) signals the termination of an action.[*] When V-了 le is suffixed to the last verb of the sentence, it may also be interpreted as conveying past tense. Here are the characteristics of V-了 le.

- V-了 le only occurs in affirmative sentences.

  我已經吃了早飯。

  我已经吃了早饭。

  wǒ yǐjing chīle zǎo fàn.
  I already ate breakfast.

  老師買了很多書。

  老师买了很多书。

  lǎoshī mǎile hěn duō shū.
  Teacher bought a lot of books.

  她昨天看了電影。

  她昨天看了电影。

  tā zuótiān kànle diànyǐng.
  She saw a movie yesterday.

---

[*] Linguists refer to this as 'perfective aspect.' For more on aspect in Mandarin see Smith, Carlota. *The Parameter of Aspect*. Dordrecht and Boston: Kluwer Academic Publishers, 1991.

▪ V-了 le can only be suffixed onto activity verbs and achievement verbs. Stative verbs are never suffixed with V-了 le. 了 le can follow a stative verb, but only if the stative verb occurs at the end of the sentence and conveys the sense of change or new information. In this case, 了 le has the meaning of S-了 le.

我喜歡豆腐了。   ☹我喜歡了豆腐。
我喜欢豆腐了。   我喜欢了豆腐。
wǒ xǐhuan dòufu le.   wǒ xǐhuanle dòufu.
I like beancurd now.

飛機票最近漲價了。
飞机票最近涨价了。
fēijī piào zuìjìn zhǎngjià le.
Airplane tickets have recently gone up in price.

▪ If a verb suffixed with V-了 le has a one-syllable object, V-了 le typically occurs after the object. If the object is two or more syllables, V-了 le occurs directly after the V.

我已經吃飯了。
我已经吃饭了。
wǒ yǐjing chī fàn le.
I already ate.

我吃了早飯了。
我吃了早饭了。
wǒ chīle zǎofàn le.
I ate breakfast.

2. Rewrite these sentences, adding V-了 where appropriate, to correspond to the meaning of the following English sentences.

1. 我看一個電影。
   我看一个电影。
   wǒ kàn yī ge diànyǐng.
   I saw a movie.

2. 我吃晚飯。
   我吃晚饭。
   wǒ chī wǎnfàn.
   I ate dinner.

3. 哥哥畢業。

   哥哥毕业。

   gēge bì yè.
   Older brother graduated.

4. 我今天早上考試。

   我今天早上考试。

   wǒ jīntiān zǎoshang kǎo shì.
   I took a test this morning.

5. 我這個星期考中文。

   我这个星期考中文。

   wǒ zhè ge xīngqī kǎo Zhōngwén.
   I took a Chinese test this week.

6. 我今天早上買兩枝鉛筆。

   我今天早上买两枝铅笔。

   wǒ jīntiān zǎoshang mǎi liǎngzhī qiānbǐ.
   This morning I bought two pencils.

7. 我們昨天晚上吃意大利菜。

   我们昨天晚上吃意大利菜。

   wǒmen zuótiān wǎnshang chī Yìdàlì cài.
   Last night we ate Italian food.

8. 他們在海邊玩一天。

   他们在海边玩一天。

   tāmen zài hǎibiān wán yītiān.
   They had fun at the beach for a whole day.

9. 我在香港住幾個月。

   我在香港住几个月。

   wǒ zài Xiānggǎng zhù jǐ ge yuè.
   I lived in Hong Kong for several months.

10. 我昨天晚上看電視看半個小時。

    我昨天晚上看电视看半个小时。

    wǒ zuótiān wǎnshang kàn diànshì kàn bàn ge xiǎoshí.
    Last night I watched television for half an hour.

11. 昨天晚上宿舍很冷。

    昨天晚上宿舍很冷。

    zuótiān wǎnshang sùshè hěn lěng.
    Last night the dormitory was very cold.

12. 我在北京看幾次京劇。

我在北京看几次京剧。

wǒ zài Běijīng kàn jǐ cì jīngjù.

I saw Beijing Opera several times in Beijing.

Non-occurrence of Events: 没有＋V méi yǒu ＋ V

V- 了 le indicates that an event occurred. It cannot be used in negative sentences. To indicate that *an event did not happen in the past*, the verb is preceded by 没 méi or 没有 méi yǒu and is not followed by 了 le. Compare the following:

我没吃早飯。

我没吃早饭。

wǒ méi chī zǎofàn.

I did not eat breakfast.

⊗ 我没吃了早飯。

我没吃了早饭。

wǒ méi chī le zǎofàn.

老師没買書。

老师没买书。

lǎoshī méi mǎi shū.

Teacher did not buy a book.

⊗ 老師没買了書。

老师没买了书。

lǎoshī méi mǎi le shū.

Note: 還没(有)/还没(有) hái méi (yǒu) + V can be translated as *not yet*.

我還没(有)吃早飯。

我还没(有)吃早饭。

wǒ hái méi (yǒu) chī zǎofàn.

I have not eaten breakfast yet.

老師還没(有)買書。

老师还没(有)买书。

lǎoshī hái méi (yǒu) mǎi shū.

Teacher has not bought a book yet.

3. Rewrite these sentences in Mandarin in negative form to indicate that the event did not occur. Translate your sentences into English.

1. 我昨天在公園裏跑步了。

我昨天在公园里跑步了。

wǒ zuótiān zài gōngyuán lǐ pǎo bù le.

I ran in the park yesterday.

2. 我妹妹買了毛衣。

我妹妹买了毛衣。

wǒ mèimei mǎi le máoyī.

My younger sister bought a sweater.

3. 我姐姐買了鞋子。

   我姐姐买了鞋子。

   wǒ jiějie mǎi le xiézi.

   My older sister bought shoes.

4. 妹妹今天穿了她的毛衣。

   mèimei jīntiān chuān le tā de máoyī.

   Younger sister wore her sweater today.

5. 弟弟昨天給他的女朋友寫信了。

   弟弟昨天给他的女朋友写信了。

   dìdi zuótiān gěi tā de nǚ péngyǒu xiě xìn le.

   Yesterday younger brother wrote a letter to his girlfriend.

6. 我哥哥昨天跟朋友打球了。

   wǒ gēge zuótiān gēn péngyou dǎ qiú le.

   My older brother played ball with his friends yesterday.

7. 我昨天晚上看了電視。

   我昨天晚上看了电视。

   wǒ zuótiān wǎnshang kàn le diànshì.

   I watched television last night.

8. 我昨天給媽媽寫了電子郵件。

   我昨天给妈妈写了电子邮件。

   wǒ zuótiān gěi māma xiě le diànzi yóujiàn.

   Yesterday I wrote an email to mom.

9. 我昨天晚上洗頭了。

   我昨天晚上洗头了。

   wǒ zuótiān wǎnshang xǐ tóu le.

   Last night I washed my hair.

10. 我今天早上上了中文課。

    我今天早上上了中文课。

    wǒ jīntiān zǎoshang shàng le Zhōngwén kè.

    This morning I attended Chinese class.

Sequence: V-了 in Serial Verb Phrases

A Mandarin sentence may include a series of verb phrases or clauses which are related in terms of sequence. Here are the characteristics of the use of V-了 to mark sequence.

- V-了 occurs directly after the first verb in the series.*

  我下了課回家去。
  我下了课回家去。
  wǒ xià le kè huí jiā qù.
  After I get out of class I go home.

- The adverb 就 jiù may occur before the second verb phrase.

  我下了課(就)回家去。
  我下了课(就)回家去。
  wǒ xià le kè (jiù) huí jiā qù.
  After I get out of class I return home.

- The sequence connector 以後/以后 yǐhòu may occur at the end of the first verb

  phrase. (See Chapter 12: Phrase and Clause Connection.)

  我下了課(以後)就回家去。
  我下了课(以后)就回家去。
  wǒ xià le kè (yǐhòu)jiù huí jiā qù.
  After I get out of class I return home.

Note: Any or all of V-了, 就 jiù, and 以後/以后 yǐhòu may be omitted from
sequence sentences.

  每天都一樣。下課回家。
  每天都一样。下课回家。
  měitiān dōu yīyàng. xià kè huí jiā.
  Every day is the same. (I) get out of class and return home.

Sequence in the Past

To indicate that the entire sequence occurred in the past, V-了 must also occur in
the second verb phrase, either after the verb, or, if the verb has a one-syllable object, at
the end of the sentence.

  我下了課(就)回家去了。
  我下了课(就)回家去了。
  wǒ xià le kè (jiù)huí jiā qù le.
  After I got out of class I returned home.

---

* Some speakers permit V-了 to occur after the object of the verb.

我們吃了晚飯以後就看了電影。

我們吃了晚飯以後就看了電影。

wǒmen chī le wǎnfàn yǐhòu jiù kàn le diànyǐng.

After we ate dinner we saw a movie.

4. Translate the following sequence sentences into English. Make sure to determine whether the sentence refers to a past or non-past sequence of events.

1. 弟弟看了電影就回家。

   弟弟看了电影就回家。

   dìdi kàn le diànyǐng jiù huí jiā.

2. 我買了車就開到紐約去了。

   我买了车就开到纽约去了。

   wǒ mǎi le chē jiù kāi dào Niǔyuē qù le.

3. 我們吃了飯就上課。(上課/上课 shàng kè *attend class*)

   我们吃了饭就上课。

   wǒmen chī le fàn jiù shàng kè.

4. 客人來了我們就說「歡迎」。(歡迎/欢迎 huānyíng *welcome*)

   客人来了我们就说「欢迎」。

   kèren lái le wǒmen jiù shuō「huānyíng」.

5. 那個孩子看了狗就哭了。(狗 gǒu *dog*, 哭 kū *cry*)

   那个孩子看了狗就哭了。

   nà ge háizi kàn le gǒu jiù kū le.

6. 我昨天晚上吃了晚飯以後就睡覺了。(睡覺/睡觉 shuì jiào *sleep*)

   我昨天晚上吃了晚饭以后就睡觉了。

   wǒ zuótiān wǎnshang chī le wǎnfàn yǐhòu jiù shuì jiào le.

7. 他們回了家以後就看了電視。(電視/电视 diànshì *television*)

   他们回了家以后就看了电视。

   tāmen huí le jiā yǐhòu jiù kàn le diànshì.

8. 我姐姐買了東西以後就拿回家給我看看。(東西/东西

   我姐姐买了东西以后就拿回家给我看看。　dōngxi *things*)

   wǒ jiějie mǎi le dōngxi yǐhòu jiù ná huí jiā gěi wǒ kàn kàn.

9. 你畢了業以後做什麼？(畢業/毕业 bì yè *graduate*)

   你毕了业以后做什么？

   nǐ bì le yè yǐhòu zuò shénme?

10. 她每天起了床就喝一杯茶。(起床 qǐ chuáng *get out of bed*)
tā měitiān qǐ le chuáng jiù hē yī bēi chá.

5. Translate these into Mandarin.

1. After I take the test I will see a movie.
2. After I graduate I will go to China.
3. Yesterday, after I got out of class I went to the park.
4. I reviewed Chinese and then watched television.
5. After we get out of class let's go to the park.

Double 了 le

A sentence may contain V-了 le and S-了 le. V-了 le indicates that the action of the verb is completed. S-了 le indicates that the information presented in the sentence is a change of some kind or is new to the listener.

Q: 你想吃早飯嗎？
你想吃早饭吗？
nǐ xiǎng chī zǎofàn ma?
Do you want to eat breakfast?

A: 我已經吃了早飯(了)。
我已经吃了早饭(了)。
wǒ yǐjing chī le zǎofàn (le).
I already ate breakfast.

Q: 那本書你還在看嗎？
那本书你还在看吗？
nà běn shū nǐ hái zài kàn ma?
You're still reading that book?

A: 我已經看了一半了。明天就可以看完。
我已经看了一半了。明天就可以看完。
wǒ yǐjing kàn le yī bàn le. míngtiān jiù kéyǐ kàn wán.
I've already read half. I'll finish it tomorrow.

V-着 zhe

The verb suffix V-着 zhe marks the duration or continuity of a situation.* V-着 zhe serves as a suffix on activity verbs and on achievement verbs which have resulting states. (See Chapter 3: Verbs and Verb Phrases.)

Here are the primary functions of V-着 zhe.

- V-着 zhe signals that an activity is ongoing. In this case, the verb may be preceded by 在 zài, 正 zhèng, or 正在 zhèng zài. The sentence may be

* Linguists refer to the meaning conveyed by V-着 zhe as 'imperfective aspect.'

concluded with the final particle 呢 ne. Note that 着 zhe, 在 zài, 正 zhèng and 呢 ne are all optional and may be omitted. Chinese speakers vary in their use of these words.

他正開着車。
他正开着车。
tā zhèng kāizhe chē.
He is driving the car.

他在開着車呢。
他在开着车呢。
tā zài kāizhe chē ne.
He is driving a car.

- V-着 zhe emphasizes the duration or unchanging nature of a situation.

孩子在地板上坐着。
háizi zài dìbǎn shàng zuòzhe.
The children are sitting on the floor.

貓在沙發上躺着。
猫在沙发上躺着。
māo zài shāfā shàng tǎngzhe.
The cat is lying on the sofa.

牆上掛着一張山水畫兒。
墙上挂着一张山水画儿。
qiáng shàng guàzhe yī zhāng shānshuǐ huàr.
There is a landscape painting hanging on the wall.

- V-着 zhe signals that two situations occur at the same time.

他們看着電視吃東西。
他们看着电视吃东西。
tāmen kànzhe diànshì chī dōngxi.
They are watching television and eating.

- V-着 zhe signals that a situation is background to a more important event.

老師讓學生站着念書。
老师让学生站着念书。
lǎoshī ràng xuésheng zhànzhe niàn shū.
The teacher made the students recite standing up.

她拉着孩子的手過馬路。

她拉着孩子的手过马路。

tā lāzhe háizi de shǒu guò mǎlù.

Holding the child's hand, she crosses the street.

我們握着手談話。

我们握着手谈话。

wǒmen wòzhe shǒu tán huà.

Shaking hands, we chatted.

那個媽媽背着孩子做飯。

那个妈妈背着孩子做饭。

nà ge māma bēizhe háizi zuò fàn.

The mother cooked holding the child on her back.

6. Translate these Mandarin sentences into English.

1. 我在吃着飯呢。

  我在吃着饭呢。

  wǒ zài chīzhe fàn ne.

2. 他正唱着歌呢。

  tā zhèng chàngzhe gē ne.

3. 他正玩着球呢。

  tā zhèng wánzhe qiú ne.

4. 小明正做着功課。

  Xiǎo Míng zhèng zuòzhe gōngkè.

5. 安静！老師正在説話呢。

  安静！老师正在说话呢。

  ānjìng! lǎoshī zhèng zài shuō huà ne.

6. 老師坐着跟學生説話。

  老师坐着跟学生说话。

  lǎoshī zuòzhe gēn xuésheng shuō huà.

7. 爸爸看着書吃早飯。

  爸爸看着书吃早饭。

  bàba kànzhe shū chī zǎofàn.

8. 錢太太拿着書走到圖書館去了。

  钱太太拿着书走到图书馆去了。

  Qián tàitai názhe shū zǒu dào túshūguǎn qù le.

9. 學生常聽着音樂做功課。

 学生常听着音乐做功课。

 xuésheng cháng tīngzhe yīnyuè zuò gōngkè.

10. 媽媽喝着咖啡看報紙。

 妈妈喝着咖啡看报纸。

 māma hēzhe kāfēi kàn bàozhǐ.

V-過/过 guo

In addition to functioning as a full verb, 過/过 guo can serve as a verb suffix that indicates that the speaker has performed an activity before. V-過/过 guo is sometimes called the *experiential* suffix, since it indicates that the subject has had the experience of performing the action some time in the past.[*]

The following are the characteristics of V-過/过 guo:

- V-過/过 guo can serve as a suffix on verbs which describe repeatable events.

Repeatable Event	**Non-Repeatable Event**
我來過這裏。	⊗我忘過你的名字。
我来过这里。	我忘过你的名字。
wǒ láiguo zhèlǐ.	wǒ wàngguo nǐde míngzi.
I've come here before.	*I've forgotten your name before.*
我吃過中國飯。	⊗我認識過他。
我吃过中国饭。	我认识过他。
wǒ chīguo Zhōngguo fàn.	wǒ rènshiguo tā.
I have eaten Chinese food before.	*I've met him before. (You can only MEET someone for the first time once.)*
那個電影我已經看過了。	⊗他死過。
那个电影我已经看过了。	他死过。
nà ge diànyǐng wǒ yǐjing kànguo le.	tā sǐguo.
That movie I've seen already.	*He has died before.*
我去過中國。	
我去过中国。	
wǒ qùguo Zhōngguo.	
I have been to China before.	

---

[*] See Li, Charles and Sandra Thompson. Mandarin Chinese: A Functional Reference Grammar. Berkeley: University of California Press, 1981, p. 226.

- V-過/过 guo indicates that V occurred at a time removed from present time.

  Compare the meaning contributed by 過/过 guo and 了 le in the following

  sentences.

他斷過他的大腿。	他斷了他的大腿。
他断过他的大腿。	他断了他的大腿。
tā duànguo tā de dàtuǐ.	tā duànle tā de dàtuǐ.
He broke his leg before (sometime in the past and it is now healed.)	*He broke his leg (and at the time of speaking it is still broken.)*

- V-過/过 guo can occur in negative, as well as affirmative sentences.

  我沒去過中國。

  我没去过中国。

  wǒ méi qùguo Zhōngguo.
  I have never been to China before.

  In affirmative sentences with V-過/过 guo, the adverb 已經/已经 yǐjing *already*

  or 曾經/曾经 céngjīng *already* may occur before the verb phrase. (See Chapter 4:

  Adverbs.) In negative sentences, the adverb 還/还 hái may occur before the negated

  verb phrase, indicating *not yet*.

  我已經去過中國。

  我已经去过中国。

  wǒ yǐjing qùguo Zhōngguo.
  I have already been to China before.

  我還沒去過中國。

  我还没去过中国。

  wǒ hái méi qùguo Zhōngguo.
  I have not been to China yet.

- V-過/过 guo can occur with V-了 le. When they both occur, 過/过 guo precedes

  了 le.

  我看過了那部電影。

  我看过了那部电影。

  wǒ kànguo le nà bù diànyǐng.
  I have seen that movie.

7. Translate the following Mandarin sentences into English.

    1. 我已經看過那本書。我不要再看了。

      我已经看过那本书。我不要再看了。

      wǒ yǐjing kànguo nà běn shū. wǒ bú yào zài kàn le.

    2. 媽媽學過日語，可是她没去過日本。

      妈妈学过日语，可是她没去过日本。

      māma xuéguo Rìyǔ, kěshì tā méi qùguo Rìběn.

    3. 我没吃過法國飯。

      我没吃过法国饭。

      wǒ méi chīguo Fǎguo fàn.

    4. 你開過車嗎？

      你开过车吗？

      nǐ kāiguo chē ma?

    5. 我們在中國的時候坐過公共汽車。

      我们在中国的时候坐过公共汽车。

      wǒmen zài Zhōngguó de shíhou zuòguo gōnggòng qìchē.

    6. 我没去過老師的家。你去過嗎？

      我没去过老师的家。你去过吗？

      wǒ méi qùguo lǎoshī de jiā. nǐ qùguo ma?

    7. 我没看過中國電影。

      我没看过中国电影。

      wǒ méi kànguo Zhōngguó diànyǐng.

    8. 我曾經用過毛筆寫字。

      我曾经用过毛笔写字。

      wǒ céngjīng yòngguo máobǐ xiě zì.

8. Answer the following questions truthfully in Mandarin. use 過/过 guo in all of your answers.

    1. Have you been to China before?

    2. Have you eaten Beijing duck before? (北京烤鴨 /北京烤鸭 Běijīng kǎoyā *Beijing roast duck*)

    3. Have you played frisbee before? (玩飛盤/玩飞盘 wán fēipán *play frisbee*)

    4. Have you seen the Great Wall before? (萬里長城/万里长城 Wànlǐ Chángchéng *the Great Wall*)

5. Have you sung karaoke before? (唱卡拉 OK chàng kǎlā OK *sing karaoke*)

6. Have you cooked Chinese food before? (做中國飯/做中国饭 zuò Zhōngguó fàn *cook Chinese food*)

7. Have you read a Chinese newspaper before? (看中文報紙/看中文报纸 kàn Zhōngwén bàozhǐ *read Chinese newspaper*)

8. Have you driven a sportscar before? (開跑車/开跑车 kāi pǎochē *drive sportscar*)

9. Have you drunk green tea before? (喝綠茶/喝绿茶 hē lǜ chá *drink green tea*)

10. Have you seen Beijing Opera before? (看京劇/看京剧 kàn jīngjù *see Beijing Opera*)

CHAPTER 7

The Resultative Structure and Potential Suffixes

THE RESULTATIVE STRUCTURE

Activity verbs (e.g. 看 kàn *to read/to look*, 寫/写 xiě *to write*, 聽/听 tīng *to listen*, 買/买 mǎi *to shop*) refer to open-ended actions without a specified result or conclusion. To indicate the result or conclusion of an activity, a resultative suffix (RV-suffix) is added to the activity verb. The verb that is formed is a 'resultative verb.' (For more on activity verbs see Chapter 3: Verbs and Verb Phrases.)

Activity Verb +	RV-Suffix	Resultative Verb
看 kàn *to read/to look*	完 wán *to finish*	看完 kànwán *to read to the point of finishing:* *to finish reading*
聽/听 tīng *to listen*	懂 dǒng *to understand*	聽懂/听懂 tīngdǒng *to listen to the point of understanding:* *to understand by hearing*

RV-suffixes are achievement verbs or stative verbs. Any verb whose meaning describes the result of an activity can function as an RV-suffix. Here is a list of some commonly occurring suffixes.

Common RV-Suffixes

到	dào	*acquire, obtain possession*
完	wán	*finish*
見/见	jiàn	*perceive*
懂	dǒng	*understand*
好	hǎo	*reach a successful conclusion*
錯/错	cuò	*do incorrectly*
着	zháo	*acquire (like 到 dào)*
掉	diào	*to disappear or fall down*
起來/起来	qǐlai	*to raise up; to begin to do*
住	zhù	*to stick*
開/开	kāi	*to open*
飽/饱	bǎo	*to be full*

夠	gòu	*to be enough*
乾淨/干净	gānjìng	*to be clean*
醉	zuì	*to be drunk*
上	shàng	*on; to go up*
下	xià	*down; to go down*

那件事情我都忘掉了。

nà jiàn shìqing wǒ dōu wàngdiào le.

I completely forgot about that matter.

我買錯了課本。

我买错了课本。

wǒ mǎicuò le kèběn.

I bought the wrong textbook.

他把衣服洗乾淨了。

他把衣服洗乾淨了。

tā bǎ yīfu xǐ gānjìng le.

He washed the clothes clean.

我們説好了明天早上六點出發。

我们说好了明天早上六点出发。

wǒmen shuōhǎo le míngtiān zǎoshang liù diǎn chūfā.

We've agreed to leave tomorrow morning at 6 a.m.

她把門開開了。

她把门开开了。

tā bǎ mén kāikai le.

She opened the door.

你吃飽了嗎?

你吃饱了吗?

nǐ chībǎo le ma?

Are you full? Did you eat until you were full?

Resultative Verbs are Indivisible Words

The verb + resultative suffix forms a resultative verb, a single, indivisible word.

Aspectual suffixes must go at the end of the resultative verb, following the RV-suffix:

我昨天晚上看完了那本書。	⊗我昨天晚上看了完那本書。
我昨天晚上看完了那本书。	我昨天晚上看了完那本书。
wǒ zuótiān wǎnshang kànwán le nà běn shū.	wǒ zuótiān wǎnshang kàn le wán nà běn shū.
I finished that book last night.	

新的詞彙我都記住了。

新的词汇我都记住了。

xīn de cíhuì wǒ dōu jìzhu le.

*I memorized all of the new
vocabulary.*

⊗新的詞彙我都記了住。

新的词汇我都记了住。

xīn de cíhuì wǒ dōu jì le zhu.

Resultative Verbs and Negation

In negative form, resultative verbs typically describe events which did not occur.

Therefore, they are negated by 没 or 没有. (See Chapter 6: The Suffixes 了 le, 着 zhe,

and 過/过 guo.)

老師説的話，我都沒聽懂。

老师说的话，我都没听懂。

lǎoshī shuō de huà, wǒ dōu méi tīngdǒng.

I didn't understand at all what the teacher said.

你今天上了課嗎？我没看到你。

你今天上了课吗？我没看到你。

nǐ jīntiān shàng le kè ma? wǒ méi kàndào nǐ.

Did you got to class today? I didn't see you.

1. Select the correct resultative verb to complete each sentence.

  1. 我妹妹學得很好。中文書她都 ＿＿＿ 了。(看見，看完，看懂)

     我妹妹学得很好。中文书她都 ＿＿＿ 了。(看见，看完，看懂)

     wǒ mèimei xué de hěn hǎo. Zhōngwén shū tā dōu ＿＿＿ le.

     (kànjian, kàn wán, kàndǒng)

     *My younger sister studies well. She completely understands her Chinese
books.*

  2. 我還沒 ＿＿＿ 中英字典。(買到，買錯，買起來)

     我还没 ＿＿＿ 中英字典。(买到，买错，买起来)

     wǒ hái méi ＿＿＿ Zhōngyīng zìdiǎn. (mǎidào, mǎicuò, mǎiqilai)

     I still haven't bought a Chinese English dictionary.

  3. 對不起。我 ＿＿＿ 了你的名字。(寫完，寫好，寫錯)

     对不起。我 ＿＿＿ 了你的名字。(写完，写好，写错)

     duìbuqǐ. wǒ ＿＿＿ le nǐ de míngzi. (xiěwán, xiěhǎo, xiěcuò)

     I'm sorry. I wrote your name wrong.

  4. 這本書我還沒 ＿＿＿ 。(看完，看到，看見)

     这本书我还没 ＿＿＿ 。(看完，看到，看见)

     zhè běn shū wǒ hái méi ＿＿＿. (kànwán, kàndào, kànjian)

     I still haven't finished reading this book.

5. Q: 你 ___ 了那個小鳥嗎？ A: ___ 了。(看完，看到，看見)

   你 ___ 了那个小鸟吗？　___ 了。(看完，看到，看见)

   nǐ ___ le nà ge xiǎo niǎo ma? ___ le. (kànwán, kàndào, kànjian)

   Q: Did you see that little bird?　A: I saw it.

6. 我們 ___ 了那個中國電影。(看到，看好，看懂)

   我们 ___ 了那个中国电影。(看到，看好，看懂)

   wǒmen ___ le nà ge Zhōngguó diànyǐng. (kàndào, kànhǎo, kàndǒng)

   We understood (by watching) the Chinese movie.

7. 我的錢都 ___ 了。(用好，用到，用完)

   我的钱都 ___ 了。(用好，用到，用完)

   wǒ de qián dōu ___ le. (yònghǎo, yòngdào, yòngwán)

   My money is all used up.

8. 你 ___ 了你朋友的家嗎？ (找到，找着，找完)

   你 ___ 了你朋友的家吗？ (找到，找着，找完)

   nǐ ___ le nǐ péngyou de jiā ma? (zhǎodào, zhǎozháo, zhǎowán)

   Did you find your friend's house?

9. 我的化學課本都沒 ___ 。(看懂，看完，看到)

   我的化学课本都没 ___ 。(看懂，看完，看到)

   wǒ de huàxué kèběn dōu méi ___ . (kàndǒng, kànwán, kàndào)

   I did not understand my chemistry textbook at all.

10. 老師叫我們把書 ___ 。(打起來，打開，打着)

   老师叫我们把书 ___ 。(打起来，打开，打着)

   lǎoshī jiào wǒmen bǎ shū ___ . (dǎqilai, dǎkāi, dǎzháo)

   Teacher told us to open up our books.

2. Answer each question in complete Mandarin sentences in the affirmative or negative as indicated.

1. 你找到了你的手錶嗎？

   你找到了你的手錶嗎？

   nǐ zhǎodào le nǐ de shóubiǎo ma?

   Did you find your watch?

   NO:

2. 你聽懂了老師的話嗎？

   你听懂了老师的话吗？

   nǐ tīngdǒng le lǎoshī de huà ma?

   Did you understand what the teacher said?

   YES:

3. 你把那個字寫錯了嗎？

   你把那个字写错了吗？

   nǐ bǎ nà ge zì xiěcuò le ma?
   YES:

4. 你寫完了那封信嗎？

   你写完了那封信吗？

   nǐ xiěwán le nà fēng xìn ma?
   Did you finish writing the letter?
   YES:

5. 你做完了作業嗎？

   你做完了作业吗？

   nǐ zuòwán le zuòyè ma?
   Did you finish doing your homework?
   NO:

6. 你買到了新的大衣嗎？

   你买到了新的大衣吗？

   nǐ mǎidào le xīn de dàyī ma?
   Did you buy a new overcoat?
   YES:

7. 你吃飽了嗎？

   你吃饱了吗？

   nǐ chībǎo le ma?
   Are you full? Did you eat until full?
   NO:

8. 你把你的行李收拾完了嗎？

   你把你的行李收拾完了吗？

   nǐ bǎ nǐde xíngli shōushí wán le ma?
   Did you finish packing your suitcases?
   YES:

9. 你找到了那個新的中國飯館嗎？

   你找到了那个新的中国饭馆吗？

   nǐ zhǎodào le nà ge xīn de Zhōngguó fànguǎn ma?
   Did you find that new Chinese restaurant?
   NO:

10. 你記住了那首詩嗎？

你记住了那首诗吗？

nǐ jìzhu le nà shǒu shī ma?

Did you memorize that poem?

   YES:

The Potential Form of Resultative Verbs

得 dé and 不 bù may occur between the activity verb and the RV-suffix to indicate the potential form of the resultative verb. Note that 得 and 不 occur in neutral tone in these expressions.

The Meaning of the Potential Form

- 得 de indicates that it is possible to achieve the result or conclusion specified by the RV-suffix:

這件衣服很大，你一定穿得上。

这件衣服很大，你一定穿得上。

zhè jiàn yīfú hěn dà, nǐ yīdìng chuāndeshàng.

This article of clothing is very big. You can certainly put it on.

那本書不太長，我想你一天看得完。

那本书不太长，我想你一天看得完。

nà běn shū bú tài cháng, wǒ xiǎng nǐ yītiān kàndewán 。

That book isn't very long. I think you can finish reading it in one day.

- 不 bù indicates that it is not possible to achieve the result or conclusion specified by the RV-suffix:

他説得太快，我聽不懂。

他说得太快，我听不懂。

tā shuō de tài kuài, wǒ tīngbudǒng.

He speaks too fast. I don't understand (by listening).

飯太多，我們可能吃不完。

饭太多，我们可能吃不完。

fàn tài duō, wǒmen kěnéng chībuwán.

There is too much food. We might not be able to finish eating it.

Note: Some resultative endings only occur in potential form:

V-得及 dejí *to be in time to V*

V-不及 bují *to not be in time to V*

快一點。還來得及上課。

快一点。还来得及上课。

kuài yīdiǎn. hái láidejí shàng kè.
Hurry up. We can still make it in time for class.

已經九點了。我們來不及看電影。

已经九点了。我们来不及看电影。

yǐjing jiǔ diǎn le. wǒmen láibují kàn diànyǐng.
It's already 9 o'clock. We won't be in time to see the movie.

V-得起 deqǐ *able to afford to V*

V-不起 buqǐ *unable to afford to V*

我買不起那個牌子的手錶。

我买不起那个牌子的手表。

wǒ mǎibuqǐ nà ge páizi de shóubiǎo.
I can't afford to buy that brand of watch.

我吃不起龍蝦。

我吃不起龙虾。

wǒ chībuqǐ lóngxiā.
I can't afford to eat lobster.

你住得起紐約市嗎？

你住得起纽约市吗？

nǐ zhùdeqǐ Niǔyuē shì ma?
Can you afford to live in New York City?

Note the special meaning of 看不起 kànbuqǐ *to look down on,* and the more restricted 看得起 kàndeqǐ *to show respect for.*

他看不起別人。

tā kànbuqǐ biéren.
He looks down on other people.

你這樣做，看得起誰？

你这样做，看得起谁？

nǐ zhèyàng zuò, kàndeqǐ shéi?
When you behave this way, who do you show respect for?

The Potential Form in Verb-NEG-Verb Questions

Resultative verbs in the potential form can be used in V-NEG-V questions. As with all V-NEG-V questions, the affirmative form precedes the negative form.

他的話，你聽得懂聽不懂？

他的话，你听得懂听不懂？

tā de huà, nǐ tīngdedǒng tīngbudǒng?

Can you understand what he says?

3. Complete these sentences with the appropriate resultative verb.

1. 他説得太快。我 _____ 。

   他说得太快。我 _____ 。

   tā shuō de tài kuài. wǒ _____ .

   He speaks too fast. I don't understand (by listening).

2. 書店没有這本書了。我 _____ 。

   书店没有这本书了。我 _____ 。

   shūdiàn méi yǒu zhè běn shū le. wǒ _____ .

   The bookstore doesn't have this book anymore. I can't buy it.

3. 你在圖書館 _____ 吧！

   你在图书馆 _____ 吧！

   nǐ zài túshūguǎn _____ ba!

   You can borrow it at the library!

4. 人太多。我怕你們 _____ 。

   人太多。我怕你们 _____ 。

   rén tài duō. wǒ pà nǐmen _____ .

   There are too many people. I'm afraid you won't be able to sit down.

5. 這些字太小。我 ___ 。

   这些字太小。我 ___ 。

   zhèxiē zì tài xiǎo. wǒ ___ .

   These characters are too small. I can't see (can't read) them.

6. 弟弟在哪兒？我們都 ___ 他。

   弟弟在哪儿？我们都 ___ 他。

   dìdi zài nǎr? wǒmen dōu ___ tā.

   Where is younger brother? We can't find him.

7. 我們一定 ___ 十個比薩餅。(比薩餅/比萨饼 bǐsà bǐng *pizza pies*)

   我们一定 ___ 十个比萨饼。

   wǒmen yīdìng ___ shí ge bǐsà bǐng。

   We certainly can't finish eating 10 pizzas.

8. 我 ___ 林肯車。

我 ___ 林肯车。

wǒ ___ Línkěn chē.

I can't afford a Lincoln Continental.

9. 我 ___ 外國人的名字。

我 ___ 外国人的名字。

wǒ ___ wàiguórén de míngzi.

I can't remember foreigners' names.

10. 你 ___ 黑板嗎？

你 ___ 黑板吗？

nǐ ___ hēibǎn ma?

Can you see the blackboard?

The Potential Form in Directional Expressions

得 de and 不 bù may be used in directional expressions to indicate the potential

form. When they are used, they occur between the verb of motion and the directional

suffix. (See also Chapter 9: Location, Directional Movement, and Distance.)

門太窄，這個沙發我們可能搬不進去。

门太窄，这个沙发我们可能搬不进去。

mén tài zhǎi. zhè ge shāfā wǒmen kěnéng bānbujìnqu.

The door is too narrow. We might not be able to move the sofa in.

4. Complete these sentences by adding the appropriate RV-ending to the verb. The RV-
ending in each sentence is a directional expression.

1. 我累了。走 _____ 。

wǒ lèi le. zǒu _____.

I'm too tired. I can't walk back.

2. 那個人太高。他進_____飛機的門。

那个人太高。他进_____飞机的门。

nà ge rén tài gāo. tā jìn _____ fēijī de mén.

That man is too tall. He cannot enter the airplane's door.

(movement is away from the speaker)

3. 那本字典太重。我拿_____。

那本字典太重。我拿_____。

nà běn zìdiǎn tài zhòng. wǒ ná_____.

That dictionary is too heavy. I can't pick it up.

4. 那座山太高。我們一定爬_____。(爬 pá *to climb*)

那座山太高。我们一定爬_____。

nà zuò shān tài gāo. wǒmen yīdìng pá_____.

That mountain is too tall. We certainly cannot climb up it.

5. 公園的門太低。車子開_____。

公园的门太低。车子开_____。

gōngyuán de mén tài dī. chēzi kāi_____.

The park gate is too low. Cars cannot drive in.

THE POTENTIAL SUFFIXES: -得了 deliǎo *able to* and -不了 buliǎo *unable to*

The potential suffixes -得了 deliǎo *able to* and -不了 buliǎo *unable to* follow activity verbs and achievement verbs. Notice that 得 and 不 occur in neutral tone in these expressions.

The Meaning of the Potential Suffixes

- -得了 deliǎo indicates that it is possible to perform the action described by the verb:

  她很有本事。將來做得了大事。

  她很有本事。将来做得了大事。

  tā hěn yǒu běnshi. jiānglái zuòdeliǎo dà shì.

  She has a lot of talent. In the future she will be able to do big things.

  我怎么能忘得了你的名字？

  wǒ zěnme néng wàngdeliǎo nǐde míngzi?

  How could I forget your name?

- -不了 buliǎo indicates that it is not possible to perform the action described by the verb:

  我開不了大卡車。

  我开不了大卡车。

  wǒ kāibuliǎo dà kǎchē.

  I am unable to drive a truck.

Compare the meaning of the potential suffixes with that of RV-suffixes.

Potential suffixes indicate that the action of the first verb may or may not happen.

RV-suffixes indicate that the result may or may not be obtained.

V + Resultative Suffix
V occurs; result is possible or not

這件事我今天 做得完。

这件事我今天 做得完。

zhè jiàn shì wǒ jīntiān zuòdewán.
I am able to finish this work today.

這件事我做不完。

这件事我做不完。

zhè jiàn shì wǒ zuòbuwán.
I am unable to finish this work.

V + Potential Suffix
Subject may or may not be able to do V

這件事我一定做得了。

这件事我一定做得了。

zhè jiàn shì wǒ yīdìng zuòdeliǎo.
I am definitely able to do this work.

這件事太複雜。恐怕我做不了。

这件事太复杂。恐怕我做不了。

zhè jiàn shì tài fùzá. kǒngpà wǒ
zuòbuliǎo.
*This matter is too confusing. I am afraid
I am unable to do it.*

5. Translate these sentences into English.

1. 我沒有錢。買不了東西。

   我没有钱。买不了东西。

   wǒ méi yǒu qián. mǎibuliǎo dōngxi.

2. 沒有筷子。我們吃不了飯。(筷子 kuàizi *chopsticks*)

   没有筷子。我们吃不了饭。

   méi yǒu kuàizi. wǒmen chībuliǎo fàn.

3. 那個門很重。孩子一定開不了。(重 zhòng *heavy*)

   那个门很重。孩子一定开不了。

   nà ge mén hěn zhòng. háizi yīdìng kāibuliǎo.

4. 我們吃不了這麼多餃子。(餃子/饺子 jiǎozi *dumplings*)

   我们吃不了这么多饺子。

   wǒmen chībuliǎo zhème duō jiǎozi.

5. 她幫不了你的忙。(幫忙/帮忙 bāng máng *to help someone*)

   她帮不了你的忙。

   tā bāngbuliǎo nǐ de máng.

6. 他沒有經驗。辦不了這件事。(經驗/经验 jīngyàn *experience*)

   他没有经验。办不了这件事。(辦事/办事 bàn shì *to do work*)

   tā méi yǒu jīngyàn. bànbuliǎo zhè jiàn shì.

7. 你拿不了這麼多東西。(拿 ná *to take; to hold*)

   你拿不了这么多东西。

   nǐ nábuliǎo zhème duō dōngxi.

8. 你又買了雨衣嗎？你穿得了這麼多嗎？（穿 chuān *to wear*）

你又买了雨衣吗？你穿得了这么多吗？

nǐ yòu mǎi le yǔyī ma? nǐ chuāndeliǎo zhème duō ma?

CHAPTER 8

Questions and Question Words

QUESTIONS

Yes-No Questions

Asking Yes-No Questions

There are three common forms for yes-no questions: S 嗎/吗 ma, V-NEG-V, and 是否 shìfǒu + VP. S 嗎/吗 ma is the most neutral form of the yes-no questions. V-NEG-V and 是否 shìfǒu +V ask for a choice between two alternatives, one affirmative and one negative.

S 嗎/吗 ma

The question is in the form of a declarative sentence with the particle 嗎/吗 ma at the end:

Declarative Sentence	嗎/吗 ma Question
他是學生。	他是學生嗎?
他是学生。	他是学生吗?
tā shì xuésheng.	tā shì xuésheng ma?
He is a student.	*Is he a student?*
他會說中文 。	他會說中文嗎?
他会说中文 。	他会说中文吗?
tā huì shuō Zhōngwén.	tā huì shuō Zhōngwén ma?
He can speak Chinese.	*Can he speak Chinese?*
她上大學。	她上大學嗎?
她上大学。	她上大学吗?
tā shàng dàxué.	tā shàng dàxué ma?
She attends college.	*Does she attend college?*

Verb-NEG-Verb

In most Verb-NEG-Verb questions, the verb is followed directly by the negated verb.

她<u>是不是</u>大學生？
她<u>是不是</u>大学生？
tā <u>shì bú shì</u> dàxuéshēng?
<u>Is</u> she a college student?

他<u>會不會</u>說中文？
他<u>会不会</u>说中文？
tā <u>huì bú huì</u> shuō Zhōngwén?
<u>Can</u> he speak Chinese?

她<u>上</u>不<u>上</u>大學？
她<u>上</u>不<u>上</u>大学？
tā <u>shàng</u> bú <u>shàng</u> dàxué?
Does she <u>attend</u> college?

If the verb phrase consists of a series of verbs, the first verb in the series is repeated in the question. Note that some verbs always occur as the first verb of a series of verbs. These include the stative verbs 會/会 huì, 能 néng, and 可以 kéyǐ, the obligation verbs 該/该 gāi, 應該/应该 yīnggāi, and 應當/应当 yīngdāng, and other verbs such as 願意/愿意 yuànyì *to be willing*, and 敢 gǎn *to dare*.

你今天晚上<u>去</u>不<u>去</u>看電影？
你今天晚上<u>去</u>不<u>去</u>看电影？
nǐ jīntiān wǎnshang qù bú qù kàn diànyǐng?
Are you <u>going</u> to see a movie tonight?

你<u>敢</u>不<u>敢</u>吃生魚片？
你<u>敢</u>不<u>敢</u>吃生鱼片？
nǐ <u>gǎn</u> bù <u>gǎn</u> chī shēngyú piàn?
Do you <u>dare</u> eat raw fish (sashimi)?

你<u>喜歡</u>不<u>喜歡</u>吃日本菜？
你<u>喜欢</u>不<u>喜欢</u>吃日本菜？
nǐ <u>xǐhuan</u> bù <u>xǐhuan</u> chī Rìběn cài?
Do you <u>like</u> to eat Japanese food?

你<u>會</u>不<u>會</u>說中文？
你<u>会</u>不<u>会</u>说中文？
nǐ <u>huì</u> bú <u>huì</u> shuō Zhōngwen?
<u>Can</u> you speak Chinese?

你願意不願意跟他結婚？

你愿意不愿意跟他结婚？

nǐ <u>yuànyì</u> bú <u>yuànyì</u> gēn tā jiéhūn?

Are you <u>willing</u> to marry him?

If the verb is a two-syllable stative verb, a Verb-NEG-Verb question can be formed by repeating the first syllable:

你喜不喜歡吃日本菜？

你喜不喜欢吃日本菜？

nǐ <u>xǐ</u> bù <u>xǐ</u>huan chī Rìběn cài?

Do you <u>like</u> to eat Japanese food?

For questions referring to non-past situations, if the verb is 是 shì or 有 yǒu or 會/会 huì, Verb + NEG may also occur after the object.

你是學生不是？

你是学生不是？

nǐ <u>shì</u> xuésheng <u>bú shì</u>?

<u>Are</u> you a student?

你有錢沒有？

你有钱没有？

nǐ <u>yǒu</u> qián <u>méi yǒu</u>?

Do you <u>have</u> money?

你會說中文不會？

你会说中文不会？

nǐ <u>huì</u> shuō Zhōngwen <u>bú huì</u>?

<u>Can</u> you speak Mandarin?

Marker of Negation

If the verb is 有 yǒu the marker of negation must be 沒有 méi yǒu.

你有沒有錢？

你有没有钱？

nǐ yǒu méi yǒu qián?

Do you have money?

For all other verbs, *in sentences referring to non-past situations*, negation is 不 bù:

你是不是學生？

你是不是学生？

nǐ shì bú shì xuésheng?

Are you a student?

你吃不吃肉？

nǐ chī bù chī ròu?

Do you eat meat?

If the verb is an activity verb or achievement verb and *the sentence refers to an event in past time*, negation is 沒 méi or 没有 méi yǒu. Notice that the affirmative verb is typically followed by 了 le or 過/过 guo. 了 le never follows the negated verb. (See Chapter 6: The Suffixes 了 le, 着 zhe, and 過/过 guo.)

你吃了沒有？

nǐ chī le méi yǒu?

Have you eaten?

Note: If the sentence refers to a situation in past time, Verb-NEG-Verb questions typically take the form: <u>Verb + Object</u> 没有 méi yǒu.

你<u>看</u>過那個電影<u>沒有</u>？

你<u>看</u>过那个电影<u>没有</u>？

nǐ <u>kàn</u>guo nà ge diànyǐng <u>méi yǒu</u>?

Have you <u>seen</u> that movie?

<u>是否</u> shìfǒu

是否 shìfǒu occurs immediately before the VP. The form is more formal and literary than the other yes-no question forms.

明天你<u>是否</u>願意和我一起去機場接白老師？

明天你<u>是否</u>愿意和我一起去机场接白老师？

míngtiān nǐ <u>shìfǒu</u> yuànyi hé wǒ yīqǐ qù jīchǎng jiē Bái lǎoshī?

Are you willing to go to the airport with me tomorrow to pick up Professor Bai?

你<u>是否</u>去中國開會？

你<u>是否</u>去中国开会？

nǐ <u>shìfǒu</u> qù Zhōngguó kāi huì?

Are you going to China to attend a meeting?

Answering Yes-No questions

Answering 'Yes'

There is no word for 'yes' in Mandarin. The following are the most common ways to answer a yes-no question in the affirmative.

- Repeat the first verb in the verb phrase:

Q: 你是學生嗎？
你是学生吗？
nǐ shì xuéshēng ma?
Are you a student?

A: 是。
shì.
Yes. (literally: 'am')

Q: 他會說中文嗎？
他会说中文吗？
tā huì shuō Zhōngwen ma?
Can he speak Chinese?

A: 會。
会。
huì.
Yes

Q: 你喜歡不喜歡吃日本菜？
你喜欢不喜欢吃日本菜？
nǐ xǐhuan bù xǐhuan chī Rìběn cài?
Do you like to eat Japanese food?

A: 喜歡
喜欢
xǐhuan
Yes

- Restate the entire sentence in declarative form:

Q: 你是學生嗎？
你是学生吗？
nǐ shì xuéshēng ma?
Are you a student?

A: 我是學生。
我是学生。
wǒ shì xuéshēng.
I am a student.

Q: 他會說中文嗎？
他会说中文吗？
tā huì shuō Zhōngwen ma?
Can he speak Chinese?

A: 他會說中文。
他会说中文。
tā huì shuō Zhōngwen.
He can speak Chinese?

Q: 你喜歡不喜歡吃日本菜？
你喜欢不喜欢吃日本菜？
nǐ xǐhuan bù xǐhuan chī Rìběn cài?
Do you like to eat Japanese food?

A: 我喜歡吃日本菜。
我喜欢吃日本菜。
wǒ xǐhuan chī Rìběn cài.
I like to eat Japanese food.

If the question form is 嗎/吗 ma or 是否 shìfǒu, it can also be answered with 是的 shì de *it is the case.*

Q: 他<u>會</u>説中文嗎？   A: 是的 。

他<u>会</u>说中文吗？   <u>shì</u> de

tā <u>huì</u> shuō Zhōngwen ma?   <u>Yes</u>.

Can he speak Chinese?

Q: 你<u>餓</u>嗎？   A: 是的 。

你<u>饿</u>吗？   <u>shì</u> de

nǐ <u>è</u> ma?   <u>Yes</u>.

Are you <u>hungry</u>?

Q: 你是否<u>説</u>中文？   A: 是的 。

你是否<u>说</u>中文？   <u>shì</u> de

nǐ shìfǒu <u>shuō</u> Zhōngwén?   <u>Yes</u>.

Do you <u>speak</u> Chinese?

If the main verb in the question is 是 shì, the question can also be answered with 對/对 duì *correct*.

Q: 你是中國人嗎？   A: 對

你是中国人吗？   对

nǐ shì Zhōngguó rén ma?   duì.

Answering 'No'

A 'no' answer includes the marker of negation 不 bù or 没 méi. If the verb is 有 yǒu, negation is always 没有 méi yǒu.

Q: 你<u>有</u>錢嗎？   A: 没有 。

你<u>有</u>钱吗？   méi yǒu.

nǐ <u>yǒu</u> qián ma?   *No.*

Do <u>you</u> have money?

If the main verb is an activity verb or an achievement verb, and negation indicates that the event did not happen in the past, the marker of negation is always 没 méi. The negative answer to V 了 le- and V-過/过 guo questions is always 没 méi + verb or 没有 méi yǒu. (See Chapter 6: The Suffixes 了 le, 着 zhe, and 過/过 guo.)

Q: 你已經吃了晚飯嗎？   A: 没有 。

你已经吃了晚饭吗？   méi yǒu.

nǐ yǐjing chī le wǎnfàn ma?   *No.*

Have you already eaten dinner?

Otherwise, negation is 不 bù.

Q: 你上大學嗎?
　　你上大学吗?
　　nǐ shàng dàxué ma?
　　Do you attend college?

A: 不上。
　　bú shàng.
　　No.

A 'no' answer may take a long form or a short form. The short form is much more natural in most situations.

The long answer

A long negative answer is a restatement of the question in negative form.

Q: 你有錢嗎?
　　你有钱吗?
　　nǐ yǒu qián ma?
　　Do you have money?

A: 我沒有錢。
　　我没有钱。
　　wǒ méi yǒu qián.
　　I don't have money.

Q: 你上大學嗎?
　　你上大学吗?
　　nǐ shàng dàxué ma?
　　Do you attend college?

A: 我不上大學。
　　我不上大学。
　　wǒ bú shàng dàxué.
　　I don't attend college.

The short answer

In response to all forms of yes-no questions:

If negation is 不 bù, the short 'no' answer is 不 bù + the first verb of the verb phrase.

Q: 你忙嗎?
　　你忙吗?
　　nǐ máng ma?
　　Are you busy?

A: 不忙。
　　bù máng.
　　not busy.

Q: 你忙不忙?
　　nǐ máng bù máng?
　　Are you busy?

A: 不忙。
　　bù máng.
　　not busy.

Q: 你會説英文嗎?
　　你会说英文吗?
　　nǐ huì shuō Yīngwén ma?
　　Can you speak English?

A: 不會。
　　不会。
　　bú huì.
　　can't.

Q: 你會不會説英文?
　　你会不会说英文?
　　nǐ huì bú huì shuō Yīngwén?
　　Can you speak English?

A: 不會。
　　不会。
　　bú huì.
　　can't.

Q: 你是否會説英文？
你是否会说英文？
nǐ shìfǒu huì shuō Yīngwén?
Can you speak English?

A: 不會。
不会。
bú huì.
can't.

Q: 你願意跟他結婚嗎？
你愿意跟他结婚吗？
nǐ yuànyì gēn tā jiéhūn ma?
Are you willing to marry him?

A: 不願意。
不愿意。
bú yuànyì.
not willing.

Q: 你願意不願意跟他結婚？
你愿意不愿意跟他结婚？
nǐ yuànyì bú yuànyì gēn tā jiéhūn?
Are you willing to marry him?

A: 不願意。
不愿意。
bú yuànyì.
not willing.

Q: 你是否願意跟他結婚。
你是否愿意跟他结婚。
nǐ shìfǒu yuànyì gēn tā jiéhūn.
Are you willing to marry him?

A: 不願意。
不愿意。
bú yuànyì.
not willing.

Q: 你敢吃生魚片嗎？
你敢吃生鱼片吗？
nǐ gǎn chī shēngyú piàn ma?
Do you dare to eat sashimi?

A: 不敢。
bù gǎn.
don't dare.

Q: 你敢不敢吃生魚片？
你敢不敢吃生鱼片？
nǐ gǎn bù gǎn chī shēngyú piàn?
Do you dare to eat sashimi?

A: 不敢。
bù gǎn.
don't dare.

Q: 我們該給小費嗎？
我们该给小费吗？
wǒmen gāi gěi xiǎofèi ma?
Should we give a tip.

A: 不該。
不该。
bù gāi.
shouldn't.

Q: 我們該不該給小費？
我们该不该给小费？
wǒmen gāi bù gāi gěi xiǎofèi?
Should we give a tip.

A: 不該。
不该。
bù gāi.
shouldn't.

If negation is 沒 méi, the short negative answer is 沒有 méi yǒu.

你有錢嗎 ?   沒有。

你有钱吗 ?   méi yǒu.

nǐ yǒu qián ma?   *No.*

Do you have money?

1. Write a yes-no question for each of the following answers. Use the question form presented after each answer.

    1. 我很喜歡吃中國飯。(嗎/吗 *ma*)

       我很喜欢吃中国饭。

       wǒ hěn xǐhuan chī Zhōngguo fàn.

       I like to eat Chinese food very much.

    2. 我是學生。 (Verb-NEG-Verb)

       我是学生。

       wǒ shì xuésheng.

       I am a student.

    3. 我家在加州。(嗎/吗 *ma*)

       wǒ jiā zài Jiāzhōu.

       My home is in California.

    4. 我會用筷子吃飯。(Verb-NEG-Verb)

       我会用筷子吃饭。

       wǒ huì yòng kuàizi chī fàn.

       I can use chopsticks to eat.

    5. 我有一點累。(嗎/吗 *ma*)

       我有一点累。

       wǒ yǒu yīdiǎn lèi.

       I am a little tired.

    6. 我會説漢語。(Verb-NEG-Verb)

       我会说汉语。

       wǒ huì shuō Hànyǔ.

       I can speak Chinese.

    7. 她有男朋友。(Verb-NEG-Verb)

       tā yǒu nán péngyou.

       She has a boyfriend.

8. 我去過中國。 (Verb-NEG-Verb)

   我去过中国。

   wǒ qùguo Zhōngguó.
   I went to China before.

9. 我看過那個電影。 (Verb-NEG-Verb)

   我看过那个电影。

   wǒ kànguo nà ge diànyǐng.
   I saw that movie before.

10. 那本書很有意思。 (Verb-NEG-Verb)

    那本书很有意思。

    nà běn shū hěn yǒu yìsi.
    That book is very interesting.

11. 我對中國歷史有興趣。 (是否 shìfǒu)

    我对中国历史有兴趣。

    wǒ duì Zhōngguó lìshǐ yǒu xìngqù.
    I am interested in Chinese history.

12. 我吃飽了。   (Verb-NEG-Verb)

    我吃饱了。

    wǒ chībǎo le.
    I've eaten until full. (I'm full.)

2. Answer "yes" to each of the following questions. Provide a short answer and a long answer.

1. 你是美國人嗎？

   你是美国人吗？

   nǐ shì Měiguo rén ma?
   Are you an American?

2. 你會不會開車？

   你会不会开车？

   nǐ huì bú huì kāi chē?
   Can you drive a car?

3. 你去過中國嗎？

   你去过中国吗？

   nǐ qùguo Zhōngguo ma?
   Have you been to China?

4. 我可以不可以借你的車？

   我可以不可以借你的车？

   wǒ kéyǐ bù kéyǐ jiè nǐ de chē?
   Can I borrow your car?

5. 你要不要買那件毛衣？

   你要不要买那件毛衣？

   nǐ yào bú yào mǎi nàjiàn máoyī?
   Do you want to buy that sweater?

6. 你有没有錢？

   你有没有钱？

   nǐ yǒu méi yǒu qián?
   Do you have any money?

7. 你願意跟我去買東西嗎？

   你愿意跟我去买东西吗？

   nǐ yuànyi gēn wǒ qù mǎi dōngxi ma?
   Are you willing to go shopping with me?

8. 你會不會説漢語？

   你会不会说汉语？

   nǐ huì bú huì shuō Hànyǔ?
   Can you speak Chinese?

9. 你喜不喜歡吃冰淇淋？

   你喜不喜欢吃冰淇淋？

   nǐ xǐ bù xǐhuan chī bīngqilín?
   Do you like to eat ice cream?

10. 你看過那個電影没有？

    你看过那个电影没有？

    nǐ kànguo nà ge diànyǐng méi yǒu?
    Have you seen that movie?

Content Questions

Content questions use the following question words and question phrases:

誰/谁	shéi	*who*
什麼/什么	shénme	*what*
什麼時候/什么时候	shénme shíhòu	*when (lit: what time)*
哪兒？/哪儿？ *	nǎr?	*where*
哪裏？/哪里？	nálǐ?	*where*
哪？	nǎ?	*which*
什麼地方/什么地方	shénme dìfang	*where*
幾/几	jǐ	*how many*
多少	duōshǎo	*how many, how much*
如何	rúhé	*how*
怎麼/怎么	zěnme	*how*
爲什麼/为什么	wèi shénme	*why*

Content questions are answered by replacing the question word with the appropriate answer. In Mandarin, the word order of content questions and their answers is identical. The question word goes where the answer goes.

她是誰？ 她是谁？ tā shì <u>shéi</u>? *Who is she?*	她是張老師。 她是张老师。 tā shì <u>Zhāng lǎoshī</u>. *She is Professor Zhang.*
那是什麼？ 那是什么？ <u>nà</u> shì shénme? *What is that?*	那是字典。 那是字典。 <u>nà</u> shì <u>zìdiǎn</u>. *That is a dictionary.*
你什麼時候吃飯？ 你什么时候吃饭？ nǐ <u>shénme shíhòu</u> chī fàn? *What time do you eat?*	我七點吃飯。 我七点吃饭。 wǒ <u>qīdiǎn</u> chī fàn. *I eat at <u>7</u>.*
你去哪兒？ 你去哪儿？ nǐ qù <u>nǎr</u>? *Where are you going?*	我去朋友家。 wǒ qù <u>péngyou jiā</u>. *I'm going to <u>a friend's house</u>.*

* 哪兒？/哪儿？ nǎr? and 哪裏？/哪里？ nálǐ? are regional variations of the same word. They have identical meaning.

你去**什麼**地方 ?   我去<u>朋友家</u>。
你去**什么**地方 ?   我去<u>朋友家</u>。
nǐ qù <u>shénme dìfang</u>?   wǒ qù <u>péngyou jiā</u>.
Where are you going?   *I'm going to a friend's house.*

你<u>幾歲</u> ?   我<u>十四歲</u>。
你<u>几岁</u> ?   我<u>十四岁</u>。
nǐ <u>jǐ</u> suī?   wǒ <u>shísì</u> suì.
How old are you?   *I'm fourteen.*

這本書<u>多少錢</u> ?   這本書<u>八塊</u>錢。
这本书<u>多少钱</u> ?   这本书<u>八块</u>钱。
zhè běn shū <u>duōshǎo</u> qián? zhè běn shū <u>bā kuài</u> qián.
How much money is this book? *This book is eight dollars.*

If the question word is 怎麼/怎么 zěnme, the answer may be either a short phrase

or a longer description of a process.

這個字<u>怎麼</u>寫 ?   這個字<u>這樣</u>寫。
这个字<u>怎么</u>写 ?   这个字<u>这样</u>写。
zhè ge zì <u>zěnme</u> xiě?   zhè ge zì <u>zhèyàng</u> xiě.
How do you write this character? *This character is written <u>this way</u>.*

If the question word phrase is 做什麼/做什么 zuò shénme, the answer replaces

both the verb and the object noun phrase.

你昨天晚上<u>做了什麼</u> ?   我<u>看了電影</u>。
你昨天晚上<u>做了什么</u> ?   我<u>看了电影</u>。
nǐ zuótiān wǎnshang <u>zuò le shénme</u>? wǒ <u>kàn le diànyǐng</u>.
What did you <u>do</u> last night? *I <u>saw a movie</u>.*

爲什麼/为什么 wèi shénme *why* questions are answered with an explanation.

The sentence often begins with 因爲/因为 yīnwei *because*. (For more about 因爲/因为

yīnwei, see Chapter 12: Phrase and Clause Connection.)

你<u>爲什麼</u>學中文 ?   <u>因爲</u>我要去中國。
你<u>为什么</u>学中文 ?   <u>因为</u>我要去中国。
nǐ <u>wèi shénme</u> xué Zhōngwen? <u>yīnwei</u> wǒ yào qù Zhōngguo.
Why do you study Mandarin?   *<u>Because</u> I want to go to China.*

The following question words, built upon the character 何 hé, are used in formal,

literary contexts. All occur directly before a VP.

何必	hébì	*What need is there for VP?*
何妨	héfáng	*What is the harm in VP?* *Why not VP?*
何時/何时	hé shí	*When VP? VP at what time?*
何故	hé gù	*Why VP? VP for what reason?*
何為/何为	héwéi	*What is NP?*
何嘗/何尝	hécháng	*It isn't the case that VP*

你何必那麼緊張？
你何必那么紧张？
nǐ hébì nàme jǐnzhāng?
Why are you so nervous?

你何妨不去作那件事？
你何妨不去作那件事？
nǐ héfáng bú qù zuò nà jiàn shì?
Why don't you try and do it (that thing)?

你何時跟我走？*
你何时跟我走？
nǐ héshí gēn wǒ zǒu?
When will you go with me?

早知道你下午來找我，我何故上午去你那兒？
早知道你下午来找我，我何故上午去你那儿？
zǎo zhīdao nǐ xiàwǔ lái zhǎo wǒ, wǒ hégù shàngwǔ qù nǐ nàr?
I knew you were coming to see me this afternoon. Why would I go to your place this morning?

我不明白何為滾石音樂，何為現代音樂。
我不明白何为滚石音乐，何为现代音乐。
wǒ bù míngbai héwéi gǔnshí yīnyuè, héwéi xiàndài yīnyuè.
I don't understand what hard rock music is and what modern music is.

我何嘗不想去中國。我就沒有錢。
我何尝不想去中国。我就没有钱。
wǒ hécháng bù xiǎng qù Zhōngguó. wǒ jiù méi yǒu qián.
It is not that I don't want to go to China. I just don't have the money.

---

*From 一無所有/一无所有 yīwú suóyǒu 'Nothing to My Name' by Cui Jian, 1986.

Questioning a Situation

怎麼樣/怎么样 zěnmeyàng *how about it*

怎麼樣/怎么样 zěnmeyàng is used to ask a general question about a noun or noun phrase:

這本書怎麼樣？
这本书怎么样？
zhè běn shū zěnmeyàng?
How is this book?

中文課怎麼樣？
中文课怎么样？
Zhōngwén kè zěnme yàng?
How is Chinese class?

The negated expression indicates that there is nothing extraordinary about the noun or noun phrase.

Q: 那個電影怎麼樣？   A: 不怎麼樣。
那个电影怎么样？   不怎么样。
nà ge diànyǐng zěnmeyàng?   bù zěnmeyàng.
How is that movie?   *Not much. (Nothing special.)*

怎麼（一）回事/怎么（一）回事 zěnme(yī) huí shì *what's going on?*

怎麼（一）回事/怎么（一）回事 zěnme(yī) huí shì is used to ask a question about a situation:

這是怎麼回事？
这是怎么回事？
zhè shì zěnme huí shì?
What's going on?

他不知道是怎麼回事。
他不知道是怎么回事。
tā bù zhīdao shì zěnme huí shì.
He didn't know what was going on.

Rhetorical Questions

Rhetorical questions are those for which the answer is obvious and for which no response is expected. In Mandarin, rhetorical expressions can be expressed using the phrase: 難道/难道 nándào *do you mean to say that ...* [*]

他有女朋友了。難道你不知道嗎？
他有女朋友了。难道你不知道吗？
tā yǒu nǚ péngyou le. nándào nǐ bù zhīdao ma?
He has a girlfriend now. Do you mean to say that you didn't know?

我聽説美國人都會跳舞。難道你不會嗎？
我听说美国人都会跳舞。难道你不会吗？
wǒ tīngshuō Měiguó rén dōu huì tiào wǔ. nándào nǐ bú huì ma?
I heard that all Americans can dance. Do you mean to say that you can't?

For a rhetorical response to a situation one can use the following expression:

可不是嗎？/可不是吗？kěbushìma?
Precisely, Naturally, You're telling me? You don't say?

王：你明天已經二十一歲了，可以喝酒了。
王：你明天已经二十一岁了，可以喝酒了。
Wáng: nǐ míngtiān yǐjing èrshíyī suì le, kéyǐ hē jiǔ le.
Wang: You're 21 tomorrow. You can drink.

李：可不是嗎！
李：可不是吗！
Lǐ: kěbushìma!
Li: You're telling me?

3. Write the question for each of these answers, questioning the phrase that is in square brackets. Translate your questions into English.

1. 我是〔陳麗麗〕。
   我是〔陈丽丽〕。
   wǒ shì〔Chén lì lì〕.
   I am Lili Chen.

2. 我每天〔七點鐘〕吃早飯。
   我每天〔七点钟〕吃早饭。
   wǒ měitiān〔qī diǎn zhōng〕chī zǎofàn.
   I eat breakfast every day at 7 o'clock.

---

[*] This expression is also included in Chapter 14: Speaker Perspective

3. 我昨天買了〔兩本〕書。
   我昨天买了〔两本〕书。
   wǒ zuótiān mǎi le〔liǎng běn〕shū.
   I bought two books yesterday.

4. 我明天跟〔朋友〕去看電影。
   我明天跟〔朋友〕去看电影。
   wǒ míngtiān〔gēn péngyou〕qù kàn diànyǐng.
   Tomorrow I am going with friends to see a movie.

5. 我們〔坐車〕去。
   我们〔坐车〕去。
   wǒmen〔zuò chē〕qù.
   We are going by car.

6. 電影票〔七塊五毛〕錢。
   电影票〔七块五毛〕钱。
   diànyǐng piào〔qī kuài wú máo〕qián.
   Movie tickets are $7.50.

7. 我喜歡看〔美〕國電影。
   我喜欢看〔美〕国电影。
   wǒ xǐhuan kàn〔Měi〕guo diànyǐng.
   I like to watch American movies.

8. 我們晚上〔八點多鐘〕回家。
   我们晚上〔八点多钟〕回家。
   wǒmen wǎnshang〔bā diǎn duō zhōng〕huí jiā.
   We'll return home tonight after 8 p.m.

9. 〔我妹妹〕跟我們去。
   〔我妹妹〕跟我们去。
   〔wǒ mèimei〕gēn wǒmen qù.
   My younger sister is going with us.

10. 我每天晚上吃〔兩〕碗飯。
    我每天晚上吃〔两〕碗饭。
    wǒ měitiān wǎnshang chī〔liǎng〕wǎn fàn.
    Every evening I eat two bowls of rice.

11. 我姐姐〔昨天〕買了新的大衣。
    我姐姐〔昨天〕买了新的大衣。
    wǒ jiějie〔zuótiān〕mǎi le xīn de dàyī.
    My older sister bought a new overcoat yesterday.

12. 我最喜歡〔這〕件毛衣。

我最喜欢〔这〕件毛衣。

wǒ zuì xǐhuan〔zhè〕jiàn máoyī.

I like this sweater best.

13. 這雙鞋子是在〔意大利〕買的。

这双鞋子是在〔意大利〕买的。

zhè shuāng xiézi shì zài〔Yìdàlì〕mǎi de.

These shoes were bought in Italy.

14. 我是〔二〕月〔五〕號生的。

我是〔二〕月〔五〕号生的。

wǒ shì〔èr〕yuè〔wǔ〕hào shēng de.

I was born February 5th.

15. 這個學校一共有〔兩千五百個〕學生。

这个学校一共有〔两千五百个〕学生。

zhè ge xuéxiào yīgòng yǒu〔liǎng qiān wǔ bǎi ge〕xuésheng.

This school has 2,500 students altogether.

4. Complete each of these sentences with one of the following words:

如何	rúhé	*how?*
怎麼樣/怎么样	zěnmeyàng	*how about it?*
怎麼（一）回事/	zěnme(yī)	*what's going on?*
怎么（一）回事	huí shì?	
怎麼/怎么	zěnme	*how?*
爲什麼/为什么	wèi shénme	*why?*
可不是嗎/可不是吗	kěbushìma	*How could it be otherwise? What do you think? Absolutely!*
難道/难道	nándào	*do you mean to say that*

1. Q: 那家飯館的菜 ___ ?   A: 不錯。

那家饭馆的菜 ___ ?   不错。

nà jiā fànguǎn de cài ___ ?   bú cuò.

Q: How is the food in that restaurant?   A: Not bad.

2. 她是你大學的朋友。___ 你不記得她了嗎？

她是你大学的朋友。___ 你不记得她了吗？

tā shì nǐ dàxué de péngyou. ___ nǐ bú jìde tā le ma?

She is your college friend. Do you mean to say you don't remember her?

3. Q:你在中國吃了中國飯嗎？　　　　　　A: ___ ！

　　你在中国吃了中国饭吗？　　　　　　　　 ___ ！

　　nǐ zài Zhōngguó chī le Zhōngguó fàn ma?　　___ ！

Q: Did you eat Chinese food in China?　　　　*A: What do you think?*

4. 我___ 不想跟你一起去中國？

　我___ 不想跟你一起去中国？

　wǒ ___ bù xiǎng gēn nǐ yīqǐ qù Zhōngguó.

How could I not want to go with you to China?

5. Q:美國孩子花很多錢嗎？

　　美国孩子花很多钱吗？

　　Měiguó háizi huā hěn duō qián ma?

Q: Do American kids spend a lot of money?

　A: ___ 。才上大學就要買車。

　　 ___ 。才上大学就要买车。

　　 ___. cái shàng dàxué jiù yào mǎi chē.

A: Absolutely. They just begin to attend college and already want to buy cars.

6. 她 ___ ？一天待在屋子裏都不願意出去！

　她 ___ ？一天待在屋子里都不愿意出去！

　tā ___. yī tiān dài zài wūzi lǐ dōu bú yuànyi chūqu!

What's up with her? Spending all day in her room and not willing to go out!

QUESTION WORDS AS INDEFINITES

Question words may have indefinite meaning when they occur before the verb phrase and are followed by 都 dōu or 也 yě. Notice that when a question word occurs in a phrase that is the object of the verb, the entire phrase must occur before the verb.

- 都 dōu is used in affirmative sentences:

誰/谁 shéi + 都 dōu + Verb = *everyone, anyone*

誰都可以來。

谁都可以来。

shéi dōu kéyǐ lái.

Anyone can come.

誰都喜歡吃中國飯。

谁都喜欢吃中国饭。

shéi dōu xǐhuan chī Zhōngguó fàn.

Everyone likes to eat Chinese food.

什麼時候/什么时候 shénme shíhòu + 都 dōu + Verb = *always, any time*

> 他什麼時候都在家。
> 他什么时候都在家。
> tā shénme shíhòu dōu zài jiā.
> *He is always home.*

什麼/什么 shénme + 都 dōu + Verb = *everything, anything*

> 弟弟什麼都吃。
> 弟弟什么都吃。
> dìdi shénme dōu chī.
> *Younger brother eats everything.*

哪兒/哪儿 nǎr + 都 dōu + Verb = *everywhere, anywhere*

> 我哪兒都去過。
> 我哪儿都去过。
> wǒ nǎr dōu qùguo.
> *I've been everywhere.*

■ 也 yě is used in negative sentences.

什麼/什么 shénme + 也 yě + Verb = *nothing/not anything*

> 弟弟什麼也不吃。
> 弟弟什么也不吃。
> dìdi shénme yě bù chī.
> *Younger brother eats nothing. (Younger brother doesn't eat anything.)*

什麼地方/什么地方 shénme dìfang + 也 yě + Verb = *nowhere/not anywhere*

> 他什麼地方也沒去過。
> 他什么地方也没去过。
> tā shénme dìfang yě méi qùguo.
> *He hasn't been anywhere.*

什麼時候/什么時候 shénme shíhòu + 也 yě + Verb = *never*

> 他什麼時候也不在家。
> 他什么时候也不在家。
> tā shénme shíhòu yě bú zài jiā.
> *He is never at home.*

Other Words with Indefinite Meaning

幾/几 jǐ

The word 幾/几 jǐ is usually understood as a question word.

你有幾塊錢？
你有几块钱？
nǐ yǒu jǐ kuài qián?
How many dollars do you have?

However, when 幾/几 jǐ is used in an affirmative sentence, it may have an indefinite sense. Notice that it may have indefinite sense without a following 都 dōu or 也 yě.

我有幾塊錢。
我有几块钱。
wǒ yǒu jǐ kuài qián.
I have several dollars.

到處/到处 dàochù *everywhere*

到處/到处 dàochù *everywhere* is an indefinite expression which is never used as a question word. It is typically followed by 都 dōu.

北京到處都有自行車。
北京到处都有自行车。
Běijīng dàochù dōu yǒu zìxíng chē.
There are bicycles everywhere in Beijing.

5. Write an answer in Mandarin to each question in the following conversations using a question word in its indefinite sense.

1. Q: 你想到哪兒去旅行？
   你想到哪儿去旅行？
   nǐ xiǎng dào nǎr qù lǚxíng?
   A: *Anyplace is okay.*

2. Q: 你什麼時候有空？
   你什么时候有空？
   nǐ shénme shíhòu yǒu kòng?
   A: *I always have free time.*

3. Q: 你喜歡喝咖啡嗎？

   你喜欢喝咖啡吗？

   nǐ xǐhuan hē kāfēi ma?
   A: *Everyone likes to drink coffee.*

4. Q: 你今天晚上要看什麼電影？

   你今天晚上要看什么电影？

   nǐ jīntiān wǎnshang yào kàn shénme diànyǐng?
   A: *Any movie is okay.*

5. Q: 你想什麼時候看電影？

   你想什么时候看电影？

   nǐ xiǎng shénme shíhòu kàn diànyǐng?
   A: *Any time is okay.*

6. Q: 你什麼時候有空？

   你什么时候有空？

   nǐ shénme shíhòu yǒu kòng?
   A: *I never have free time.*

7. Q: 你認識張大偉嗎？

   你认识张大伟吗？

   nǐ rènshi Zhāng Dàwěi ma?
   A: *Everyone knows him.*

8. Q: 我們什麼時候吃冰淇淋？

   我们什么时候吃冰淇淋？

   wǒmen shénme shíhòu chī bīngqilín?
   A: *Anytime is okay.*

9. Q: 你喜歡在哪兒做作業？

   你喜欢在哪兒做作业？

   nǐ xǐhuan zài nǎr zuò zuòyè?
   A: *Any quiet place is okay.*   (安靜/安静 ānjìng *quiet*)

10. Q: 你爬得上那座山嗎？   (爬山 pá shān *climb a mountain*)

    你爬得上那座山吗？

    nǐ pádeshàng nà zuò shān ma?
    A: *No one can climb that mountain.*

Question Words in Parallel Phrases

<u>Question Word 就 jiù Question Word</u>

Parallel phrases are phrases that occur in sequence in a sentence, in which each phrase has the same grammatical structure and theme. When a question word occurs in each of the phrases of a parallel structures, it has indefinite meaning.

誰想吃誰就吃。
谁想吃谁就吃。
shéi xiǎng chī, shéi jiù chī.
Whoever wants to eat, eat.

你要到哪兒去就到哪兒去。
你要到哪儿去就到哪儿去。
nǐ yào dào nǎr qù jiù dào nǎr qù.
Go wherever you want.

你要吃多少就吃多少。
你要吃多少就吃多少。
nǐ yào chī duōshǎo jiù chī duōshǎo.
Eat as much as you want.

你要怎麼寫就怎麼寫。
你要怎么写就怎么写。
nǐ yào zěnme xiě jiù zěnme xiě.
Write however you want.

6. These conversations use question words in parallel phrases. Translate them into English.

1. Q: 這件事情應該怎麼做？
這件事情应该怎么做？
zhè jiàn shìqing yīnggāi zěnme zuò?

A: 你要怎麼做就怎麼做。
你要怎么做就怎么做。
nǐ yào zěnme zuò jiù zěnme zuò.

2. Q: 我們請誰吃飯？
我们请谁吃饭？
wǒmen qǐng shéi chī fàn?

A: 你要請誰就請誰。

你要请谁就请谁。

nǐ yào qǐng shéi jiù qǐng shéi.

3. Q: 我們給母親買什麼東西？

我们给母亲买什么东西？

wǒmen gěi mǔqīn mǎi shénme dōngxī?

A: 你要買什麼就買什麼。

你要买什么就买什么。

nǐ yào mǎi shénme jiù mǎi shénme.

4. Q: 我們到哪兒去？

我们到哪儿去？

wǒmen dào nǎr qù?

A: 你要到哪兒去我們就到哪兒去。

你要到哪儿去我们就到哪儿去。

nǐ yào dào nǎr qù wǒmen jiù dào nǎr qù.

5. Q: 小費要給多少錢？   (小費/小费 xiǎofèi tip)

小费要给多少钱？

xiǎofèi yào gěi duōshǎo qián?

A: 你要給多少就給多少。

你要给多少就给多少。

nǐ yào gěi duōshǎo jiù gěi duōshǎo.

6. 趙：這個字怎麼寫？

赵：这个字怎么写？

Zhào: zhè ge zì zěnme xiě?

王：你要怎麼寫就怎麼寫。

王：你要怎么写就怎么写。

Wáng: nǐ yào zěnme xiě jiù zěnme xiě.

趙：不行啊。每個字都有固定的筆畫！

赵：不行啊。每个字都有固定的笔画！

Zhào: bù xíng a. měi ge zì dōu yǒu gùdìng de bǐhuà!

Zhao: That's not okay! Every character has a definite stroke order!

7. Q: 你弟弟在哪兒？

你弟弟在哪兒？

nǐ dìdi zài nǎr?

A: 大概跟哥哥一塊兒。哥哥到哪兒去弟弟就到哪兒去。

大概跟哥哥一块儿。哥哥到哪儿去弟弟就到哪儿去。

dàgài gēn gēge yī kuàr. gēge dào nǎr qù dìdi jiù dào nǎr qù.

8. Q: 你今天晚上跟誰跳舞？

你今天晚上跟谁跳舞？

nǐ jīntiān wǎnshang gēn shéi tiào wǔ?

A: 我要跟誰跳舞就跟誰跳舞。

我要跟谁跳舞就跟谁跳舞。

wǒ yào gēn shéi tiào wǔ jiù gēn shéi tiào wǔ.

CHAPTER 9

Location, Directional Movement, and Distance

LOCATION

Location Words and Possible Suffixes

		- 頭/头-tou	-面 -mian	- 邊/边 -bian	- 間/间 -jiān
裏/里 lǐ	*in*	✓	✓	✓	
外 wài	*out*	✓	✓	✓	
上 shàng	*on, above*	✓	✓	✓	
下 xià	*under*	✓	✓	✓	
右 yòu*	*right*		✓	✓	
左 zuǒ*	*left*		✓	✓	
前 qián	*front*	✓	✓	✓	
後/后 hòu	*back/behind*	✓	✓	✓	
對/对 duì*	*across from*		✓		
旁 páng*	*next to*			✓	
中 zhōng*	*in between*				✓

No Suffix:

內 nèi	*in*

Compass Directions					
		- 頭/头-tou	- 面-mian	- 邊/边-bian	- 間/间 -jiān
東/东 dōng	*east*		✓	✓	
南 nán	*south*		✓	✓	
西 xī	*west*		✓	✓	
北 běi	*north*		✓	✓	

---

*Suffix usually occurs.

No Suffix:

東北/东北 dōngběi	*northeast*
西北 xīběi	*northwest*
東南/东南 dōngnán	*southeast*
西南 xīnán	*southwest*

Note: Most directional words consist of a base form and a suffix. When the directional word is two syllables in length (for example, 西北 xīběi *northwest*), no suffix is used.

Notice that for the interim directions *northeast, northwest, southeast,* and *southwest,* the Chinese order of direction words is the opposite of the English order. The compass directions are recited in the following order: 東南西北/东南西北 dōng nán xī běi *east south west north* (in contrast to English: *north, east, south, west*).

Location Phrases

Locations always assume a reference point. Here, the box is the reference point, and the location phrases describe points around the box.

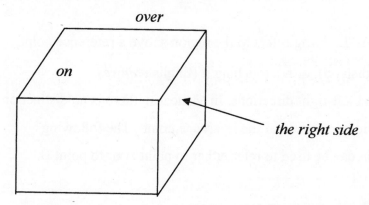

- In English, location phrases occur before the reference point:
  over the box, on the box, etc.

- In Mandarin, location phrases occur *after* the reference point, in the following pattern:

Reference Point 的 de location phrase

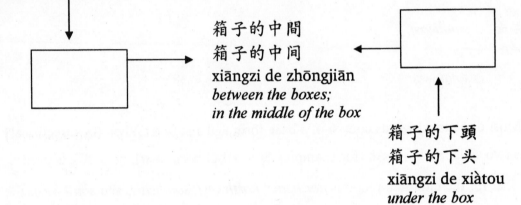

箱子的上頭
箱子的上头
xiāngzi de shàngtou
over/above the box

箱子的中間
箱子的中间
xiāngzi de zhōngjiān
between the boxes;
in the middle of the box

箱子的下頭
箱子的下头
xiāngzi de xiàtou
under the box

Note: If the location phrase is one syllable in length, 的 de is typically omitted:

箱子的裏頭
箱子的里头
xiāngzi de lǐtou
inside the box
→
箱子裏
箱子里
xiāngzilǐ
inside the box

Notice the difference in meaning between some Mandarin location expressions and their English counterparts:

- 上 shàng: In Mandarin, 上 shàng refers to the region above a reference point, either touching it (English *on*), or not touching it (English *above*).

- Compass directions and left-right directions: In Mandarin, there is no distinction between a location inside or outside of the reference point. The following expression in Mandarin can be used to refer either to point A or to point B.

城的北邊
城的北边
chéng de běibian
A: the north side of the city OR B: *outside the city in the region to the north.*

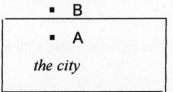

Location Phrases as NP Modifiers

Location phrases can serve as modifiers of NPs. When they do, they follow the same rule as all other NP modifiers: they precede the head noun. Location phrases which serve as modifiers are followed by 的 de:

Modified NP	**Location Phrase**
北邊的山	山的北邊
北边的山	山的北边
běibiān de shān	shān de běibiān
the mountains to the north	*to the north of the mountains*

1. Describe locations as instructed. (房子 fángzi *house*, 湖 hú *lake*, 山 shān *mountain*)

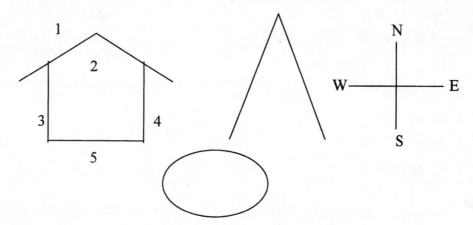

1. Describe the location of number 1 with respect to the house.

2. Describe the location of number 2 with respect to the house.

3. Describe the location of number 3 with respect to the house.

4. Describe the location of number 4 with respect to the house.

5. Describe the location of number 5 with respect to the house.

6. What is the compass direction of the mountain with respect to the house?

7. What is the compass direction of the mountain with respect to the lake?

8. What is the compass direction of the lake with respect to the house?

9. What is the compass direction of the lake with respect to the mountain?

10. Where is the lake with respect to the mountains in the picture below?

2. Translate these phrases into English. Some of these phrases describe locations, and some are nouns with locations as modifiers.

1. 右邊的人
右边的人
yòubian de rén

2. 房子的後頭
房子的后头
fángzi de hòutou

3. 中間的房子
中间的房子
zhōngjiān de fángzi

4. 房子的中間
房子的中间
fángzi de zhōngjiān

5. 西邊的湖
西边的湖
xībian de hú

6. 公園的北邊
公园的北边
gōngyuán de běibiān

7. 北邊的公園
北边的公园
běibiān de gōngyuán

8. 前頭的那個女孩子
前头的那个女孩子
qiántou de nà ge nǚ háizi

9. 那個女孩子的前頭
那个女孩子的前头
nà ge nǚ háizi de qiántou

10. 學校的東邊
学校的东边
xuéxiào de dōngbian

在 zài and Spatial Location

The verb that indicates spatial location is 在 zài: *to be located*.

弟弟在房子裏。
弟弟在房子里。
dìdi zài fángzi lǐ.
Younger brother is (located) in the house.

圖書館在大學路的北邊。
图书馆在大学路的北边。
túshūguǎn zài dàxué lù de běibiān.
The library is (located) north of College Road.

A Note on 在 zài and 是 shì

While 在 zài can be translated as *be*, it is distinct in meaning from the verb 是 shì *be*. 是 shì joins two Noun Phrases and indicates a relationship of identity between them. (Chapter 3: Verbs and Verb Phrases.) The relationship indicated by 在 zài is that of location.

是 shì	在 zài
弟弟是學生。	弟弟在公園裏。
弟弟是学生。	弟弟在公园里。
dìdi shì xuésheng.	dìdi zài gōngyuán lǐ.
Younger brother is a student.	*Younger brother is (located) in the park.*

A Note on 在 zài and 有 yǒu

在 zài and 有 yǒu may both occur in descriptions involving location. 在 zài is a verb used to indicate the location of an object. 有 yǒu is a verb used to indicate the existence of an object. Notice the meanings they contribute in the following sentences.

(在)公園裏有湖。
(在)公园里有湖。
(zài) gōngyuán lǐ yǒu hú.
Located in the park there is a lake.

湖在公園裏。
湖在公园里。
hú zài gōngyuán lǐ.
The lake is located in the park.

有湖在公園裏。

有湖在公园里。

yǒu hú zài gōngyuán lǐ.

There is a lake located in the park.

Since both 有 yǒu and 在 zài are verbs, they can both be negated.

公園裏<u>沒有</u>湖。

公园里<u>没有</u>湖。

gōngyuán lǐ <u>méi yǒu</u> hú.

In the park there is no lake.

湖<u>不在</u>公園裏。

湖<u>不在</u>公园里。

hú <u>bú zài</u> gōngyuán lǐ.

The lake is not in the park. (It is someplace else.)

3. In complete sentences, describe the location of the lake with respect to the park(s) in each of the following pictures. Use compass locations for 2, 3, 4, and 5.

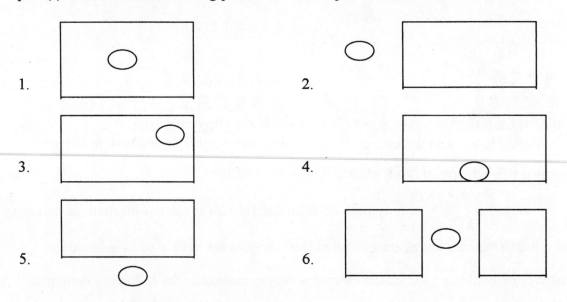

4. Translate the following locations into English.

1. 在我的旁邊

在我的旁边

zài wǒ de pángbiān

2. 在老師的左邊

在老师的左边

zài lǎoshī de zuǒbian

3. 國外
   国外
   guówài

4. 那個人的右面
   那个人的右面
   nà ge rén de yòumiàn

5. 在你的前頭
   在你的前头
   zài nǐ de qiántou

6. 桌子上有一本書。
   桌子上有一本书。
   zhuōzi shàng yǒu yī běn shū.

7. 房子的後頭有人。
   房子的后头有人。
   fángzi de hòutou yǒu rén.

8. 房子裏沒有人。
   房子里没有人。
   fángzi lǐ méi yǒu rén.

9. 我弟弟在那兩個女孩子的中間。
   我弟弟在那两个女孩子的中间。
   wǒ dìdi zài nà liǎng ge nǚ háizi de zhōngjiān.

10. 圖書館在你的前頭。
    图书馆在你的前头。
    túshūguǎn zài nǐ de qiántou.

DIRECTIONAL MOVEMENT

Directional Movement Expressions

In Mandarin, directional movement is expressed as follows.

Mover+ Movement Verb+ Direction+ Reference Point+ Speaker Perspective: 來 lái or 去 qù

他	走	進	屋子	來了。
他	走	进	屋子	来了。
tā	zǒu	jìn	wūzi	lái le.
He	*walked*	*into*	*the room*	*(towards the speaker).*

他	走	進	屋子	去了。
他	走	进	屋子	去了。
tā	zǒu	jìn	wūzi	qù le.
He	*walked*	*into*	*the room*	*(away from the speaker).*

Common Directional Words

進/进	jìn	*into*
到	dào	*at (final destination of movement)*
出	chū	*out of*
過/过	guò	*pass/go by*
上	shàng	*up*
下	xià	*down*
往	wǎng	*towards*
回	huí	*return back*

Common Movement Verbs

走	zǒu	*walk*
跑	pǎo	run
開/开	kāi	*drive*
飛/飞	fēi	*fly*
跳	tiào	*skip; jump; dance*
爬	pá	*climb*
游	yóu	*swim*

Speaker Perspective: 來 lái and 去 qù

來 lái and 去 qù reflect the perspective of the speaker or addressee regarding the direction of the movement. 來 lái indicates movement towards the speaker or addressee. 去 qù indicates movement away from the speaker or addressee.

媽媽走進屋子來了。

妈妈走进屋子来了。

māma zǒu jìn wūzi lái le.

Mom walked into the room.

(The speaker is in the room and the direction of mom's movement is towards the speaker.)

媽媽走進屋子去了。

妈妈走进屋子去了。

māma zǒu jìn wūzi qù le.

Mom walked into the room.

(The speaker is outside of the room and the direction of mom's movement is away from the speaker.)

Omission of the Reference Point

While a reference point is always implied in directional movement, the reference point itself may be omitted from the sentence:

媽媽走進來了。

妈妈走进来了。

māma zǒu jìn lái le.

Mom walked in.

他跑出去了。

tā pǎo chū qu le.

He ran out.

Note: Sentences with 往 wǎng and 到 dào must include a reference point:

她跑到公園去了。

她跑到公园去了。

tā pǎo dào gōngyuán qù le.

She ran to the park.

☹她跑到去了。

tā pǎo dào qù le.

他開往海邊去了。

他开往海边去了。

tā kāi wǎng hǎibiān qù le.

He drove towards the ocean.

☹他開往去了。

他开往去了。

tā kāi wǎng qù le.

Human or Animal Reference Points

Nouns, NPs, or pronouns with human or animal reference cannot serve as reference points in directional expressions unless they are followed by a specifier:

請到我這兒來。

请到我这儿来。

qǐng dào wǒ zhèr lái.

Please come to me.

☹請到我來。

请到我来。

qǐng dào wǒ lái.

她跑到李老師那兒去了。

她跑到李老师那儿去了。

tā pǎo dào Lǐ lǎoshī nàr qù le.

She ran to (where) Professor Li (is).

☹她跑到李老師去了。

她跑到李老师去了。

tā pǎo dào Lǐ lǎoshī qù le.

Directional Expressions as Resultative Endings

When a verb of motion is followed by a directional expression, the directional expression may function as a resultative ending, indicating the result of the movement. 得 de and 不 bù may occur between the verb of movement and the directional ending to add potential meaning. (See Chapter 7: The Resultative Structure and Potential Suffixes.)

山很高。你爬得上去嗎？
山很高。你爬得上去吗？
shān hěn gāo. nǐ pádeshàng qù ma?
The mountain is very tall. Can you climb it?

湖太大了。我游不過去。
湖太大了。我游不过去。
hú tài dà le. wǒ yóubuguò qù.
The lake is too wide. I can't swim across.

5. Translate these Mandarin sentences with directional expressions into English.

1. 她爬上山去了。
   tā pá shàng shān qù le.

2. 他從那個門跑出來了。
   他从那个门跑出来了。
   tā cóng nà ge mén pǎo chū lái le.

3. 他每天都從這邊跑上去。
   他每天都从这边跑上去。
   tā měitiān dōu cóng zhèbiān pǎo shàng qù.

4. 我的錢他都拿走了。
   我的钱他都拿走了。
   wǒ de qián tā dōu ná zǒu le.

5. 妹妹拿來了很多東西。
   妹妹拿来了很多东西。
   mèimèi ná lái le hěn duō dōng xī.

6. 這本書，請你拿回圖書館去。
   这本书，请你拿回图书馆去。
   zhè běn shū, qǐng nǐ ná huí túshūguǎn qù.

7. 他每天下午走到郵局去寄信。(郵局/邮局 yóujú *post office*,

   他每天下午走到邮局去寄信。 寄信 jì xìn *mail letter*)

   tā měitiān xiàwǔ zǒu dào yóujú qù jì xìn.

8. 請你帶來你的漢語課本。

   请你带来你的汉语课本。

   qǐng nǐ dàilái nǐ de Hànyǔ kèběn.

9. 他走回家去了。

   他走回家去了。

   tā zǒu huí jiā qù le.

10. 他不想走進屋子裏去。

    他不想走进屋子里去。

    tā bù xiǎng zǒu jìn wūzi lǐ qù.

Relocation Verbs

Relocation verbs describe moving an item to a new location. The item that is relocated occurs in the sentence as the object of the verb 把 bǎ. (See Chapter 10: The 把 bǎ Construction.)

妹妹把車開回家了。

妹妹把车开回家了。

mèimei bǎ chē kāi huí jiā le.

Younger sister drove the car home.

他把我的錢拿走了。

他把我的钱拿走了。

tā bǎ wǒde qián názǒu le.

He took my money away.

Common Relocation Verbs

開/开	kāi	*to drive*
拿	ná	*to bring/to take*
拉	lā	*to pull*
推	tuī	*to push*
運/运	yùn	*to transport*
搬	bān	*to move*
帶/带	dài	*to bring/to take*
背	bēi	*to carry on one's back*
放	fàng	*to put, to place*
掉	diào	*to drop*

6. Complete these sentences in Mandarin to match the meaning of the English sentences. Each Mandarin sentence includes a directional expression. Additional exercises using 把 bǎ and directional expressions are found in Chapter 10: The 把 bǎ Construction.

1. 她把 ___ 背___ ___ 了。
   tā bǎ ___ bēi ___ ___ le.
   She carried the child home on her back.

2. 我們把 ___ 搬 ___ ___ ___ 去了。
   我们把 ___ 搬 ___ ___ ___ 去了。
   wǒmen bǎ ___ bān ___ ___ ___ qù le.
   We moved the table into the room.

3. 爸爸把 ___ 放 ___ ___ ___ 。
   爸爸把 ___ 放 ___ ___ ___ 。
   bàba bǎ ___ fàng ___ ___ ___.
   Dad put the newspaper on the table.

4. 誰把 ___ 掉 ___ ___ ___ ?
   谁把 ___ 掉 ___ ___ ___ ?
   shéi bǎ ___ diào ___ ___ ___?
   Who dropped the cup on the floor?

5. 我們不能把 ___ 開 ___ ___ 去。
   我们不能把 ___ 开 ___ ___ 去。
   wǒmen bù néng bǎ ___ kāi ___ ___ qù.
   We can't drive the car into the park.

6. 我明天要把 ___ 開 ___ ___ 去。

   我明天要把 ___ 开 ___ ___ 去。

   wǒ míngtiān yào bǎ ___ kāi ___ ___ qù.
   Tomorrow I want to drive the car to Mr. Wang's place.

7. 我把 ___ 從 ___ ___ ___ 來了。

   我把 ___ 从 ___ ___ ___ 来了。

   wǒ bǎ ___ cóng ___ ___ ___ lái le.
   I pulled younger brother out of (out from) the water.

8. 你什麼時候把 ___ 開 ___ ___ 來?

   你什么时候把 ___ 开 ___ ___ 来?

   nǐ shénme shíhòu bǎ ___ kāi ___ ___ lái?
   When are you driving the car to my house?

9. 我明天要把 ___ 帶 ___ ___ 去。

   我明天要把 ___ 带 ___ ___ 去。

   wǒ míngtiān yào bǎ ___ dài ___ ___ qù.
   Tomorrow I have to take little brother to school.

10. 車壞了!我們只好把 ___ 推 ___ ___ 了。

    车坏了!我们只好把 ___ 推 ___ ___ 了。

    chē huài le! wǒmen zhǐ hǎo bǎ ___ tuī ___ ___ le.
    The car is broken! The best thing we can do is push it home.

DISTANCE

Expressing Distance

A 離/离 B distance
   lí

A 離/离 B 遠/远 ~ 近
   lí   yuǎn jìn

我家離學校三英里路(遠)。*

我家离学校三英里路(远)。

wǒ jiā lí xuéxiào sān yīng lǐ lù (yuǎn).
My house is 3 miles from school.

---

* Mandarin speakers from Taiwan tend to include 遠/远 yuǎn and not 路 lù.

我家離學校很遠。

我家离学校很远。

wǒ jiā lí xuéxiào hěn yuǎn.

My house is very far from school.

我家離學校很近。

我家离学校很近。

wǒ jiā lí xuéxiào hěn jìn.

My house is very close to school.

Note: 離/离 lí *from* is used to indicate distance, and is never used to indicate the starting point of movement. To indicate movement from a place, use 從 cóng *from.*

從這兒到郵局怎麼走？

从这儿到邮局怎么走？

cóng zhèr dào yóujú zěnme zǒu?

How do you go from here to the post office?

Negating Distance

我家離這兒不很遠。

我家离这儿不很远。

wǒ jiā lí zhèr bù hěn yuǎn.

My house is not very far from here.

我家離這兒不近。

我家离这儿不近。

wǒ jiā lí zhèr bú jìn.

My house is not close to here.

我家離這兒不到三英里路。

我家离这儿不到三英里路。

wǒ jiā lí zhèr bú dào sān yīng lǐ lù.

My house is not three miles from here.

To indicate a correction about a distance, use 不是 bú shì as follows:

錢：王老師的家離這兒三英里路。

王老师的家离这儿三英里路。

Wáng lǎoshī de jiā lí zhèr sān yīng lǐ lù.

Qian: Teacher Wang's house is 3 miles from here.

毛：王老師的家離這兒不是三英里路。是三十英里路。

王老师的家离这儿不是三英里路。是三十英里路。

Wáng lǎoshī de jiā lí zhèr bú shì sān yīng lǐ lù. shì sānshí yīng lǐ lù.

Mao: Teacher Wang's house is not 3 miles from here. It's 30 miles from here.

Questioning Distance

你家離這兒多遠？

你家离这儿多远？

nǐ jiā lí zhèr duō yuǎn?

How far is your house from here?

你家離這兒有幾英里路？

你家离这儿有几英里路？

nǐ jiā lí zhèr yǒu jǐ yīng lǐ lù?

How many miles from here is your house?

你家離這兒近嗎？

你家离这儿近吗？

nǐ jiā lí zhèr jìn ma?

Is your house close to here?

你家離這兒遠嗎？／遠不遠？

你家离这儿远吗？／远不远？

nǐ jiā lí zhèr yuǎn ma?/yuǎn bù yuǎn?

Is your house far from here?

7. Answer the questions in full sentences based on the information in parentheses.

圖書館離書店多遠？

图书馆离书店多远？

túshūguǎn lí shūdiàn duō yuǎn?

1. (20 miles)
2. (2 miles)
3. (18 miles)
4. (100 miles)
5. (6 ½ miles)

公園離你家遠嗎？

公园离你家远吗？

gōngyuán lí nǐ jiā yuǎn ma?

6. no
7. yes
8. extremely far
9. not too far
10. very close

8. Put these phrases in the correct order to make well-formed sentences. The English translations are included.

1. 法國離不遠意大利。

   法国离不远意大利。

   Fǎguó lí bù yuǎn Yìdàlì.
   France is not far from Italy.

2. 美國很遠離中國。

   美国很远离中国。

   Měiguó hěn yuǎn lí Zhōngguó.
   America is very far from China.

3. 紐約兩百英里路差不多離波士頓。

   纽约两百英里路差不多离波士顿。

   Niǔyuē liǎng bǎi yīng lǐ lù chàbuduō lí Bōshìdùn.
   New York is about 200 miles from Boston.

4. 多遠澳大利亞離英國？

   多远澳大利亚离英国？

   duō yuǎn Aòdàlìyà lí Yīngguó?
   How far is Australia from England?

5. 加州遠離佛羅里達州嗎？

   加州远离佛罗里达州吗？

   Jiāzhōu yuǎn lí Fúluólǐdá zhōu ma?
   Is California far from Florida?

6. 很加拿大近離美國。

   很加拿大近离美国。

   hěn Jiānádà jìn lí Měiguó.
   Canada is very close to the U.S.

7. 墨西哥不太遠離得州。

   墨西哥不太远离得州。

   Mòxīgē bú tài yuǎn lí Dézhōu.
   Mexico is not too far from Texas.

8. 芝加哥不到密西根離一百英里路。

   芝加哥不到密西根离一百英里路。

   Zhījiāgē bú dào Mìxīgēn lí yī bǎi yīng lǐ lù.
   Chicago isn't 100 miles from Michigan.

9. 日本離很近韓國。

日本离很近韩国。

Rìběn lí hěn jìn Hánguó.
Japan is very close to South Korea.

10. 相當遠喀麥隆巴西離。

相当远喀麦隆巴西离。

xiāngdāng yuǎn Kāmàilóng Bāxīlí.
Cameroon is rather far from Brazil.

CHAPTER 10

The 把 bǎ Construction

把 bǎ occurs in the following structure:

Subject NP₁ 把 bǎ NP₂ VP

While 把 bǎ has no direct equivalent in English, sentences with 把 bǎ may be paraphrased as:

Subject NP₁ takes NP₂ and does VP with it.

The properties of the 把 bǎ construction are as follows:

- The VP following 把 bǎ + NP must describe a completed action or an action with duration. Therefore, 把 bǎ may occur with the following verbs and verb phrases:

Achievement verbs, since they refer to completed actions (see also Chapter 3: Verbs and Verb Phrases):

我把他們的名字都忘了。真不好意思。
我把他们的名字都忘了。真不好意思。
wǒ bǎ tāmen de míngzi dōu wàng le. zhēn bù hǎo yìsi.
I forgot all of their names. How embarrassing.

他把我的書丟掉了。
他把我的书丢掉了。
tā bǎ wǒ de shū diūdiào le.
He lost my book. (He took my book and lost it.)

Activity verbs with duration emphasized or implied:

你再把這個問題想一想。
你再把这个问题想一想。
nǐ zài bǎ zhè ge wèntí xiǎng yī xiǎng.
Think about that problem for awhile.

請把你的作業改一改。
请把你的作业改一改。
qǐng bǎ nǐ de zuòyè gǎi yī gǎi.
Please correct your homework.

190

Activity verbs with resultative verb endings (see also Chapter 7: The Resultative

Structure and Potential Suffixes):

弟弟把蛋糕吃完了。
dìdi bǎ dàngāo chīwán le.
Younger brother ate up the cake.

我把那個字念錯了。
我把那个字念错了。
wǒ bǎ nà ge zì niàncuò le.
I read that character wrong.

Relocation verbs with directional complements (see also Chapter 9: Location,

Directional Movement, and Distance):

請把書拿出來。
请把书拿出来。
qǐng bǎ shū náchūlái.
Please take the books out.

他把車開上山去了。
他把车开上山去了。
tā bǎ chē kāi shàng shān qù le.
*He drove the car up the mountain. (He took the car and drove it up the
mountain.)*

- In the 把 bǎ construction, NP₂ must refer to a specific object or concept. A NP

  may acquire a specific reference in context. The specifiers 這/这 zhè and 那 nà

  can also be used to mark a NP as specific.

我把這本書看完了。   ⊗我把書看完了。
我把这本书看完了。   我把书看完了。
wǒ bǎ zhè běn shū kànwán le.   wǒ bǎ shū kànwán le.
I finished reading this book.   *I finished reading a book.*

- The verb may act on a portion of NP₂. The 'part' occurs after verb.

弟弟把蛋糕吃了一半。
dìdi bǎ dàngāo chīle yī bàn.
Younger brother ate half the cake.

他把這本書看了幾頁。
他把这本书看了几页。
tā bǎ zhè běn shū kànle jǐ yè.
He read a few pages of the book.

■ 把 bǎ cannot be followed by a verb suffix.

我把書放在桌子上了。   ☹我把着書放在桌子上了。

我把书放在桌子上了。   我把着书放在桌子上了。

wǒ bǎ shū fàng zài zhuōzi shàng le.   wǒ bǎzhe shū fàng zài zhuōzi
I put the books on the table.   shàng le.

弟弟把餅乾都吃完了。   ☹弟弟把了餅乾都吃完了。

弟弟把饼干都吃完了。   弟弟把了饼干都吃完了。

dìdi bǎ bǐnggān dōu chīwán le.   dìdi bǎ le bǐnggān dōu chīwán le.
Younger brother ate up the cookies.

1. Translate these sentences into English: 把 bǎ with a verb with completed action.

1. 他把照相機借給我用。(照相機/照相机 zhàoxiàngjī *camera*)

   他把照相机借给我用。

   tā bǎ zhàoxiàngjī jiè gěi wǒ yòng.

2. 王明把巧克力送給他女朋友。(巧克力 qiǎokèlì *chocolates*)

   王明把巧克力送给他女朋友。

   Wáng Míng bǎ qiǎokèlì sòng gěi tā nǚ péngyou.

3. 媽媽把那張畫兒掛在牆上。(掛 guà *hang*, 牆 qiáng *wall*)

   妈妈把那张画儿挂在墙上。

   māma bǎ nà zhāng huàr guà zài qiáng shàng.

4. 別把杯子放在電視上面。(杯子 bēizi *cup*,

   别把杯子放在电视上面。   電視/电视 diànshì *television*)

   bié bǎ bēizi fàng zài diànshì shàngmian.

5. 我的狗把我的作業吃掉了。 (狗 gǒu *dog*,

   我的狗把我的作业吃掉了。   作業/作业 zuòyè *homework*)

   wǒ de gǒu bǎ wǒ de zuòyè chīdiào le.

6. 我把自行車擦乾淨了。(擦乾淨/擦干净 cā gānjìng *wipe clean*)

   我把自行车擦干净了。

   wǒ bǎ zìxíngchē cā gānjìng le.

7. 我弟弟把他的車碰壞了。(碰壞/碰坏 pèng huài *crashed*)

   我弟弟把他的车碰坏了。

   wǒ dìdi bǎ tā de chē pèng huài le.

8. 我把那張照片放大了。 (照片 zhàopiàn *photo*, 放大 fang dà *enlarge*)

   我把那张照片放大了。

   wǒ bǎ nà zhāng zhàopiàn fang dà le.

9. 請你把門拉開。

请你把门拉开。

qǐng nǐ bǎ mén lākāi.

10. 他們不到一個小時就把行李都收拾好了。(行李 xíngli *suitcase*)

他们不到一个小时就把行李都收拾好了。(收拾 shōushí *pack*)

tāmen bú dào yī ge xiǎoshí jiù bǎ xíngli dōu shōushí hǎo le.

11. 你能不能把這件衣服洗乾淨？(洗乾淨/洗干净 xǐ gānjìng

你能不能把这件衣服洗干净？   *wash clean*)

nǐ néng bu néng bǎ zhè jiàn yīfu xǐ gānjìng?

2. Translate these sentences into English: 把 bǎ with verbs involving movement and relocation. (See Chapter 9: Location, Directional Movement, and Distance, for a list of relocation verbs.)

1. 他把車開進公園去了。

他把车开进公园去了。

tā bǎ chē kāi jìn gōngyuán qù le.

2. 我把孩子背回家了。

wǒ bǎ háizi bēi huí jiā le.

3. 學生把東西都拿到高教授家去了。

学生把东西都拿到高教授家去了。

xuésheng bǎ dōngxi dōu ná dào Gāo jiàoshòu jiā qù le.

4. 我得把書都還回圖書館去。(還/还 huán *to return*)

我得把书都还回图书馆去。

wǒ děi bǎ shū dōu huán huí túshūguǎn qù.

5. 弟弟把我的車開到學校去了。

弟弟把我的车开到学校去了。

dìdi bǎ wǒde chē kāi dào xuéxiào qù le.

6. 你要把東西運到哪兒去？

你要把东西运到哪儿去？

nǐ yào bǎ dōngxī yùn dào nǎr qù?

7. 請把書架搬到書房裏去。

请把书架搬到书房里去。

qǐng bǎ shūjià bān dào shūfáng lǐ qù.

8. 請你們把書帶來。

   請你们把书带来。

   qǐng nǐmen bǎ shū dài lái.

9. 請把狗拉到外頭去。

   请把狗拉到外头去。

   qǐng bǎ gǒu lā dào wàitou qù.

10. 請把我的字典拿來。

    请把我的字典拿来。

    qǐng bǎ wǒ de zìdiǎn ná lái.

11. 她把男朋友推到門外面去了。

    她把男朋友推到门外面去了。

    tā bǎ nán péngyou tuī dào mén wàimian qù le.

3. What did they do with their Chinese book? Translate each person's explanation into a complete Chinese sentence. Use 把 bǎ in each sentence.

   1. 妹妹 mèimei: *I took the book home.*

   2. 媽媽 māma: *I read half.*

   3. 姐姐 jiějie: *I finished reading it.*

   4. 哥哥 gēge: *I loaned it to my younger brother.*

   5. 弟弟 dìdi: *I lost it.*

CHAPTER 11

Comparisons

MORE THAN

比 bǐ *more than*

NP₁ 比 bǐ NP₂ SV*
NP₁ is more SV than NP₂

汽水比茶貴。
汽水比茶贵。
qìshuǐ bǐ chá guì.
Soda is more expensive than tea.

寫字比説話難。
写字比说话难。
xiě zì bǐ shuō huà nán.
Writing is harder than speaking

做得對比做得快還要好。
做得对比做得快还要好。
zuòdeduì bǐ zuòdekuài hái yào hǎo.
Doing it correctly is even better than doing it fast.

Modification of 比 bǐ comparisons

- SV 一點/一点 SV yīdiǎn *a little more SV*

哥哥比弟弟高一點。
哥哥比弟弟高一点。
gēge bǐ dìdi gāo yīdiǎn.
Older brother is a little taller than younger brother.

---

* Comparison structures compare NPs. Notice that verbs and verb + object sequences may also function as NPs. Linguists say that these verb constructions are 'nominalized' when they function in this way.

195

- SV 得多 SV de duō *a lot more SV*

哥哥比弟弟高得多。
gēge bǐ dìdi gāo de duō.
Older brother is a lot taller than younger brother.

1. Using the 比 bǐ comparison structure, compare "A" and "B" with respect to the property "C" in complete sentences.

	A	**B**	**C**
1.	中文 Zhōngwén *Chinese*	英文 Yīngwén *English*	難/难 nán *difficult*
2.	餃子/饺子 jiǎozi *dumplings*	比薩 比萨 bǐsà *pizza*	好吃 hǎo chī *good to eat*
3.	文學/文学 wénxué *literature*	數學/数学 shùxué *math*	有意思 yǒu yìsi *interesting*
4.	妹妹 mèimei *younger sister*	弟弟 dìdi *younger brother*	用功 yònggōng *hardworking*
5.	孩子 háizi *children*	大人 dàren *adults*	多 duō *more*

更 SV   gèng SV *even more SV*

更 gèng is an intensifier and goes directly before a SV. It compares a NP with another NP which has been mentioned in the discourse.

哥哥比弟弟高。
gēge bǐ dìdi gāo.
Older brother is taller than younger brother.

姐姐更高。
jiějie gèng gāo.
Older sister is even taller.

可樂比茶貴。
可乐比茶贵。
kělè bǐ chá guì.
Cola is more expensive than tea.

礦泉水更貴。
矿泉水更贵。
kuàngquán shuǐ gèng guì.
Mineral water is even more expensive.

最 zuì SV *most SV*

最 zuì is an intensifier and immediately precedes a SV. It is the marker of

'superlative' comparison in Mandarin.

哥哥最高。
gēge zuì gāo.
Older brother is the tallest.

可樂最貴。
可乐最贵。
kělè zuì guì.
Cola is the most expensive.

最好不過了/最好不过了 zuì hǎo búguò le *nothing is better than that*

馬老師：我們今天出去吃飯，好嗎？
马老师：我们今天出去吃饭，好吗？
Mǎ lǎoshī: wǒmen jīntiān chū qù chī fàn, hǎo ma?
Teacher Ma: Today we'll eat out, okay?

羅老師：最好不過了。
罗老师：最好不过了。
Luó lǎoshī: zuì hǎo búguò le.
Teacher Luo: Nothing is better than that.

2. Add 比 bǐ, 更 gèng, or 最 zuì to make sentences from each group of words to best
match the English translations.

1. 貓，狗，小。老鼠，小。
猫，狗，小。老鼠，小。
māo, gǒu, xiǎo. lǎoshǔ, xiǎo.
Cats are smaller than dogs. Mice are even smaller.

2. 摩托車，自行車，貴。車子，貴。
摩托车，自行车，贵。车子，贵。
mótuōchē, zìxíngchē, guì. chēzi, guì.
*Motorcycles are more expensive than bicycles. Cars are even more
expensive.*

3. 餅乾，水果，甜。巧克力，甜。
饼干，水果，甜。巧克力，甜。
bǐnggān, shuǐguǒ, tián. qiǎokèlì, tián.
Cookies are sweeter than fruit. Chocolate is even sweeter.

4. 姐姐，妹妹，高。哥哥，高。爸爸，高。
   jiějie, mèimei, gāo. gēge, gāo. bàba, gāo.
   *Older sister is taller than younger sister. Older brother is even taller. Dad
   is the tallest.*

5. 她是我校 ___ 聰明的學生。
   她是我校 ___ 聪明的学生。
   tā shì wǒ xiào ___ cōngming de xuésheng.
   She is the smartest student in my school.

6. 她是我 ___ 好的朋友。
   tā shì wǒ ___ hǎo de péngyou
   She is my best friend.

LESS THAN

<u>没有 méi yǒu   *not as much as*</u>

   NP₁ 没有 NP₂ SV
      méi yǒu
   NP₁ is not as SV as NP₂

   茶沒有可樂貴。
   茶没有可乐贵。
   chá méi yǒu kělè guì.
   Tea is not as expensive as soda.

   說話沒有寫字難。
   说话没有写字难。
   shuō huà méi yǒu xiě zì nán.
   Speaking is not as hard as writing.

Modification of 没有 méi yǒu comparisons

■ 那麼/那么 nàme + SV or 這麼/这么 zhème + SV

   那麼(高)/那么(高) nàme gāo   *that (tall)*
   這麼(高)/这么(高) zhème gāo   *this (tall)*

   那麼/那么 nàme and 這麼/这么 zhème often need not be translated into

   English.

   茶沒有可樂那麼貴。
   茶没有可乐那么贵。
   chá méi yǒu kělè nàme guì.
   Tea is not as expensive as cola.

我没有你那麽聰明。

我没有你那么聪明。

wǒ méi yǒu nǐ nàme cōngming.

I am not as smart as you.

不如 bùrú *not equal to*

不如 bùrú is used in formal written or spoken discourse as follows:

NP₁ 不如 bùrú NP₂

NP₁ is not equal to NP₂

説不如做。

说不如做。

shuō bùrú zuò.

Speaking is not as good as doing.

NP₁ 不如 bùrú NP₂ (SV)

NP₁ is not equal to NP₂ (in terms of the SV)

我不如他聰明。

我不如他聪明。

wǒ bùrú tā cōngming.

I am not as smart as he is.

與其/与其 VP₁ 不如 VP₂   yǔqí VP₁ bùrú VP₂   *VP₁ is not as good as VP₂*

與其學日文不如學中文。

与其学日文不如学中文。

yǔqí xué Rìwén bùrú xué Zhōngwén.

Studying Japanese is not as good as studying Chinese.

3. Convert the following 比 bǐ comparisons to 没有 méi yǒu comparisons keeping the meaning constant, following the example.

Example

他比我聰明。　　　　　　　　　　我没有他那麽聰明。

他比我聪明。 ⟶ 我没有他那么聪明。

tā bǐ wǒ cōngming.　　　　　　wǒ méi yǒu tā nàme cōngming.

He is smarter than I am.　　　　*I am not as smart as he is.*

1. 姐姐比弟弟高。

jiějie bǐ dìdi gāo.

Older sister is taller than younger brother.

2. 我上午比下午忙。

wǒ shàngwǔ bǐ xiàwǔ máng.

I am busier in the morning than in the afternoon.

3. 西瓜比南瓜甜。

xīguā bǐ nánguā tián.

Watermelon is sweeter than pumpkin.

4. 俄國比德國冷。

俄国比德国冷。

Èguó bǐ Déguó lěng.

Russia is colder than Germany.

5. 太平洋比大西洋大。

Tàipíngyáng bǐ Dàxīyáng dà.

The Pacific Ocean is bigger than the Atlantic Ocean.

6. 我的貓比我的狗還懶。

我的猫比我的狗还懒。

wǒ de māo bǐ wǒde gǒu hái lǎn.

My cat is even lazier than my dog.

EQUAL TO

Comparisons with 一樣/一样 yīyàng *the same*

NP₁ 跟/和 NP₂ 一樣/一样*

NP₁ gēn/hé NP₂ yīyàng

NP₁ and NP₂ are the same

這本書跟那本書一樣。

这本书跟那本书一样。

zhè běn shū gēn nà běn shū yīyàng.

This book and that book are the same.

NP₁ 跟/和 NP₂ 一樣/一样 SV

NP₁ gēn/hé NP₂ yīyàng SV

NP₁ and NP₂ are equally SV

可樂跟茶一樣貴。

可乐跟茶一样贵。

kělè gēn chá yīyàng guì.

Cola and tea are equally expensive.

---

* In 一樣/一样 yīyàng structures, 跟 gēn and 和 hé, are the most commonly used connecting words, but 像 xiàng and 同 tóng sometimes occur.

説話和寫字一樣難。

说话和写字一样难。

shuō huà hé xiě zì yīyàng nán.

Speaking and writing are equally difficult.

如 rú ... 般的 bān de ... *the same*

NP$_1$ 如 NP$_2$ 般的 SV

NP$_1$ rú NP$_2$ bān de SV

NP$_1$ has the same SV quality as NP$_2$

湖裏的水如鏡子般的清。

湖里的水如镜子般的清。

hú lǐ de shuǐ rú jìngzi bān de qīng.

The water in the lake is as clear as a mirror.

(好)像(hǎo)xiàng ... 似的 sì de *to be like*

NP$_1$ (好)像 NP$_2$ 似的

NP$_1$ (hǎo)xiàng NP$_2$ sì de

NP$_1$ is like NP$_2$

她好像很累似的。

tā hǎoxiàng hěn lèi sìde.

She seems very tired.

NOT EQUAL TO

Comparisons with 不一樣/不一样 bù yīyàng *not the same*

NP$_1$ 跟/和 NP$_2$ 不一樣/不一样 NP$_1$ gēn/ hé NP$_2$ bù yīyàng

NP$_1$ and NP$_2$ are not the same

饅頭跟麪包不一樣。

馒头跟面包不一样。

mántou gēn miànbāo bù yīyàng.

Steamed buns and bread are not the same.

網球和羽毛球不一樣。

网球和羽毛球不一样。

wǎngqiú hé yǔmáoqiú bù yīyàng.

Tennis and badminton are not the same.

NP$_1$ 跟/和 NP$_2$ 不一樣/不一样 SV

NP$_1$ gēn/ hé NP$_2$ bù yīyàng SV

NP$_1$ and NP$_2$ are not the same SV

美國車的價錢跟日本車的價錢不一樣貴。

美国车的价钱跟日本车的价钱不一样贵。

Měiguó chē de jiàqián gēn Rìběn chē de jiàqián bù yīyàng guì.

American cars and Japanese cars are not equally expensive.

紅燒豆腐和家常豆腐不一樣辣 。

红烧豆腐和家常豆腐不一样辣 。

hóngshāo dòufu hé jiācháng dòufu bù yīyàng là.

Red cooked beancurd and home style beancurd are not equally spicy.

不等於/不等于 bù děngyú *not equivalent to*

媽媽，爸爸不給你錢不等於他們不愛你。

妈妈，爸爸不给你钱不等于他们不爱你。

māma, bàba bù gěi nǐ qián bù děngyú tāmen bú ài nǐ.

Mom and dad not giving you money doesn't mean they don't love you.

他很瘦不等於他身體不好。

他很瘦不等于他身体不好。

tā hěn shòu bù děngyú tā shēntǐ bù hǎo.

His being thin doesn't mean that he is not healthy.

4. Use the parenthesized patterns to compare each of the following noun phrases with respect to the specified property.

1. 這件毛衣，那件毛衣，貴（一樣）

   这件毛衣，那件毛衣，贵（一样）

   zhè jiàn máoyī, nà jiàn máoyī, guì (yīyàng)

   This sweater and that sweater are equally expensive.

2. 男孩子，女孩子，聰明（一樣）

   男孩子，女孩子，聪明（一样）

   nán háizi, nǚháizi, cōngming (yīyàng)

   Boys and girls are equally smart.

3. 小狗，小貓，可愛（一樣）

   小狗，小猫，可爱（一样）

   xiáogǒu, xiǎomāo, kě'ài (yīyàng)

   Puppies and kittens are equally cute.

4. 電腦，計算機，有用（不一樣）

   电脑，计算机，有用（不一样）

   diànnǎo, jìsuànjī, yǒuyòng (bù yīyàng)

   Computers and calculators are not equally useful.

5. 朋友，家裏人（不一樣）
朋友，家里人（不一样）
péngyou, jiālǐ rén (bù yīyàng)
Friends and family are not the same.

6. 叉子，筷子，方便（一樣）
叉子，筷子，方便（一样）
chāzi, kuàizi, fāngbiàn (yīyàng)
Forks and chopsticks are equally convenient.

7. 高跟鞋，球鞋，舒服（不一樣）
高跟鞋，球鞋，舒服（不一样）
gāogēnxié, qiúxié, shūfu (bù yīyàng)
High heeled shoes and sneakers are not equally comfortable.

8. 飛盤，足球，好玩（一樣）
飞盘，足球，好玩（一样）
fēipán, zúqiú, hàowán (yīyàng)
Frisbee and soccer are equally fun.

9. 萬里長城，埃及的金字塔，有名（一樣）
万里长城，埃及的金字塔，有名（一样）
Wànlǐ Chángchéng, Āijí de jīnzìtǎ, yǒumíng (yīyàng)
The Great Wall and Egypt's pyramids are equally famous.

10. 法語，漢語，難（不一樣）
法语，汉语，难（不一样）
Fǎyǔ, Hànyǔ, nán (bù yīyàng)
French and Chinese are not equally difficult.

INCLUDING THE ACTIVITY IN THE COMPARISON

Comparison sentences may also include the activity verb for which two NPs are compared. When the activity verb is included, the verb is followed by 得 de, and Verb + 得 de occur either right before the stative verb or right before the comparison word.

比 bǐ Comparisons

Verb + 得 de occurs right before the stative verb:

哥哥比弟弟说得快。
哥哥比弟弟说得快。
gēge bǐ dìdi shuō de kuài.
Older brother speaks faster than younger brother.

<u>Verb + 得 de occurs right before the comparison word:</u>

哥哥説得比弟弟快。

哥哥说得比弟弟快。

gēge shuō de bǐ dìdi kuài.
Older brother speaks faster than younger brother.

If the object of the action verb is also included in the sentence, verb + object must precede verb + 得 de. (For more on this kind of modification, see Chapter 3: Verbs and Verb Phrases.)

NP₁ 比 NP₂ <u>Verb + Object</u> <u>Verb 得</u> Stative Verb

哥哥比弟弟説話説得快。

哥哥比弟弟说话说得快。

gēge bǐ dìdi shuō huà shuō de kuài.
Older brother speaks faster than younger brother.

NP₁ <u>Verb + Object</u> <u>Verb 得</u> 比 NP₂ Stative Verb

哥哥説話説得比弟弟快。

哥哥说话说得比弟弟快。

gēge shuō huà shuō de bǐ dìdi kuài.
Older brother speaks faster than younger brother.

没有 méi yǒu Comparisons

NP₁ 没有 NP₂ <u>Verb + Object</u> <u>Verb 得</u> (那麽/那么 nàme) Stative Verb

弟弟没有哥哥説話説得(那麽)快。

弟弟没有哥哥说话说得(那么)快。

dìdi méi yǒu gēge shuō huà shuō de (nàme) kuài.
Younger brother doesn't speak as fast as older brother.

NP₁ <u>Verb + Object</u> <u>Verb 得</u> 没有 NP₂ Stative Verb

弟弟説話説得没有哥哥(那麽)快。

弟弟说话说得没有哥哥(那么)快。

dìdi shuō huà shuō de méi yǒu gēge (nàme) kuài.
Younger brother doesn't speak as fast as older brother.

一樣/一样 yīyàng Comparisons

NP₁ 跟/和 NP₂ <u>Verb + Object</u> <u>Verb 得</u> 一樣/一样 Stative Verb

弟弟跟哥哥説話説得一樣快。

弟弟跟哥哥说话说得一样快。

dìdi gēn gēge shuō huà shuō de yīyàng kuài.

Younger brother speaks as fast as older brother.

NP₁ <u>Verb + Object</u> <u>Verb</u> 得 跟/和 NP₂ 一樣/一样 Stative Verb

弟弟説話説得和哥哥一樣快。

弟弟说话说得和哥哥一样快。

dìdi shuō huà shuō de hé gēge yīyàng kuài.

Younger brother speaks as fast as older brother.

5. A. In full sentences, compare 弟弟 dìdi and 妹妹 mèimei with respect to each of the following properties. Use the comparison structure in parenthesis following each property.

	弟弟 dìdi	妹妹 mèimei	哥哥 gēge
1. intelligence (比)	*more*	*less*	*even more*
2. speed (没有)	*faster*	*slower*	
3. height (比)	*taller*	*shorter*	*even taller*
4. eating speed (比)	*faster*	*slower*	*even faster*
5. speaking speed (没有)	*slower*	*faster*	
6. length of study (一樣/样)	*the same*	*the same*	
7. eating quantity (比)	*more*	*less*	*even more*
8. reading speed (一樣/样)	*the same*	*the same*	

B. In four complete sentences each using the word 更 gèng, describe the four qualities in which older brother surpasses younger sister and younger brother.

9.

10.

11.

12.

6. Answer each question using 没有 méi yǒu as in the following example. Translate your answer into English.

Q: 弟弟跟妹妹一樣高嗎？   A: 不。弟弟没有妹妹那麼高。

弟弟跟妹妹一样高吗？   不。弟弟没有妹妹那么高。

dìdi gēn mèimei yīyàng gāo ma?   bù. dìdi méi yǒu mèimei nàme gāo.

Q: *Are younger brother and younger*   A: *No. Younger brother is not as tall as*

sister equally tall?   *younger sister.*

1. 巧克力和紅豆一樣好吃嗎？

   巧克力和红豆一样好吃吗？

   qiǎokèlì hé hóngdòu yīyàng hǎo chī ma?

   Are chocolate and red beans equally delicious?

2. 老師跟學生一樣忙嗎？

   老师跟学生一样忙吗？

   lǎoshī gēn xuésheng yīyàng máng ma?

   Are teachers and students equally busy?

3. 自行車和摩托車一樣快嗎？

   自行车和摩托车一样快吗？

   zìxíngchē hé mótuō chē yīyàng kuài ma?

   Are bicycles and motorcycles equally fast?

4. 太極拳跟空手道一樣難嗎？

   太极拳跟空手道一样难吗？

   tàijíquán gēn kōngshǒudào yīyàng nán ma?

   Are taijiquan and karate equally difficult?

5. 金子和銀子一樣漂亮嗎？

   金子和银子一样漂亮吗？

   jīnzi hé yínzi yīyàng piàoliang ma?

   Are gold and silver equally beautiful?

6. 手機和電腦一樣有用嗎？

   手机和电脑一样有用吗？

   shǒujī hé diànnǎo yīyàng yǒuyòng ma?

   Are cell phones and computers equally useful?

7. 狗像馬一樣快嗎？

   狗像马一样快吗？

   gǒu xiàng mǎ yīyàng kuài ma?

   Are dogs and horses equally fast?

8. 廣東菜和四川菜一樣辣嗎？

   广东菜和四川菜一样辣吗？

   Guǎngdōng cài hé Sìchuān cài yīyàng là ma?

   Are Cantonese food and Sichuan food equally hot and spicy?

9. 日本跟中國一樣大嗎？

   日本跟中国一样大吗？

   Rìběn gēn Zhōngguó yīyàng dà ma?

   Are Japan and China equally big?

10. 冬天跟春天一樣美嗎？

冬天跟春天一样美吗？

dōngtiān gēn chūntiān yīyàng měi ma?

Are winter and spring equally pretty?

7. **Complete these sentences in Mandarin to match the English translations.**

1. 中國人，美國人，喝茶，多

中国人，美国人，喝茶，多

Zhōngguó rén, Měiguó rén, hē chá, duō

Chinese people drink more tea than American people.

2. 我姐姐，寫字，我，漂亮

我姐姐，写字，我，漂亮

wǒ jiějie, xiě zì, wǒ, piàoliang

My older sister writes characters prettier than I do.

3. 我，我哥哥，玩飛盤，多

我，我哥哥，玩飞盘，多

wǒ, wǒ gēge, wán fēipán, duō

I don't play frisbee as much as my older brother.

4. 媽媽，做菜，爸爸，好

妈妈，做菜，爸爸，好

māma, zuò cài, bàba, hǎo

Mom cooks better than dad.

5. 哥哥，爸爸，唱歌，好

gēge, bàba, chàng gē, hǎo

Older brother sings as well as dad.

6. 我的馬，跑，別的馬，快

我的马，跑，别的马，快

wǒ de mǎ, pǎo, bié de mǎ, kuài

My horse runs faster than other horses.

CHAPTER 12

Phrase and Clause Connection

Phrases and clauses which occur in sequence are often related in particular ways: in terms of temporal sequence, contrast, cause-and-effect, etc. This chapter presents the Mandarin connecting words that are commonly used to indicate phrase and clause relationships.

IMPORTANT FEATURES OF PHRASE AND CLAUSE CONNECTION

- Mandarin has a strong *narrative presupposition*: the order of events or situations in the discourse typically follows the order of events or situations in the real world.

- Connecting words are not used as frequently as they are in English. Often, the relationship between phrases or clauses that occur in sequence are implied rather than specified with a connecting word. The context of the sentence usually provides the information needed to interpret the relationship between the phrases or clauses.

- Mandarin connecting words often occur in pairs, in which one word may occur in each of the connected phrases or clauses. Since connecting words are optional, one or both of the connecting words may be absent.
  Examples of paired connectives include:

雖然/虽然 ...可是	suīrán ... kěshì	*although ... but*
因爲/因为 ... 所以	yīnwei... suóyǐ	*because ... therefore*
要是 ... 就	yàoshi ... jiù	*if ... then*
不但 ... 而且	búdàn ... érqiě	*not only ... but also*

- In Mandarin, the order of clauses linked by connecting words is generally fixed: the 雖然/虽然 suīrán clause must occur before the 可是 kěshì clause, the 因爲/因为 yīnwei clause must occur before the 所以 suóyǐ clause, etc. As the two English sentences below illustrate, the relative position of English clauses linked by connecting words is relatively free.

  > *Because I got up late I didn't eat breakfast.* =
  > *I didn't eat breakfast because I got up late.*

208

ADDITION

Words that Link Nouns or Noun Phrases

跟 gēn, 和 hé, 同 tóng, *and* 與/与 yǔ

All of these connecting words translate as *and* in English, and all connect NPs. 跟 gēn and 和 hé, are by far the most commonly used of these connectors. 同 tóng is more common in southern China, and 與/与 yǔ occurs in formal, literary language.

弟弟和妹妹都喜歡吃甜的東西。
弟弟和妹妹都喜欢吃甜的东西。
dìdi hé mèimei dōu xǐhuan chī tián de dōngxi.
Younger brother and younger sister both like to eat sweet things.

我跟他已經認識了很久。
我跟他已经认识了很久。
wǒ gēn tā yǐjing rènshi le hěn jiǔ.
He and I have already known each other for a long time.

我每天早上喝咖啡和果汁。
wǒ měitiān zǎoshang hē kāfēi hé guǒzhī.
Every morning I drink coffee and fruit juice.

我看過《茶與同情》那個電影。
我看过《茶与同情》那个电影。
wǒ kànguo "Chá yǔ Tóngqíng," nà ge diànyǐng.
I've seen that movie "Tea and Sympathy."

Note: 跟 gēn, 和 hé, 同 tóng and 與/与 yǔ do not link verbs or VPs.

🙁媽媽收拾房子和做菜。
妈妈收拾房子和做菜。
māma shōushí fángzi hé zuò cài.
Mom straightens up the house and cooks.

Words that link Verb Phrases*

也 yě *also*

弟弟喜歡聽音樂，也喜歡打球。
弟弟喜欢听音乐，也喜欢打球。
dìdi xǐhuan tīng yīnyuè, yě xǐhuan dǎ qiú.
Little brother likes to listen to music and also likes to play ball.

---

* See Chapter 4: Adverbs, for additional discussion of 也 yě and 還/还 hái.

還/还 hái *in addition, still*

弟弟已經吃了二十個餃子，還想多吃一些。

弟弟已经吃了二十个饺子，还想多吃一些。

dìdi yǐjing chīle èrshí ge jiǎozi, hái xiǎng duō chī yī xiē.

Little brother has already eaten 20 dumplings and still wants to eat more.

Note: 還沒有/还没有 hái méi yǒu *means 'not yet'*

另外 lìngwài *in addition*

妹妹買了一雙鞋子，另外還買了一雙襪子。

妹妹买了一双鞋子，另外还买了一双袜子。

mèimei mǎi le yīshuāng xiézi, lìngwài hái mǎi le yīshuāng wàzi.

Little sister bought a pair of shoes, and in addition bought a pair of socks.

弟弟吃了飯，另外還吃了麵包。

弟弟吃了饭，另外还吃了面包。

dìdi chīle fàn, lìngwài hái chīle miànbāo.

Younger brother ate rice and in addition also ate bread.

而 ér *and/but*

而 ér is a literary expression used to connect VPs related in terms of addition or

contrast.

這個東西物美而價廉。

这个东西物美而价廉。

zhè ge dōngxi wù měi ér jià lián.

(As for) this item, it is attractive and the price is cheap.

這個東西貴而不實用。

这个东西贵而不实用。

zhè ge dōngxi guì ér bù shíyòng.

This item is expensive and impractical.

Paired Connecting Words that Link VPs

也 … 也 … yě … yě … *both … and …*

他們每天晚上也唱歌也跳舞。

他们每天晚上也唱歌也跳舞。

tāmen měitiān wǎnshang yě chàng gē yě tiào wǔ.

Every night they sing and dance.

又 ... 又 ...　yòu ... yòu ...　*both ... and ...*

他又高又壯。

他又高又壮。

tā yòu gāo yòu zhuàng.
He is both tall and strong.

一邊/一边 ... 一邊/一边 ...　yībiān ... yībiān ...

on the one hand ... on the other hand ...　(both ... and ...)

他一邊寫字一邊聽音樂。

他一边写字一边听音乐。

tā yībiān xiě zì yībiān tīng yīnyuè.
He's writing and listening to music.

不但 ... 而且 ...　búdàn ... érqiě ...　*not only ... but also ...*

那個學生不但很聰明而且很用功。

那个学生不但很聪明而且很用功。

nà ge xuésheng búdàn hěn cōngming érqiě hěn yònggōng.
That student is not only very smart but is also very hardworking.

她不但漂亮而且很和氣。

她不但漂亮而且很和气。

tā búdàn piàoliang érqiě hěn héqi.
She's not only pretty, she's also very nice.

不僅/不仅 ... 而且 ...　bù jǐn ... ér qiě ...　*not only ... but also ...*

他不僅聰明而且用功。

他不仅聪明而且用功。

tā bùjǐn cōngming érqiě yònggōng.
He is not only smart, he's also hardworking.

既 ... 又 ...　jì ... yòu ...　*both ... and ...*

春天既漂亮又舒服。

chūntiān jì piàoliang yòu shūfu.
Springtime is both beautiful and comfortable.

DISJUNCTION

Words That Link Verb Phrases

還是/还是 háishi *or*

- 還是/还是 háishi is used in questions that ask the listener to chose between two

  alternatives.

  你坐火車去還是坐飛機去？
  你坐火车去还是坐飞机去？
  nǐ <u>zuò huǒchē qù</u> háishi <u>zuò fēijī qù</u>?
  Are you going by train or by plane?

- 是 shì may occur before the first of two linked VPs.

  是喝茶好還是喝水好？
  是喝茶好还是喝水好？
  shì <u>hē chá hǎo</u> háishi <u>hē shuǐ hǎo</u>?
  Is it good to drink tea or is it good to drink water?(i.e. which is better?)

  When the main verb of the verb phrase is 是 shì, it may be omitted from the
  second verb phrase so that 還是/还是 háish occurs directly before the NP:

  他是大學生還是中學生？
  他是大学生还是中学生？
  tā <u>shì dàxuéshēng</u> háishi <u>zhōngxuéshēng</u>?
  Is he a college student or a high school student?

  When answering a 還是/还是 háishi question that asks about preference or

opinion, it is possible to include 還是/还是 háishi before the selected alternative:

  還是喝水好。
  还是喝水好。
  háishi hē shuǐ hǎo.
  It is better to drink water.

或者 huòzhě

- 或者 huòzhě is used in declarative sentences to indicate two alternatives, both of

  which are possible or acceptable.

  看電影或者聽音樂都好。
  看电影或者听音乐都好。
  kàn diànyǐng huòzhě tīng yīnyuè dōu hǎo.
  Watching a movie or listening to music is okay.

找工作，去上海或者去北京都行。

找工作，去上海或者去北京都行。

zhǎo gōngzuò, qù Shànghǎi huòzhě qù Běijīng dōu xíng.
To find a job, going to Shanghai or Beijing is okay.

她今天來或者明天來。

她今天来或者明天来。

tā jīntiān lái huòzhě míngtiān lái.
She is coming today or tomorrow.

Words That Link Noun Phrases

不是 …   就是 …   búshi   …   jiù shì   …   *if not ... then ...*

每天都有人來找我。不是小王就是小李。

每天都有人来找我。不是小王就是小李。

měitiān dōu yǒu rén lái zhǎo wǒ. búshi xiǎo Wáng jiù shì xiǎo Lǐ.
Every day someone comes looking for me. If it isn't little Wang it's little Li.

1. Fill in the blanks in the story with the appropriate connecting words where possible to convey addition (*and* connection) or disjunction (*or* connection). Sometimes more than one choice is acceptable. Some blanks must be kept empty. An English translation is provided for each sentence.

    1. 城西邊有一所房子。房子 ＿＿ 大 ＿＿老。沒有人住。

        城西边有一所房子。房子 ＿＿ 大 ＿＿老。没有人住。

        chéng xībian yǒu yī suǒ fángzi. fángzi ＿＿ dà ＿＿ lǎo. méi yǒu rén zhù.
        There is a house on the west side of town. The house is big and old. No one lives there.

    2. 有人說房子裏有鬼。＿＿ 說如果你要跟鬼做朋友，你得拿飯進去 ＿＿ 給鬼吃。

        有人说房子里有鬼。＿＿ 说如果你要跟鬼做朋友，你得拿饭进去 ＿＿ 给鬼吃。

        yǒu rén shuō fángzi lǐ yǒu guǐ. ＿＿ shuō rúguǒ nǐ yào gēn guǐ zuò péngyou, nǐ děi ná fàn jìnqu ＿＿ gěi guǐ chī.
        Some people say there are ghosts in the house. And they say that if you want to be friends with the ghosts, you have to take food inside and give it to the ghosts to eat.

    3. 妹妹 ＿＿ 我都聽說了這個故事，＿＿ 想要看看鬼。

        妹妹 ＿＿ 我都听说了这个故事，＿＿ 想要看看鬼。

        mèimei ＿＿ wǒ dōu tīngshuō le zhè ge gùshì, ＿＿ xiǎng yào kàn kàn guǐ.
        Younger sister and I heard this story and wanted to see the ghosts.

4. 我們問媽媽「鬼喜歡吃什麼？」她説他們喜歡吃米飯，＿＿ 喜
   歡吃餃子＿＿ 豆腐。

   我们问妈妈「鬼喜欢吃什麽？」她说他们喜欢吃米饭，＿＿ 喜
   欢吃饺子＿＿ 豆腐。

   wǒmen wèn māma   " guǐ xǐhuan chī shénme?" tā shuō tāmen xǐhuan
   chī mǐ fàn,___ xǐhuan chī jiǎozi ___ dòufu.
   *We asked Mom "what do ghosts like to eat?" Mom said they eat rice, and
   they eat jiaozi (dumplings), and they eat doufu (beancurd).*

5. 他們 ＿＿ 喜歡吃麵，＿＿＿ 喜歡喝酒 ＿＿ 可樂。
   他们 ＿＿ 喜欢吃面，＿＿＿ 喜欢喝酒 ＿＿ 可乐。
   tāmen ＿＿ xǐhuan chī miàn, ＿＿＿ xǐhuan hē jiǔ ___ kělè.
   *They also like to eat noodles, and they like to drink wine, and they like to
   drink cola.*

6. 所以我們做了紅燒豆腐，＿＿ 包了很多餃子。
   所以我们做了红烧豆腐，＿＿ 包了很多饺子。
   suóyǐ wǒmen zuò le hóngsháo dòufu, ＿＿＿ bāo le hěn duō jiǎozi.
   So we made red-cooked beancurd and wrapped a lot of jiaozi.

7. ＿＿ 我們 ＿＿ 買了酒 ＿＿ 可樂。
   ＿＿ 我们 ＿＿ 买了酒 ＿＿ 可乐。
   ＿＿ wǒmen ＿＿ mǎi le jiǔ ___ kělè.
   And we bought wine and cola.

8. 等到天黑了，我們 ＿＿＿ 到那所房子去了。
   等到天黑了，我们 ＿＿＿ 到那所房子去了。
   děng dào tiān hēi le, wǒmen ＿＿＿ dào nà suǒ fángzi qù le.
   We waited until the day turned dark and we went to that house.

9. 進了房子，＿＿ 妹妹就問「你想鬼今天會喝酒 ＿＿ 喝可樂？」
   进了房子，＿＿ 妹妹就问「你想鬼今天会喝酒 ＿＿ 喝可乐？」
   jìn le fángzi, ___ mèimei jiù wèn "nǐ xiǎng guǐ jīntiān huì hē jiǔ ___ hē
   kělè? "
   *We entered the house and younger sister asked "do you think the ghosts will
   drink the wine or drink the cola today?"*

10. 忽然我們聽見一個聲音，好像跟人説話一樣：
    忽然我们听见一个声音，好像跟人说话一样：
    hūrán wǒmen tīngjiàn yī ge shēngyīn, hǎoxiàng gēn rén shuō huà
    yīyàng:
    Suddenly we heard a sound, like a person speaking.

「 酒 ＿＿ 可樂都好。＿＿ 我們 ＿＿ 喜歡喝水。」

「 酒 ＿＿ 可乐都好。＿＿ 我们 ＿＿ 喜欢喝水。」

" jiǔ ___ kělè dōu hǎo. ___ wǒmen ___ xǐhuan hē shuǐ."

"Wine or cola are both okay. And we also like to drink water."

11. 餃子＿＿ 酒都掉在地上。

饺子＿＿ 酒都掉在地上。

jiǎozi ___ jiǔ dōu diào zài dì shàng.

The jiaozi and the wine fell to the ground.

12. 我們跑出房子去了，＿＿ 跑回家了。

我们跑出房子去了，＿＿ 跑回家了。

wǒmen pǎo chū fángzi qù le, ___ pǎo huí jiā le.

We ran out of the house and ran home.

13. 第二天回房子裏 ＿＿ 一看。

第二天回房子里 ＿＿ 一看。

dì èr tiān huí fángzi lǐ ___ yī kàn.

The next day we returned to the house and looked.

14. 在房子後頭找到了幾個酒瓶，＿＿ 全都是空的。

在房子后头找到了几个酒瓶，＿＿ 全都是空的。

zài fángzi hòutou zhǎodào le jǐ ge jiǔ píng, ___ quán dōu shì kōng de.

But behind the house we found several wine bottles, and they were all empty.

15. ＿＿ 地上 ＿＿ 有一封信說「謝謝你們給我們菜 ＿＿ 酒。我們
以後再見！」

＿＿ 地上 ＿＿ 有一封信说「谢谢你们给我们菜 ＿＿ 酒。我们
以後再见！」

___ dì shàng ___ yǒu yī fēng xìn shuō " xièxie nǐmen gěi wǒmen cài
___ jiǔ. wǒmen yǐhòu zài jiàn!"

*And on the ground was a letter which said "Thank you for giving us food
and wine. We will see you later."*

SEQUENCE AND SIMULTANEITY

Narrative Sequence

以後/以后 yǐhòu *after*

以後/以后 yǐhòu can be used in two different ways: as a *clause-final*

connector, and as a *clause-initial* connector. These uses are illustrated here.

Clause-final 以後/以后 yǐhòu

S_1 以後/以后, S_2. S_1 yǐhòu, S_2.   *after S_1, S_2.*

The characteristics of clause-final 以後/以后 yǐhòu are as follows:

- Clause-final 以後/以后 yǐhòu occurs at the end of the first clause. Note that its equivalent in English, the word *'after,'* occurs at the beginning of its clause.

  你來了<u>以後</u>，我們就吃飯。
  你来了<u>以后</u>，我们就吃饭。
  nǐ lái le yǐhòu, wǒmen jiù chī fàn.
  After you arrive, we will eat.

- V-了 le may occur immediately after the verb in the first VP.

  她畢了業以後就找工作。*
  她毕了业以后就找工作。
  tā bì le yè yǐhòu jiù zhǎo gōngzuò.
  After she graduates she will look for a job.

- 就 jiù or, less commonly, 才 cái may occur immediately before the second VP. When 才 cái occurs, it reflects the speaker's perception that the sequence took longer than expected or was in some way difficult to achieve. This relationship can often be expressed in English with the expression *only then* or *only after*. For more on 就 jiù and 才 cái see Chapter 4: Adverbs.

  她畢了業以後就買車。
  她毕了业以后就买车。
  tā bì le yè yǐhòu jiù mǎi chē.
  After she graduates she will buy a car.

  她畢了業以後才買車。
  她毕了业以后才买车。
  tā bì le yè yǐhòu cái mǎi chē.
  Only after she graduates will she buy a car.

- The order of clauses or VPs in clause-final 以後/以后 yǐhòu sentences is fixed. The 以後/以后 yǐhòu clause must come first.

  弟弟看完了書以後就睡覺了。
  弟弟看完了书以后就睡觉了。
  dìdi kànwán le shū yǐhòu jiù shuì jiào le.
  Younger brother finished reading the book and went to sleep.

---

*Some native speakers of Mandarin treat 畢業/毕业 bìyè as a single verb and others consider it a verb + object. Here it is used as a verb + object, with 了 le occurring directly after the verb 畢/毕 bì.

⊗弟弟睡覺了看完了書以後。

弟弟睡觉了看完了书以后。

dìdi shuì jiào le kànwán le shū yǐhòu.

Clause-initial 以後/以后 yǐhòu

S₁, 以後/以后 S₂.   S₁, yǐhòu S₂.   *S₁, afterwards S₂.*

我們先做功課，以後再看電視。

我们先做功课，以后再看电视。

wǒmen xiān zuò gōngkè, yǐhòu zài kàn diànshì.
First we'll do homework, (and) afterwards we will watch television.

現在不努力，以後會後悔的。

现在不努力，以后会后悔的。

xiànzài bù nǔlì, yǐhòu huì hòuhuǐ de.
If you are not hard-working now, later you will regret it.

Clause-initial 以後/以后 yǐhòu is not associated with any special uses of 了 le

or 就 jiù or 才 cái. Grammatically, it is a sentence adverb. See Chapter 4: Adverbs.

然後/然后 ránhòu   *afterwards*

他學習中文，然後就到中國去了。

他学习中文，然后就到中国去了。

tā xuéxí Zhōngwén, ránhòu jiù dào Zhōngguó qù le.
He studied Chinese. Later he went to China.

然後/然后 ránhòu is a clause-initial connector. It is equivalent in meaning and

usage to clause-initial 以後/以后 yǐhòu.

後來/后来 hòulái   *afterwards*

他在大學念法律，後來就當法官了。

他在大学念法律，后来就当法官了。

tā zài dàxué niàn fǎlǜ, hòulái jiù dāng fǎguān le.
When he was in college he studied law. Afterwards he became a judge.

後來/后来 hòulái is a clause-initial connector. It is equivalent in meaning and

usage to 以後/以后 yǐhòu and 然後/然后 ránhòu.

一 ... 就 ...   yī ... jiù   *as soon as ...*

我一看就知道他是一個明星。

我一看就知道他是一个明星。

wǒ yī kàn jiù zhīdao tā shì yī ge míngxīng.

As soon as I saw him I knew he was a star.

先 ... 後/后 ...   xiān ... hòu ...   *first ... afterwards ...*

你炒菜的時候先放油後放菜。

你炒菜的时候先放油后放菜。

nǐ chǎo cài de shíhou xiān fàng yóu hòu fàng cài.

When you stir-fry vegetables, first you put in the oil and then you put in the vegetables.

先 ... 再 ...   xiān ...   zài..   *first ... afterwards ...*

我們先吃飯再聊天吧。

我们先吃饭再聊天吧。

wǒmen xiān chī fàn zài liáo tiān ba.

Let's first eat and then chat.

2. Put the phrases in these sentences in the proper order to match the English translations.

1. 以後就我了回學校去看電影。

以后就我了回学校去看电影。

yǐhòu jiù wǒ le huí xuéxiào qù kàn diànyǐng.

After I see a movie I will return to school.

2. 以後我們寫字就念一本中文書了了。

以后我们写字就念一本中文书了了。

yǐhòu wǒmen xiě zì jiù niàn yī běn Zhōngwén shū le le.

After we wrote characters we read a Chinese book.

3. 學生就吃早飯以後去到公園了。

学生就吃早饭以后去到公园了。

xuéshēng jiù chī zǎofàn yǐhòu qù dào gōngyuán le.

After the students eat breakfast they will go to the park.

4. 就他們買票上車了以後了。

就他们买票上车了以后了。

jiù tāmen mǎi piào shàng chē le yǐhòu le.

After they bought the tickets they got on the bus.

5. 就我回家跑步了。 (跑步 pǎo bù *to jog*)

jiù wǒ huí jiā pǎo bù le.

After I jog I will go home.

3. Rewrite these sentences, adding 以後/以后 yǐhòu, 就 jiù, and 了 le in their proper locations as required.

1. 我畢業到中國去。

我毕业到中国去。

wǒ bìyè dào Zhōngguó qù.

After I graduate I will go to China.

2. 我哥哥畢業到中國去。

我哥哥毕业到中国去。

wǒ gēge bìyè dào Zhōngguó qù.

After older brother graduated he went to China.

3. 我吃晚飯去看電影。

我吃晚饭去看电影。

wǒ chī wǎnfàn qù kàn diànyǐng.

After I eat dinner I will see a movie.

4. 我吃晚飯看電影。

我吃晚饭看电影。

wǒ chī wǎnfàn kàn diànyǐng.

After I ate dinner I saw a movie.

5. 我考試想吃冰淇淋。

我考试想吃冰淇淋。

wǒ kǎoshì xiǎng chī bīngqilín.

After I take the test I will eat ice cream.

Reverse Sequence

以前 yǐqián *before*

S₁ 以前 yǐqián, S₂. *Before S₁, S₂.*

以前 yǐqián like 以後/以后 yǐhòu, is a clause-final connector.

The characteristics of 以前 yǐqián are as follows:

- 以前 yǐqián occurs at the end of the first clause. Note that its equivalent in English, the word *before*, occurs at the beginning of its clause.

你出國以前，先學一點外語。

你出国以前，先学一点外语。

nǐ chū guó <u>yǐqián</u>, xiān xué yīdiǎn wàiyǔ.

<u>Before</u> you go abroad, first study a foreign language for awhile.

- V-了 le cannot occur in the first clause of 以前 yǐqián sentences.

你上課以前先吃早飯吧。

你上课以前先吃早饭吧。

nǐ shàng kè yǐqián xiān chī zǎofàn ba.

Before you go to class, first eat breakfast.

⊗你上了課以前先吃早飯吧。

你上了课以前先吃早饭吧。

nǐ shàng le kè yǐqián xiān chī zǎofàn ba.

- The 以前 yǐqián clause typically comes first in 以前 yǐqián sentences.*

睡覺以前得先洗澡。

睡觉以前得先洗澡。

shuì jiào yǐqián děi xiān xǐ zǎo.

Before you go to sleep you should first get washed.

⊗洗澡，睡覺以前。

洗澡，睡觉以前。

xǐ zǎo, shuì jiào yǐqián.

4. Place these phrases in the proper order to correspond to the English translations.

1. 每天以前我都吃早飯洗澡。

   每天以前我都吃早饭洗澡。

   měitiān yǐqián wǒ dōu chī zǎofàn xǐzǎo.

   Every day before I eat I wash.

2. 以前看電影把功課先做完。

   以前看电影把功课先做完。

   yǐqián kàn diànyǐng bǎ gōngkè xiān zuòwán.

   Before you watch a movie finish your school work.

3. 我以前來中國已經學兩年的中文了。

   我以前来中国已经学两年的中文了。

   wǒ yǐqián lái Zhōngguó yǐjing xué liǎng nián de Zhōngwén le.

   Before I came to China I already studied Chinese for two years.

---

* In everyday speech, an 以前 yǐqián clause may be added to the end of a sentence as an afterthought.

4. 先去以前公園看好不好天氣。

先去以前公园看好不好天气。

xiān qù yǐqián gōngyuán kàn hǎo bù hǎo tiānqì.

Before you go to the park first see if the weather is good.

5. 以前回家請寄信到郵局去。

以前回家请寄信到邮局去。

yǐqián huí jiā qǐng jì xìn dào yóujú qù.

Before you go home please go to the post office to mail a letter.

5. Complete these sentences by adding 以前 yǐqián and 了 le where appropriate to correspond to the English translations.

1. 我去中國不會説中文。

我去中国不会说中文。

wǒ qù Zhōngguó bú huì shuō Zhōngwén.

Before I went to China I couldn't speak any Chinese.

2. 我們學漢字先學拼音。

我们学汉字先学拼音。

wǒmen xué hànzì xiān xué pīnyīn.

Before we study characters we will learn pinyin.

3. 電影開始可以説話。

电影开始可以说话。

diànyǐng kāishǐ kéyǐ shuō huà.

Before the movie begins it is okay to talk.

4. 我上大學在銀行工作一年。

我上大学在银行工作一年。

wǒ shàng dàxué zài yínháng gōngzuò yīnián.

Before I went to college I worked at a bank for a year.

5. 你回家我們先喝茶吧。

你回家我们先喝茶吧。

nǐ huí jiā wǒmen xiān hē chá ba.

Before you go home let's have a cup of tea.

Simultaneity

的時候/的时候 de shíhou *when*

The characteristics of 的時候/的时候 de shíhou sentences are as follows:

- 的時候/的时候 de shíhou occurs at the end of the first clause. Note that the English equivalent of 的時候/的时候 de shíhou, *when*, occurs at the beginning of its clause.

  哥哥開車的時候老聽音樂。
  哥哥开车的时候老听音乐。
  gēge kāi chē <u>de shíhou</u> lǎo tīng yīnyuè.
  <u>*When* older brother drives he always listens to music.</u>

- The 的時候/的时候 de shíhou clause is the first clause in the sentence.[*]

  開車的時候不許吃飯。
  开车的时候不许吃饭。
  kāi chē de shíhou bù xǔ chī fàn.
  When driving a car you are not allowed to eat.

  ☹不許吃飯，開車的時候。
  不许吃饭，开车的时候。
  bù xǔ chīfàn, kāi chē de shíhou.

Note: 的時候/的时候 de shíhou is more precise than the English word *when* in the relationship it marks. English *when* can be used to indicate either simultaneity or sequence. In Mandarin, 的時候/的时候 de shíhou is only used to indicate simultaneous situations. It cannot be used to join clauses related in terms of sequence. For sequence, you must use 以後/以后 yǐhòu. Compare the following sentences.

Sequence: *When* or *after* can be used in English. 以後/以后 yǐhòu is used in Mandarin.

  你吃完了飯以後請給我打電話。
  你吃完了饭以后请给我打电话。
  nǐ chīwán le fàn yǐhòu qǐng gěi wǒ dǎ diànhuà.
  After (when) you have finished eating, please phone me.

---

[*] In everyday speech, the 的時候/的时候 de shíhou clause is sometimes added afterwards as an afterthought.

Simultaneous situations: *When* is used in English. 的時候/的时候 de shíhou is used in

Mandarin.

> 弟弟忙的時候總是睡得很少。
> 弟弟忙的时候总是睡得很少。
> dìdi máng de shíhou zǒngshì shuì dé hěn shǎo.
> *When younger brother is busy he always sleeps very little.*

6. Translate these sentences into English.

> 1. 天氣熱的時候應該多喝水。
>   天气热的时候应该多喝水。
>   tiānqì rè de shíhou yīnggāi duō hē shuǐ.
>
> 2. 你讀書的時候最好別聽音樂。
>   你读书的时候最好别听音乐。
>   nǐ dú shū de shíhou zuì hǎo bié tīng yīnyuè.
>
> 3. 弟弟忙的時候都不吃午飯。(午飯/午饭 wǔfàn *lunch*)
>   弟弟忙的时候都不吃午饭。
>   dìdi máng de shíhou dōu bù chī wǔfàn.
>
> 4. 天氣好的時候孩子都在外頭玩。
>   天气好的时候孩子都在外头玩。
>   tiānqì hǎo de shíhou háizi dōu zài wàitou wán.
>
> 5. 我坐公共汽車的時候都復習中文字。(復習/复习 fùxí *review*)
>   我坐公共汽车的时候都复习中文字。
>   wǒ zuò gōnggòngqìchē de shíhou dōu fùxí Zhōngwén zì.

7. Put these phrases in the proper order to correspond to the English translations.

> 1. 的時候我小老騎自行車。
>   的时候我小老骑自行车。
>   de shíhou wǒ xiǎo lǎo qí zìxíngchē.
>   *When I was young I always rode my bicycle.*
>
> 2. 都爸爸吃早飯看報紙的時候。
>   都爸爸吃早饭看报纸的时候。
>   dōu bàba chī zǎofàn kàn bàozhǐ de shíhou.
>   *When dad eats breakfast he always reads the newspaper.*
>
> 3. 的時候我累不好考得。
>   de shíhou wǒ lèi bù hǎo kǎo de.
>   *When I am tired I don't do well on exams.*

4. 中國飯你吃的時候應該用筷子。
中国饭你吃的时候应该用筷子。
Zhōngguó fàn nǐ chī de shíhou yīnggāi yòng kuàizi.
When you eat Chinese food you should use chopsticks.

5. 都的時候我姐姐開車唱歌。
都的时候我姐姐开车唱歌。
dōu de shíhou wǒ jiějie kāi chē chàng gē.
When my older sister drives the car she always sings.

CONTRAST

Paired Connectors

The following contrast connectors may occur in pairs. 雖然/虽然 suīrán *although* may occur at the beginning of the first clause. The other connectors occur in the second clause, either before the subject or the VP.

雖然/虽然 suīrán *athough*	可是	kěshì	*but*
	但(是)	dànshì	
	不過/不过	búguò	

Note: As with other paired connectors, one or both of the connecting words may be omitted.

聽説那個電影很可怕，但是我還要看。
听说那个电影很可怕，但是我还要看。
tīngshuō nà ge diànyǐng hěn kěpà, dànshì wǒ hái yào kàn.
I heard that that movie is very scary, but I still want to see it.

這件衣服雖然很漂亮，可是很貴。
这件衣服虽然很漂亮，可是很贵。
zhè jiàn yīfú suīrán hěn piàoliang, kěshì hěn guì.
Although this article of clothing is pretty, it's expensive.

苦瓜很苦，不過我還喜歡吃。
苦瓜很苦，不过我还喜欢吃。
kǔguā hěn kǔ, búguò wǒ hái xǐhuan chī.
Bitter melon is very bitter, but I still like to eat it.

Adverbial Connectors

These connectors occur directly before the verb and indicate contrast. 卻 què may co-occur with other contrast connectors in the same clause.

却 què *in contrast*

> 那輛車子很貴，但他卻要買。
>
> 那辆车子很贵，但他却要买。
>
> nà liàng chēzi hěn guì, dàn tā què yào mǎi.
>
> *That car is expensive, but he still wants to buy it.*

倒是 dàoshì *contrary to one's expectation based on the context*

> 這個東西倒是很好，就是價錢太貴。
>
> 这个东西倒是很好，就是价钱太贵。
>
> zhè ge dōngxi dàoshì hěn hǎo, jiù shì jiàqian tài guì.
>
> *This thing is very good, it's just that the price is too high.*

> 那個地方我倒是想去看一看。
>
> 那个地方我倒是想去看一看。
>
> nà ge dìfang wǒ dàoshì xiǎng qù kànyikàn.
>
> *I want to go to that place and have a look.*
>
> *(You might not expect that I'd want to go there.)*

Indicating Contrast through the VP

Stative Verb 是 shì Stative Verb   *It's Stative Verb all right, but ...*

> 美國菜好是好，可是肉太多。
>
> 美国菜好是好，可是肉太多。
>
> Měiguó cài hǎo shì hǎo, kěshì ròu tài duō.
>
> *American food is good all right, but there is too much meat.*

> 這雙鞋子貴是貴但我還想買。
>
> 这双鞋子贵是贵但我还想买。
>
> zhè shuāng xiézi guì shì guì dàn wǒ hái xiǎng mǎi.
>
> *These shoes are expensive all right but I still want to buy them.*

Sentence Initial Connectors: S_1. _____ S_2

These words link two sentence or clauses. They occur at the beginning of the second sentence or clause. Note that 不過/不过 búguò can also occur directly before the VP.

不過/不过 búguò *however, nevertheless*

他歷史學得不好，不過數學學得很好。

他历史学得不好，不过数学学得很好。

tā lìshǐ xuéde bù hǎo, búguò shùxué xuéde hěn hǎo.

He is not doing well in history. However, he is doing very well in math.

然而 rán'ér *however, nevertheless*

自由好是好，然而也不能濫用自由。

自由好是好，然而也不能滥用自由。

zìyóu hǎo shì hǎo, rán'ér yě bù néng lànyòng zìyóu.

Freedom is very good, but you should not abuse freedom.

反而 fǎn'ér *on the contrary*

他小時候很用功，長大以後反而不用功了。

他小时候很用功，长大以后反而不用功了。

tā xiǎo shíhou hěn yònggōng, zhǎngdà yǐhòu fǎn'ér bú yònggōng le.

When he was young he was very hard working, but after he grew up he wasn't hardworking anymore.

反過來/反过来 fǎnguolái *conversely*

這個政策對病人不方便。反過來對醫院也没有什麼好處。

这个政策对病人不方便。反过来对医院也没有什么好处。

zhè ge zhèngcè duì bìngrén bù fāngbiàn. fǎnguolái duì yīyuàn yě méi yǒu shénme hǎochu.

This policy is not convenient for patients. Conversely, it's not particularly beneficial for the hospital either.

(要)不然 (yào)burán *otherwise*

快吃吧！要不然飯菜都涼了。

快吃吧！要不然饭菜都凉了。

kuài chī ba! yàoburán fàn cài dōu liáng le.

Hurry up and eat! Otherwise the food is going to get cold.

否則/否则 fǒuzé *otherwise*

我們趕快走吧。否則來不及了。

我们赶快走吧。否则来不及了。

wǒmen gǎnkuài zǒu ba. fǒuzé láibují le.

We'd better hurry up and go. Otherwise we won't be on time.

8. Complete each sentence by adding the appropriate contrast connector to match the English translation. For some sentences, more than one choice is possible.

    1. 我很想去看你，___ 今天没有空。

       我很想去看你，___ 今天没有空。

       wǒ hěn xiǎng qù kàn nǐ, ___ jīntiān méi yǒu kōng.

       I really want to go see you, but I have no free time today.

    2. 她要我們今天八點準時到，___ 她自己卻沒準時。

       她要我们今天八点准时到，___ 她自己却没准时。

       tā yào wǒmen jīntiān bā diǎn zhǔn shí dào, ___ tā zìjǐ què méi zhǔnshí.

       She wanted us to arrive punctually at 8, but she herself was not on time.

    3. 他很聰明，___ 他有一點懶。

       他很聪明，___ 他有一点懒。

       tā hěn cōngming, ___ tā yǒu yīdiǎn lǎn.

       He is very smart, but he is a little lazy.

    4. 我很討厭他。___，他也不喜歡我。

       我很讨厌他。___，他也不喜欢我。

       wǒ hěn tǎoyàn tā. ___, tā yě bù xǐhuan wǒ.

       I despise him. Conversely, he doesn't like me either.

    5. 學外語要每天復習，___ 學不好。

       学外语要每天复习，___ 学不好。

       xué wàiyǔ yào měitiān fùxí, ___ xuébuhǎo.

       When you study a foreign language you have to review every day. Otherwise you will not learn it well.

    6. 我去了中國，___ 沒看萬里長城。

       我去了中国，___ 没看万里长城。

       wǒ qù le Zhōngguó, ___ méi kàn Wànlǐ Chángchéng.

       I went to China, but I didn't see the Great Wall.

    7. 那個電影很多人要看。你最好早買票，___ 你也許買不到。

       那个电影很多人要看。你最好早买票，___ 你也许买不到。

       nà ge diànyǐng hěn duō rén yào kàn. nǐ zuì hǎo zǎo mǎi piào, ___ nǐ yéxǔ mǎibudào.

       Lots of people want to see that movie. You'd better buy a ticket early. Otherwise you may not be able to buy one.

8. 我送給爺爺一個鐘。爺爺 ___ 不高興，___ 非常生氣。

   我送给爷爷一个钟。爷爷 ___ 不高兴，___ 非常生气。

   wǒ sòng gěi yéye yī ge zhōng. yéye ___ bù gāoxìng, ___ fēicháng shēngqì.

   *I gave grandpa a clock. Grandpa was not only not happy, on the contrary he was really mad.**

9. 我要看王老師，___ 我找不到他的辦公室。

   我要看王老师，___ 我找不到他的办公室。

   wǒ yào kàn Wáng lǎoshī, ___ wǒ zhǎobudào tā de bàngōngshì.

   I want to see teacher Wang, but I can't find his office.

10. 他人很好，___ 他很沒意思。

    tā rén hěn hǎo, ___ tā hěn méi yìsi.

    He is a nice person, but he is really not interesting.

CONDITIONALITY

if ... then ...

      The following words can all be translated with the English conditional connector *if*.[†] The adverb 就 jiù typically occurs before the VP of the following clause.

Note: 如果 rúguǒ and 要是 yàoshi are interchangeable in meaning and are used in colloquial Mandarin. The other expressions are used in formal, literary structures.

if S_1/VP_1

如果	rúguǒ
要是	yàoshi
假如	jiǎrú
若是	ruòshì
倘若	tǎngruò
假若	jiǎruò
假使	jiáshǐ
倘使	tángshǐ
設若/设若	shèru

---

[*] In Chinese culture a clock is a symbol of the end of life. It is not appropriate to give one as a gift, especially to an older person.

[†] The English word *'if'* also introduces indirect questions: *I don't know if he knows the answer.* There is no word in Mandarin with that function.

要是你一定要買車就買吧。

要是你一定要买车就买吧。

yàoshi nǐ yīdìng yào mǎi chē jiù mǎi ba.
If you really want to buy a car, then buy one.

假如我是你，我就跟他結婚。

假如我是你，我就跟他结婚。

jiǎrú wǒ shì nǐ, wǒ jiù gēn tā jiéhūn.
If I were you, I would marry him.

假使你今天能來我就不去了。

假使你今天能来我就不去了。

jiáshǐ nǐ jīntiān néng lái wǒ jiù bú qù le.
If you can come today I won't go.

除非 chúfēi *unless, only if*

除非他的態度改變了，問題才能解決。

除非他的态度改变了，问题才能解决。

chúfēi tā de tàidu gǎibiàn le, wèntí cái néng jiějué.
Only if his attitude changes can this problem be resolved.

除非你天天做運動，要不然就會越來越胖。

除非你天天做运动，要不然就会越来越胖。

chúfēi nǐ tiāntiān zuò yùndòng, yàoburán jiù huì yuè lái yuè pàng.
Unless you exercise every day, you will get fatter and fatter.

就是 … 也 … jiùshì … yě … *even if*

就是你幫助我，我也做不完。

就是你帮助我，我也做不完。

jiùshì nǐ bāngzhù wǒ, wǒ yě zuòbuwán.
Even if you help me, I won't be able to finish.

就是你勸我，我還是不願意跟你去。

就是你劝我，我还是不愿意跟你去。

jiùshì nǐ quàn wǒ, wǒ hái shì bú yuànyi gēn nǐ qù.
Even if you urge me to do it, I still am not willing to go with you.

CAUSE-AND-EFFECT

因爲/因为… 所以 … yīnwei … suóyǐ … *because … therefore …*

因爲他人很好，所以別人都喜歡他。

因为他人很好，所以别人都喜欢他。

yīnwei tā rén hěn hǎo, suóyǐ bié ren dōu xǐhuan tā.

Since he is a good person, other people all like him.

他人很好，所以別人都喜歡他。

他人很好，所以别人都喜欢他。

tā rén hěn hǎo, suóyǐ bié ren dōu xǐhuan tā.

He is a good person, so other people all like him.

既然… (就) jìrán … (jiù) *since it is the case …*

既然你已經學過，就不必再學了 。

既然你已经学过，就不必再学了 。

jìrán nǐ yǐjing xuéguo, jiù bú bì zài xué le.

Since you have already studied (it) once, you don't have to study it again.

因此 yīncǐ *because of this*

波士頓的冬天很冷。因此需要多穿一點衣服。

波士顿的冬天很冷。因此需要多穿一点衣服。

Bōshìdùn de dōngtiān hěn lěng. yīncǐ xūyào duō chuān yīdiǎn yīfu.

Boston's winters are very cold. Therefore you need to wear more clothes.

9. Add the appropriate connecting words to complete each sentence according to its English translation.

1. ___ 你不認識這個字，就去問老師。

   ___ 你不认识这个字，就去问老师。

   ___ nǐ bú rènshi zhè ge zì, jiù qù wèn lǎoshī.

   If you don't recognize this character, go ask the teacher.

2. ___ 我是去年來這兒的，___ 我還不認識很多人。

   ___ 我是去年来这儿的，___ 我还不认识很多人。

   ___ wǒ shì qùnián lái zhèr de, ___ wǒ hái bú rènshi hěn duō rén.

   Although I came here last year, I still don't know very many people.

3. 我常跟她说話，___ 我還不知道她叫什麼名字。

   我常跟她说话，___ 我还不知道她叫什麼名字。

   wǒ cháng gēn tā shuō huà, ___ wǒ hái bù zhīdao tā jiào shénme míngzi.

   I often speak with her but I still do not know her name.

4. ___ 他很忙，___ 他很願意幫助別人。

   ___ 他很忙，___ 他很愿意帮助别人。

   ___ tā hěn máng, ___ tā hěn yuànyi bāngzhù bié ren.
   Although he is very busy, he is still willing to help other people.

5. 他才十五歲，___ 他數學學得比大學生好。

   他才十五岁，___ 他数学学得比大学生好。

   tā cái shíwǔ suì, ___ tā shùxué xué dé bǐ dàxuéshēng hǎo.
   He is only 15 years old, but he is better at math than college students.

6. 哥哥 ___ 已經上大學四年級了，___ 他還不會說外語。

   哥哥 ___ 已经上大学四年级了，___ 他还不会说外语。

   gēge ___ yǐjing shàng dàxué sì niánjí le, ___ tā hái bú huì shuō wàiyǔ.
   *Older brother is already a senior in college, but he still can't speak a
   foreign language.*

7. ___ 我家離這兒很遠，___ 我很少回家。

   ___ 我家离这儿很远，___ 我很少回家。

   ___ wǒ jiā lí zhèr hěn yuǎn, ___ wǒ hěn shǎo huí jiā.
   Since my home is very far from here, I rarely go home.

8. ___ 我去過幾次，___ 我認識路。

   ___ 我去过几次，___ 我认识路。

   ___ wǒ qùguo jǐ cì, ___ wǒ rènshi lù.
   Since I've gone (there) a few times I know the road.

9. ___ 太陽從西邊出來，___ 我不會跟你結婚的。

   ___ 太阳从西边出来，___ 我不会跟你结婚的。

   ___ tàiyáng cóng xībian chulai, ___ wǒ bú huì gēn nǐ jiéhūn de.
   Only if the sun comes up in the west will I be willing to marry you.

10. 外頭正下着大雨，___ 我們今天無法去野餐了。

    外头正下着大雨，___ 我们今天无法去野餐了。

    wàitou zhèng xiàzhe dà yǔ. ___ wǒmen jīntiān wúfǎ qù yěcān le.
    It's raining hard outside. Because of this we can't go to the picnic.

11. 你得用功一點，___ 就不能學好中文。

    你得用功一点，___ 就不能学好中文。

    nǐ děi yònggōng yīdiǎn, ___ jiù bù néng xuéhǎo Zhōngwén.
    *You have to be a little more hardworking. Otherwise you won't be able to
    master Chinese.*

12. 趕快起床吧，＿＿ 你會遲到。

赶快起床吧，＿＿ 你会迟到。

gǎnkuài qǐ chuáng ba. ＿＿ nǐ huì chídào.

Hurry up and get out of bed. Otherwise you will be late.

13. ＿＿ 你已經把作業都做好了，今天晚上可以多看一點電視。

＿＿ 你已经把作业都做好了，今天晚上可以多看一点电视。

＿＿ nǐ yǐjing bǎ zuòyè dōu zuòhǎo le, jīntiān wǎnshang kéyǐ duō kàn yīdiǎn diànshì.

Since you've already finished your homework, tonight you can watch a little more television.

14. 她不喜歡吃肉。＿＿ 你勸她吃她也不會吃。

她不喜欢吃肉。＿＿ 你劝她吃她也不会吃。

tā bù xǐhuan chī ròu. ＿＿ nǐ quàn tā chī tā yě bú huì chī.

She doesn't like to eat meat. Even if you urge her to eat it she still won't eat it.

15. ＿＿ 現在不努力，以後會後悔的。

＿＿ 现在不努力，以后会后悔的。

＿＿ xiànzài bù nǔlì, yǐhòu huì hòuhuǐ de.

If you are not hard-working now, later you will regret it.

Focusing Constructions

Focusing constructions emphasize an NP by making it prominent in some way. Mandarin has many constructions which focus the NP. Here are the most common.

Topicalization

When an NP that is not the subject occurs at the beginning of the sentence, it functions as its topic.

這本書，老師説我們都應該看。
这本书，老师说我们都应该看。
zhè běn shū, lǎoshī shuō wǒmen dōu yīnggāi kàn.
This book, the teacher said we should all read (it).

The topic may be preceded by a word which introduces it as the topic.

Topic Marker	Meaning
關於/关於 NP guānyú NP	*regarding, concerning NP*
對於/对於 NP duìyú NP	*regarding, concerning NP (formal literary)*
對 NP 來説 对 NP 来说 duì NP lái shuō	*concerning NP*
至於/至於 NP zhìyú (NP)	*regarding, concerning, as for NP (formal, literary)*

The use of these topic markers is illustrated in the following sentences.

關於出國學習的事情，我們必須考慮考慮。
关于出国学习的事情，我们必须考虑考虑。
guānyú chū guó xuéxí de shìqing, wǒmen bìxū kǎolù kǎolù.
As for the matter of leaving the country to study, we should think it over for awhile.

他很節省，對於貴重的東西都沒興趣。
他很节省，对于贵重的东西都没兴趣。
tā hěn jiéshěng, duìyú guìzhòng de dōngxi dōu méi xìngqù.
He is very thrifty. He is not interested in valuable possessions.

我們已經盡力了，至於成功還是失敗，就不重要了。

我们已经尽力了，至于成功还是失败，就不重要了。

wǒmen yǐjing jìnlì le, zhìyú chénggōng háishi shībài, jiù bú zhòngyào le.

We've already done what we could. As to whether we will succeed or fail, that is not important.

對中國人來說，面子很要緊。

对中国人来说，面子很要紧。

duì Zhōngguó rén lái shuō, miànzi hěn yàojǐn.

Face is very important to Chinese people.

是 shì ... (的 de)

The words 是 shì and 的 de can be used to focus a phrase in the sentence. The

focused phrase must occur before the verb.

- 是 shì occurs directly before the focused phrase.

- 的 de occurs immediately after the verb or at the end of the sentence, before any

  sentence-final particles.*

你是在哪儿學的中文？

你是在哪儿学的中文？

nǐ shì zài nǎr xué de Zhōngwén?

Where did you study Chinese?

你是在美國長大的嗎？

你是在美国长大的吗？

nǐ shì zài Měiguó zhǎng dà de ma?

Did you grow up in America?

---

* 的 de at the end of the sentence sometimes results in an ambiguous meaning in which 的 de can be interpreted as a marker of emphasis or as a marker of noun phrase modification.

我是在紐約買車的。

我是在纽约买车的。

wǒ shì zài Niǔyuē mǎi chē de.

It was in New York where I bought the car. OR

I am the person who bought the car in New York.

When 的 de follows the verb it is always interpreted as a marker of emphasis. That is

我是在紐約買的車。

我是在纽约买的车。

wǒ shì zài Niǔyuē mǎi de chē.

can only mean "*It was in New York where I bought the car.*"

■ 是 shì may occur alone, or it may occur with 的 de. When 是 shì and 的 de

occur together in a sentence, they focus a phrase *and* indicate that the situation

described in the sentence occurred in the past.

弟弟是在紐約上大學，不是在麻州上大學。

弟弟是在纽约上大学，不是在麻州上大学。

dìdi <u>shì</u> zài Niǔyuē shàng dàxué, bú <u>shì</u> zài Mázhōu shàng dàxué.

Younger brother attends college in New York, not in Massachusetts.

弟弟是在紐約上大學的。

弟弟是在纽约上大学的。

dìdi <u>shì</u> zài Niǔyuē shàng dàxué <u>de</u>.

Younger brother attended college in New York.

是 shì can be used to focus the subject NP, the time phrase, or the PP, including a

PP indicating location.

<u>是 shì before the subject NP:</u>

Q: 是<u>誰</u>提的這個問題？   A: 是<u>我</u>提的。

是<u>谁</u>提的这个问题？   是<u>我</u>提的。

shì <u>shéi</u> tí de zhè ge wèntí?   shì <u>wǒ</u> tí de.

Who raised this question?   *It is I who raised (it).*

<u>是 shì before the location phrase:</u>

我們是在日本認識的。

我们是在日本认识的。

wǒmen shì <u>zài Rìbĕn</u> rènshi de.

We met in Japan.

<u>是 shì before the time phrase:</u>

我是去年去中國的。

我是去年去中国的。

wǒ <u>shì qùnián</u> qù Zhōngguó de.

It was last year that I went to China.

是 shì . . . 的 de and V-了 le provide different information about past

time/completed events.

V-了 le indicates that an event occurred. (See Chapter 6: The Suffixes 了 le,

着 zhe, and 過/过 guo.)

我買了車。
我买了车。
wǒ mǎi le chē.
I bought a car.

是 shì . . . 的 de emphasizes a detail of an event that has occurred.

我是在紐約買的車。
我是在纽约买的车。
wǒ shì zài Niǔyuē mǎi de chē.
It was in New York that I bought a car.

Because 是 shì . . . 的 de and V-了 le provide different perspectives on an event,

是 shì . . . 的 de and V-了 le do not occur in the same sentence.

1. Rewrite the following sentences, using 是 shì . . . 的 de to focus the bracketed
phrase in each sentence. Translate your sentences into English.

1. 我〔今天〕買書。
   我〔今天〕买书。
   wǒ〔jīntiān〕mǎi shū.

2. 我〔在公園裏〕看到王老師。
   我〔在公园里〕看到王老师。
   wǒ〔zài gōngyuán lǐ〕kàndào Wáng lǎoshī.

3. 我〔去年〕認識陳麗麗。
   我〔去年〕认识陈丽丽。
   wǒ〔qùnián〕rènshi Chén Lìlì.

4. 我〔在車上〕買票。
   我〔在车上〕买票。
   wǒ〔zài chē shàng〕mǎi piào.

5. 我〔跟張老師〕借書。
   我〔跟张老师〕借书。
   wǒ〔gēn Zhāng lǎoshī〕jiè shū.

6. 我〔在南京〕吃豆沙包。 (豆沙包 dòushā bāo *red bean paste buns*)
   wǒ〔zài Nánjīng〕chī dòushā bāo.

7. 我〔二零零一年〕去中國。
   我〔二零零一年〕去中国。
   wǒ〔èr líng líng yī nián〕qù Zhōngguó.

8. 我〔昨天晚上〕看那個電影。

   我〔昨天晚上〕看那个电影。

   wǒ〔zuótiān wǎnshang〕kàn nà ge diànyǐng.

9. 我哥哥〔在中國〕練太極拳。 (練/练 liàn *to study, to practice*)

   我哥哥〔在中国〕练太极拳。 (太極拳/太极拳 tàijíquán

   wǒ gēge〔zài Zhōngguó〕liàn tàijíquán. *Chinese shadow boxing*)

10. 你〔幾月幾號〕生? (幾月幾號/几月几号 jǐ yuè jǐ hào

   你〔几月几号〕生?   *what month and date?*)

   nǐ〔jǐyuè jǐhào〕shēng?

2. Translate the following sentences into Mandarin, using 是 shì . . . 的 de to focus the bracketed phrase in each sentence. Note that the words "it was … that" are used as a focusing construction in English and do not get translated into Mandarin.

   1. I grew up in America. (長大/长大 zhǎng dà *to grow up*)
   2. It was [in 1985] that I graduated.
   3. I came [from China].
   4. It was [in America] that I studied Chinese.
   5. They got married in 1992. (結婚/结婚 jiéhūn *to get married*)

除了 … 以外   chúle … yǐwài

除了 chúle NP₁ 以外 yǐwài + 都 dōu *except for NP₁*

除了妹妹以外,我們都喜歡看電影。

除了妹妹以外,我们都喜欢看电影。

chúle mèimei yǐwài, wǒmen dōu xǐhuan kàn diànyǐng.
Except for younger sister, we all like to see movies.

除了 chúle NP₁ 以外 yǐwài + 也 yě *including NP₁*

除了米飯以外,他們也吃了饅頭。

除了米饭以外,他们也吃了馒头。

chúle mǐfàn yǐwài, tāmen yě chīle mántou.
Besides rice, they also ate steamed bread.

■ The full pattern includes both 除了 chúle and 以外 yǐwài. However, either 除了 chúle or 以外 yǐwài may be omitted.

茄子以外我什麼都吃。

茄子以外我什么都吃。

qiézi yǐwài wǒ shénme dōu chī.
Except for eggplant I eat anything.

除了吃，他什麼都不做。

除了吃，他什么都不做。

chúle chī, tā shénme dōu bú zuò.

Except for eating, he doesn't do anything.

3. Complete these sentences by translating the English into Mandarin. Translate the completed sentences into English.

1. 除了七月以外, August's weather is also very hot.
   chúle qīyuè yǐwài,

2. 除了咖啡以外, I also like to drink tea.
   chúle kāfēi yǐwài,

3. 除了美國飯以外, Mom can also cook Chinese food.
   除了美国饭以外,
   chúle Měiguó fàn yǐwài,

4. In addition to my younger brother, 我妹妹也結婚了。
   　　　　　　　　　　　　　　　　我妹妹也结婚了。
   　　　　　　　　　　　　　　　wǒ mèimei yě jiéhūn le.

5. 除了姐姐以外, we all went to China last year.
   chúle jiějie yǐwài,

6. Except for my name, 我把字都寫錯了。
   　　　　　　　　　　　我把字都写错了。
   　　　　　　　　　wǒ bǎ zì dōu xiěcuò le.

7. 除了弟弟以外, we all ate until we were full.
   除了弟弟以外,
   chúle dìdi yǐwài,

8. 除了這個字以外, I know all of the other characters.
   除了这个字以外,
   chúle zhè ge zì yǐwài,

9. In addition to me, 我弟弟也學漢語。
   　　　　　　　　　　我弟弟也学汉语。
   　　　　　　　　wǒ dìdi yě xué Hànyǔ.

10. Except for Zhao Ming, 我們都看過那個電影。
    　　　　　　　　　　　我们都看过那个电影。
    　　　　　　　　　wǒmen dōu kànguo nà ge diànyǐng.

連/连 NP 也/都 VP lián NP yě/dōu VP   *even NP does VP*

連/连 lián occurs before the subject. 也 yě or 都 dōu may occur right before the VP.

連弟弟也喜歡吃餅乾。
连弟弟也喜欢吃饼乾。
lián dìdi yě xǐhuan chī bǐnggān.
Even younger brother likes to eat cookies.

When the focused NP is the object of the VP, 連/连 lián plus the focused NP occur right after the subject NP and before the Verb. 也 yě or 都 dōu may be included after the focused NP, at the beginning of the VP.

弟弟連菠菜也喜歡吃。
弟弟连菠菜也喜欢吃。
dìdi lián bōcài yě xǐhuan chī.
Younger brother even likes to eat spinach.
(Literally: Younger brother even spinach likes to eat.)

4. Rewrite these sentences, using 連/连 lián to focus the bracketed phrase. The English translations are provided.

1. 我很笨。〔一個字〕都不認識。
   我很笨。〔一个字〕都不认识。
   wǒ hěn bèn. 〔yī ge zì〕dōu bú rènshi.
   I am really stupid. I don't even recognize one character.

2. 我弟弟很聰明。他聽得懂〔日語〕。
   我弟弟很聪明。他听得懂〔日语〕。
   wǒ dìdi hěn cōngming. tā tīngdedǒng〔Rìyǔ〕.
   My younger brother is very smart. He even understands Japanese.

3. 弟弟沒去過〔紐約〕。
   弟弟没去过〔纽约〕。
   dìdi méi qùguo〔Niǔyuē〕.
   Younger brother hasn't even been to New York.

4. 誰都喜歡陳麗麗。〔哥哥〕喜歡她。
   谁都喜欢陈丽丽。〔哥哥〕喜欢她。
   shéi dōu xǐhuan Chén Lìlì.〔gēge〕xǐhuan tā.
   Everyone likes Lili Chen. Even older brother likes her.

5. 我買不了電影票。我沒有〔一塊錢〕。

我买不了电影票。我没有〔一块钱〕。

wǒ mǎibuliǎo diànyǐng piào. wǒ méi yǒu〔yī kuài qián〕.

I can't buy a movie ticket. I don't even have one dollar.

6. 這些字你都寫錯了。〔你的名字〕寫錯了。

这些字你都写错了。〔你的名字〕写错了。

zhè xiē zì nǐ dōu xiěcuò le.〔nǐ de míngzi〕xiěcuò le.

*You've written all of these characters wrong. You've even written your name
wrong.*

7. 他沒說〔一句話〕。

他没说〔一句话〕。

tā méi shuō〔yī jù huà〕.

He didn't even say one word.

8. 誰都去過蘇州。〔弟弟〕去過。

谁都去过苏州。〔弟弟〕去过。

shéi dōu qùguo Sūzhōu.〔dìdi〕qùguo.

Everyone has been to Suzhou. Even younger brother has been there.

9. 她病了。不會吃〔冰淇淋〕。

她病了。不会吃〔冰淇淋〕。

tā bìng le. bú huì chī〔bīngqilín〕.

She's sick. She can't even eat ice cream.

10. 他什麼都吃。他吃〔苦瓜〕。

他什么都吃。他吃〔苦瓜〕。

tā shénme dōu chī. tā chī〔kǔguā〕.

He eats everything. He even eats bitter melon.

Passives

The structure of passive sentences in Mandarin is as follows:

〔affected object〕〔被 bèi/ 讓 ràng/ 叫 jiào NP〕〔Verb〕

When the passive marker is 叫 jiào, the verb may be preceded by 給/给 gěi.

飛機票被我丟了。

飞机票被我丢了。

fēijī piào bèi wǒ diū le.

飛機票讓我丢了。

飞机票让我丢了。

fēijī piào ràng wǒ diū le.

飛機票叫我給丢了。

飞机票叫我给丢了。

fēijī piào jiào wǒ gěi diū le.
The airplane ticket was lost by me.

Mandarin passive sentences generally imply that the event is 'bad news' for the narrator or one of the participants in the situation.

我的皮包被小偷偷走了。

wǒ de píbāo bèi xiǎotōu tōuzǒu le.
My handbag was stolen by a thief.

Activity verbs in passive sentences are often followed by Resultative Verb endings. (See Chapter 7: The Resultative Structure and Potential Suffixes.)

餅乾都被弟弟吃完了。

饼乾都被弟弟吃完了。

bǐnggān dōu bèi dìdi chīwán le.
The cookies were eaten up by younger brother.

The passive marker 被 bèi may occur without a following NP.

壞人被捕了。

坏人被捕了。

huàirén bèi bǔ le.
The bad guy was arrested.

Note: Perhaps because of its more specialized meaning as a source of 'bad news,' the use of the passive in Mandarin is relatively restricted and is much less common than in English.

5. Rearrange the phrases in each sentence to correspond to their English translations.

    1. 妹妹吃完蛋糕讓了。

      妹妹吃完蛋糕让了。

      mèimei chīwán dàngāo ràng le.
      The cake was eaten up by younger sister.

2. 人家拿走行李讓了我的。

   人家拿走行李让了我的。

   rénjiā názǒu xíngli ràng le wǒde.

   My suitcases were taken away by someone.

3. 讓火燒了房子。

   让火烧了房子。

   ràng huǒ shāo le fángzi.

   The house was burned by the fire.

4. 人家被我的車碰壞了。

   人家被我的车碰坏了。

   rénjiā bèi wǒde chē pèng huài le.

   My car was wrecked by someone.

5. 叫別的孩子嘲笑我妹妹了。

   jiào bié de háizi cháoxiào wǒ mèimei le.

   My younger sister was teased by the other children.

6. Translate these passive sentences into English.

   1. 太太被先生打了。

      tàitai bèi xiānsheng dǎ le.

   2. 老師的筆讓學生拿走了。

      老师的笔让学生拿走了。

      lǎoshī de bǐ ràng xuésheng ná zǒu le.

   3. 他的鞋子被狗咬壞了。 (咬 yǎo *to bite, to chew*)

      他的鞋子被狗咬坏了。

      tā de xiézi bèi gǒu yǎohuài le.

   4. 窗戶被弟弟打破了。(窗戶 chuānghu *window*)

      chuānghu bèi dìdi dǎpò le. 打破 dǎpò *break by hitting*)

   5. 我的小鳥叫弟弟給放走了。(小鳥/小鸟 xiǎoniǎo *little bird*,

      我的小鸟叫弟弟给放走了。 放走 fàng zǒu *release*)

      wǒ de xiǎoniǎo jiào dìdi gěi fàngzǒu le.

   6. 包裹被郵局弄丟了。   (包裹 bāoguǒ *package*, 郵局/邮局 yóujú

      包裹被邮局弄丢了。   *post office*, 弄丟 nòngdiū *to lose*)

      bāoguǒ bèi yóujú nòngdiū le.

CHAPTER 14

Speaker Perspective

Mandarin uses adverbs and sentence-final particles to convey the speaker's perspective about a situation. The most common of these are presented here.

ADVERBS AND ADVERBIAL PHRASES

Sentence-Initial Adverbs and Adverbial Phrases

These sentence-initial adverbs and adverbial phrases express the speaker's surprise, regret, or confirmation of a situation.

没想到	méi xiǎngdào	*Unexpectedly, (I) never expected that ...*
恐怕	kǒngpà	*I'm afraid that ...*
看上去	kànshang qù	*It seems that ...*
依我看	yī wǒ kàn	*From my perspective ...*
據我所知/据我所知	jù wǒ suǒ zhī	*From what I know ...*
實際上/实际上	shíjìshang	*In fact ...*
其實/其实	qíshí	*In fact ...*

没想到你會說中國話。
没想到你会说中国话。
méi xiǎngdào nǐ huì shuō Zhōngguó huà.
I never thought that you could speak Chinese.

這次的考試我恐怕考不好。
这次的考试我恐怕考不好。
zhè cì de kǎoshì wǒ kǒngpà kǎo bù hǎo.
I'm afraid I will not do well on this test.

這次考試恐怕你考得不好。
这次考试恐怕你考得不好。
zhè cì kǎoshì kǒngpà nǐ kǎode bù hǎo.
I'm afraid you did not do well on this test.

他看上去很年輕。
他看上去很年轻。
tā kànshang qù hěn niánqīng.
He appears to be very young.

or

看上去他很年輕。

看上去他很年轻。

kànshang qù tā hěn niánqīng.
He appears to be very young.

依我看這件事情很容易做。

依我看这件事情很容易做。

yī wǒ kàn zhè jiàn shìqing hěn róngyì zuò.
From my perspective this thing is easy to do.

據我所知美國人不是都很有錢。

据我所知美国人不是都很有钱。

jù wǒ suǒ zhī Měiguó rén bú shì dōu hěn yǒu qián.
From what I know Americans are not all rich.

實際上窮人也很多。

实际上穷人也很多。

shíjìshang qióng rén yě hěn duō.
In fact there are also a lot of poor people.

很多人認爲中文很難學。其實並不難。

很多人认为中文很难学。其实并不难。

hěn duō rén rènwéi Zhōngwén hěn nán xué. qíshí bìng bù nán.
Many people think that Chinese is difficult to study. In fact it isn't difficult at all.

Adverbs and Adverbial Phrases That Occur Before the Verb Phrase

The following adverbs which express speaker perspective occur before the verb phrase. They comment on the factuality, predictability, or futility of the situation. Illustrative sentences and additional exercises involving these adverbs are presented in Chapter 4: Adverbs.

明確/明确	míngquè	*clearly*
好像	hǎoxiàng	*seemingly, apparently*
顯得/显得	xiǎndé	*seemingly, apparently*
並/并	bìng *(+Negation)*	*not at all (always occurs with negation)*
居然	jūrán	*unexpectedly, to one's suprise*
竟然	jìngrán	*unexpectedly, to one's suprise*
白	bái	*in vain*
徒然	túrán	*in vain, futile*
簡直/简直	jiǎnzhí *(+Negation)*	*simply (always occurs with negation)*

1. Select an adverb from the two lists above to complete each of the following sentences to best match its English translation.

1. 你以爲他知道。___ 他一點也不知道。

   你以为他知道。___ 他一点也不知道。

   nǐ yǐwéi tā zhīdao. ___ tā yīdiǎn yě bù zhīdao.

   You think he knows. In fact he doesn't know at all.

2. 我 ___ 在哪兒見過他。

   我 ___ 在哪儿见过他。

   wǒ ___ zài nǎr jiànguo tā.

   I seem to have seen him somewhere before.

3. 他 ___ 學了三年中文。一句話也不會説。

   他 ___ 学了三年中文。一句话也不会说。

   tā ___ xué le sān nián Zhōngwén. yī jù huà yě bú huì shuō.

   He studied three years of Chinese in vain. He can't speak a word.

4. 他 ___ 一年没跟爸爸説話。

   他 ___ 一年没跟爸爸说话。

   tā ___ yīnián méi gēn bàba shuō huà.

   To my surprise he didn't speak with Dad for a year.

5. ___ 她的中文説得很好。

   ___ 她的中文说得很好。

   ___ tā de Zhōngwén shuō dé hěn hǎo.

   From what I know her Chinese is very good.

6. 他 ___ 很認真。

   他 ___ 很认真。

   tā ___ hěn rènzhēn.

   He seems to be very conscientious.

7. 她已經六十歲了。但是 ___ 她才有四十歲左右。

   她已经六十岁了。但是 ___ 她才有四十岁左右。

   tā yǐjing liùshí suì le. dànshì ___ tā cái yǒu sìshí suì zuǒyòu.

   She is already 60 years old. But she looks around 40 years old.

8. 你别説。别 ___ 費精力了。

   你别说。别 ___ 费精力了。

   nǐ bié shuō. bié ___ fèi jīnglì le.

   Don't say anything. Don't waste your effort.

9. 他 ___ 忘了女朋友的生日。

   tā ___ wàng le nǚ péngyou de shēngri.

   Totally unexpectedly, he forgot his girlfriend's birthday.

10. 他 ___ 一點也不知道。

    他 ___ 一点也不知道。

    tā ___ yīdiǎn yě bù zhīdao.

    He simply doesn't know anything.

11. 她是在中國長大的。___ 她不喜歡吃中國飯。

    她是在中国长大的。___ 她不喜欢吃中国饭。

    tā shì zài Zhōngguó zhǎng dà de. ___ tā bù xǐhuan chī Zhōngguó fàn.

    She grew up in China. Who would have thought she doesn't like to eat Chinese food.

12. ___ ， 他們兩個人的關係不太好。

    ___ ， 他们两个人的关系不太好。

    ___ , tāmen liǎng ge rén de guānxi bú tài hǎo.

    From what I can see, the relationship between the two of them is not very good.

SENTENCE FINAL PARTICLES

- Most final particles convey speaker perspective, providing information about the speaker's attitude towards the preceding sentence or about the speaker's intentions in saying or writing the sentence.[*]   In this way, Mandarin final particles often serve the same role as sentence intonation in English.

- Final particles always occur in neutral tone.

- · Nothing in the sentence goes after the final particle. It is literally the last word in the sentence.

---

[*] The final particle 嗎/吗 ma has a grammatical function. It indicates that the sentence is a yes/no question. (See Chapter 8: Questions and Question Words.)

   你是學生嗎？
   你是学生吗？
   nǐ shì xuésheng ma?
   Are you a student?

吧　ba *marker of a rhetorical question or a suggestion*

昨天的音樂會不錯吧？

昨天的音乐会不错吧？

zuótiān de yīnyuèhuì búcuò ba?

Yesterday's concert wasn't bad, was it?

他是你弟弟吧？

tā shì nǐ dìdi ba?

He must be your younger brother, right?

吃飯吧！

吃饭吧！

chī fàn ba!

Let's eat!

啊　a *marker of obviousness*

他不吃啊。

tā bù chī a.

He's not eating.

您是美國人啊。

您是美国人啊。

nín shì Měiguórén a.

You must be an American.

呀　ya *variation of* 啊*, used when the previous word ends in a vowel*

今天外頭的風好大呀！

今天外头的风好大呀！

jīntiān wàitou de fēng hǎo dà ya!

The wind outside is very big!

你踩到我的脚了呀！

nǐ cǎidào wǒ de jiǎo le ya!

You've stepped on my foot!

呢　ne *used as the marker of a yes-no questioning when asking the same question about a second subject:*

Q: 你父親母親都好嗎？   A: 他們都好，謝謝。

你父亲母亲都好吗？   他们都好，谢谢。

nǐ fùqin mǔqin dōu hǎo ma?   tāmen dōu hǎo. xièxiè.

Are your mother and father both okay?   *They are both fine, thanks.*

Q: 你爺爺呢？
你爷爷呢？
nǐ yéye ne?
How about your grandfather?

呢 ne *used to indicate a continued situation:*

他還在這兒呢。
他还在这儿呢。
tā hái zài zhèr ne.
He is still here.

他們在吃飯呢。
他们在吃饭呢。
tāmen zài chīfàn ne.
They are eating now.

嘛 ma *marker of persuasion or to emphasize the obvious*

你跟我一塊兒去嘛！
你跟我一块儿去嘛！
nǐ gēn wǒ yī kuàr qù ma!
Go with me!

是星期天嘛！辦公室當然沒人。
是星期天嘛！办公室当然没人。
shì xīngqītiān ma! bàngōngshì dāngrán méi rén.
It's Sunday. Of course there is no one in the office.

啦 la *marker of doubt, impatience, or annoyance*

好啦！好啦！我都懂啦！
好啦！好啦！我都懂啦！
hǎo la! hǎo la! wǒ dōu dǒng la!
OK! OK! I understand!

已經九點啦。他當然下班了！
已经九点啦。他当然下班了！
yǐjing jiǔ diǎn la. tā dāngrán xià bān le!
It is already 9 o'clock. Of course he's left work!

<u>喔 wo *marker of surprise, sudden realization, reminder*</u>

畢業後，別把我忘了喔！

毕业后，别把我忘了喔！

bì yè hòu, bié bǎ wǒ wàng le wo!

After you graduate, don't forget me!

<u>哦 o *marker of doubt; used for reminders*</u>

畢業後，別把我忘了哦！

毕业后，别把我忘了哦！

bì yè hòu, bié bǎ wǒ wàng le o!

After you graduate, don't forget me!

<u>咯 lo *marker of obviousness*</u>

下雨咯。

下雨咯。

xià yǔ lo.

It's raining.

2. Add the appropriate final particle to each sentence to correspond to the English translation.

   1. 時間到了。我們走 ＿＿ ！

     时间到了。我们走 ＿＿ ！

     shíjiān dào le.　wǒmen zǒu ＿ !

     The time has arrived. Let's go!

   2. 是星期日。一定得找你的朋友一起來＿＿！

     是星期日。一定得找你的朋友一起来＿＿！

     shì xīngqīrì.　yīdìng děi zhǎo nǐ de péngyou yīqǐ lái ＿＿＿ !

     It's Sunday. You should certainly get your friends together and come!

   3. 今天的天氣好冷＿＿！

     今天的天气好冷＿＿！

     jīntiān de tiānqì hǎo lěng ＿＿!

     It's really cold today!

   4. 外頭風大。快到屋子裏來＿＿！

     外头风大。快到屋子里来＿＿！

     wàitou fēng dà. kuài dào wūzi lǐ lái ＿＿!

     It's windy outside. Hurry up and come into the room!

5. 先借我二十塊錢 __ ！我明天一定會還你 __ ！

   先借我二十块钱 __ ！我明天一定会还你 __ ！

   xiān jiè wǒ èrshí kuài qián __! wǒ míngtiān yīdìng huì huán nǐ __ !

   Lend me $20. I will certainly return it to you tomorrow!

6. 請進來坐一會兒 __ ！

   请进来坐一会儿 __ ！

   qǐng jìnlái zuò yīhuìr __!

   Come on in and sit for awhile!

7. 我很想你 __ ！你也想我嗎？

   我很想你 __ ！你也想我吗？

   wǒ hěn xiǎng nǐ __!   nǐ yě xiǎng wǒ ma?

   I really miss you. Do you miss me?

8. 我從來沒去過法國 __ ！

   我从来没去过法国 __ ！

   wǒ cónglái méi qùguo Fǎguo __!

   I've never been to France before!

9. 這樣不太好 __ ？

   这样不太好 __ ？

   zhè yàng bú tài hǎo ___ ?

   Doing it this way isn't so good, huh?

10. 學中文好難！怎樣才能學好 ___ ？

    学中文好难！怎样才能学好 ___ ？

    xué Zhōngwén hǎo nán! zěnyàng cái néng xuéhǎo __ ?

    Studying Chinese is really hard! What do we have to do to finally learn it?

3. Add a final particle to each sentence in the story to best convey the meaning.

   1. 我的小貓在沙發上睡得很舒服 ___ ！

      我的小猫在沙发上睡得很舒服 ___ ！

      wǒ de xiǎomāo zài shāfā shàng shuì de hěn shūfu __!

      My little cat is sleeping comfortably on the sofa!

   2. 我看他已經睡了兩個小時了，就對他說：「起來 __ ！

      我看他已经睡了两个小时了，就对他说：「起来 __ ！

      wǒ kàn tā yǐjing shuì le liang ge xiǎoshí le, jiù duì tā shuō: "qǐlai __ !

      I see he's already been sleeping a couple of hours and I say to him: "get up!

3. 你已經睡了很久 ___！」

   你已经睡了很久 ___！」

   nǐ yǐjing shuì le hěn jiǔ ___ !"

   You've already been sleeping a long time! "

4. 小貓看了看我，好像對我説：「幹嘛？別吵 ___！」

   小猫看了看我，好像对我说：「干嘛？别吵 ___！」

   xiǎomāo kàn le kàn wǒ, hǎoxiàng duì wǒ shuō: "gànma? bié chǎo ___!"

   The little cat looked at me as if to say to me "What's the matter?
   Don't bother me!"

5. 他又繼續睡 ___。

   他又继续睡 ___。

   tā yòu jìxù shuì ___ .

   And he continued to sleep.

Answers to Exercises

Chapter 1

1. 1. 十四 shísì
2. 23
3. 二十八 èrshíbā
4. 56
5. 三十九 sānshíjiǔ
6. 74
7. 六十七 liùshíqī
8. 22
9. 九十二 jiǔshí èr
10. 18
11. 七十七 qīshíqī
12. 88
13. 二十六 èrshíliù
14. 41

2. 1. 六百七十萬
六百七十万
liù bǎi qīshí wàn
2. 51,622
3. 九百二十萬兩千〇二
九百二十万两千〇二
jiǔ bǎi èrshí wàn liǎng qiān líng èr
4. 3,842,156
5. 七萬四千
七万四千
qī wàn sì qiān
6. 490,130
7. 兩百萬
两百万
liǎng bǎi wàn
8. 2,556,902
9. 四十三萬八千零五十九
四十三万八千零五十九
sìshísān wàn bā qiān líng wǔshíjiǔ
10. 993,251

3. 1. 七十五個人左右
七十五个人左右
qīshí wǔ ge rén zuǒyòu
2. 1000 or more
3. 差不多一百個人
差不多一百个人
chàbuduō yī bǎi ge rén
4. $300 more or less

5. 七十五個人以上
七十五个人以上
qīshí wǔ ge rén yǐshàng
6. almost $300
7. 四十以下
sìshí yǐxià
8. more than $100
9. 七十五多
qīshí wǔ duō
10. 300 or fewer

4. 1. 第三 dì sān
2. 第八 dìbā
3. 第十 dìshí
4. 第二 dì èr
5. 第九十九 dì jiǔshíjiǔ
6. 5th
7. 20th
8. 9th
9. 1st
10. 4th

5. 1. liù bā sān jiǔ yī èr sān sì
liù bā sān jiǔ yāo èr sān sì
2. wǔ sān sān sì èr sān bā qī
3. bā bā sān sān yī yī yī yī
bā bā sān sān yāo yāo yāo yāo
4. yāo yāo jiǔ
5. yāo yāo sì
6. yī sān wǔ èr yī líng wǔ liù liù liù liù
yāo sān wǔ èr yāo líng wǔ liù liù liù liù

6. 1. 60%
2. 百分之十八
bǎi fēn zhī shíbā
3. 89%
4. 百分之六十六
bǎi fēn zhī liùshí liù
5. 32%
6. 百分之三十五
bǎi fēn zhī sānshí wǔ
7. 3/4
8. 十二分之十一
shí'èr fēn zhī shíyī
9. 9/10
10. 七分之四
qī fēn zhī sì
11. 1/2

252

12. 六分之五
    liù fēn zhī wǔ

7. 1. 百分之九十一。
      bǎi fēn zhī jiǔshí yī.
   2. 分之二十六。
      bā fēn zhī èrshí liù.
   3. 百分之四十九。
      bǎi fēn zhī sìshí jiǔ.
   4. 八分之七。
      bā fēn zhī qī.
   5. 十一分之十。
      shíyī fēn zhī shí.
   6. 五分之四。
      wǔ fēn zhī sì.

8. 1. .05
   2. 二點三/二点三
      èr diǎn sān
   3. 1.1003
   4. 點六六六/点六六六
      diǎn liù liù liù
   5. .86
   6. 九點七/九点七
      jiǔ diǎn qī
   7. .806
   8. 一點〇五/一点〇五
      yī diǎn líng wǔ
   9. 22.22
   10. 八點四/八点四
      bā diǎn sì

9. 1. 6 折
   2. 7.5 折
   3. 4 折
   4. 3.5 折
   5. 1 折

10. 1. $80
   2. $54
   3. $60
   4. $5
   5. 4

Chapter 2

1. 1. 他們/他们 tāmen
   2. 我們/我们 wǒmen
   3. 你 nǐ，他們/他们 tāmen
   4. 你 nǐ
   5. 我 wǒ，我自己 wǒ zì jǐ
   6. 咱們/咱们 zánmen or 我們/我们

   wǒmen
   7. 她們/她们 tāmen
   8. 我 wǒ，你 nǐ or 你們/你们 nǐmen
   9. 您 nín
   10. 你 nǐ，你 nǐ

2. 1. φ
   2. 他
   3. φ
   4. 我/φ
   5. φ

3. 1. i   6. c
   2. d or h   7. j
   3. d or h   8. e
   4. a   9. g
   5. b   10. f

4. 1. 十二枝筆/十二枝笔 shí'èr zhī bǐ
   2. 五杯茶 wǔ bēi chá
   3. 二十二個人/二十二个人
      èrshí'èr ge rén
   4. 三碗飯/三碗饭 sānwǎn fàn
   5. 兩輛車/两辆车 liǎng liàng chē
   6. 七條河/七条河 qī tiáo hé
   7. 八本書/八本书 bā běn shū
   8. 兩把椅子/两把椅子 liǎng bǎ yǐzi
   9. 四張紙/四张纸 sì zhāng zhǐ
   10. 五瓶汽水 wǔ píng qìshuǐ

5. 1. 兩天半/两天半 liǎng tiān bàn
   2. 四個半小時/四个半小时
      sì ge bàn xiǎoshí
      (四個半鐘頭/四个半钟头
      sì ge bàn zhōngtóu)
   3. 半碗飯/半碗饭 bàn wǎn fàn
   4. 一斤半米飯/一斤半米饭
      yī jīn bàn mǐfàn
   5. 三個半月/三个半月 sān ge bàn yuè
   6. 九年半 jiǔ nián bàn
   7. 十二分半(鐘/钟)
      shí èr fēn bàn (zhōng)
   8. 半本書/半本书 bàn běn shū
   9. 五瓶半汽水/五瓶半汽水
      wǔ píng bàn qìshuǐ
   10. 半年 bàn nián

6. 1. 四枝鉛筆/四枝铅笔 sì zhī qiānbǐ

2. 三個朋友/三个朋友 sān ge péngyou

3. 十七本書/十七本书 shíqī běn shū

4. 那杯茶 nà bēi chá

5. 这十年/这十年 zhè shí nián

7. 1. 25 sheets of paper
2. those 6 chairs
3. 12 months
4. these 5 days
5. those 2 people

8. 1. 一九八○年一月一號/号
yī jiǔ bā líng nián yī yuè yī hào/hào
2. July 20, 1969
3. 一七七六年七月四日
yī qī qī liù nián qī yuè sì rì
4. December 31, 1999
5. 二零零二年十月五日
èr líng líng èr nián shí yuè wǔ rì
6. November 25, 2003
7. 一九九七年二月十四日
yī jiǔ jiǔ qī nián èr yuè shí sì rì
8. May 8, 1945
9. 一九七零年八月十六日
yī jiǔ qī líng nián bā yuè shíliù rì
10. November 19, 1863

9. 1. 兩點過一刻/两点过一刻
liǎng diǎn guò yīkè
2. 10:55
3. 四點差一刻/四点差一刻
sì diǎn chà yīkè
4. 5:17
5. 八點差十分/八点差十分
bā diǎn chà shí fēn   OR
差十分八點/差十分八點
chà shí fēn bā diǎn
6. 12:30
7. 八點過二十分/八点过二十分
bā diǎn guò èrshí fēn
8. 5:58
9. 四點十分/四点十分
sì diǎn shí fēn
10. 8:59

10. 1. 十八塊兩毛五分錢
十八块两毛五分钱
shíbā kuài liǎng máo wǔ fēn qián
2. $49.84
3. 五百一十九塊三毛一分錢

五百一十九块三毛一分钱
wǔ bǎi yīshí jiǔ kuài sān máo yī fēn qián
4. $235.40
5. 一百一十七塊六毛二
一百一十七块六毛二
yī bǎi yīshí qī kuài liù máo èr
6. $726

11. 1. 我的中文書
我的中文书
wǒ de Zhōngwén shū

2. 中國出的書
中国出的书
Zhōngguó chū de shū

3. 很甜的水果
hěn tián de shuíguǒ

4. 你姐姐的男朋友
nǐ jiějie de nán péngyou

5. 我喜歡做的事
我喜欢做的事
wǒ xǐhuan zuò de shì

6. 人口多的國家
人口多的国家
rénkǒu duō de guójiā

7. 在美國製造的車
在美国制造的车
zài Měiguó zhìzào de chē

8. 跟你說話的那個女孩子
跟你说话的那个女孩子
gēn nǐ shuō huà de nà ge nǚ háizi

9. 麻州某城市的一個大學
麻州某城市的一个大学
Mázhōu mǒu chéngshì de yī ge dàxué

10. 很難的中文考試
很难的中文考试
hěn nán de Zhōngwén kǎoshì

12. 1. that very interesting movie
2. this very expensive pair of earrings made in Japan
3. my two older brothers
4. a few books about China
5. this very complicated Chinese character

6. a very expensive watch
7. the book that I read
8. students who took the exam yesterday
9. a red pen
10. students who study Chinese

13. 1. a cook
2. a patient OR a doctor
3. a driver
4. a rich person
5. a poor person
6. an airline passenger
7. a barber
8. a clerk
9. a tailor
10. a student

Chapter 3

1. 1. 張明很高。
张明很高。
Zhāng Míng hěn gāo.

2. 張明很胖。
张明很胖。
Zhāng Míng hěn pàng.

3. 張明很聰明。
张明很聪明。
Zhāng Míng hěn cōngming.

4. 張明很用功。
张明很用功。
Zhāng Míng hěn yònggōng.

5. 張明很謙虛。
张明很谦虚。
Zhāng Míng hěn qiānxū.

6. 張明不矮。
张明不矮。
Zhāng Míng bù ǎi.

7. 張明不瘦。
张明不瘦。
Zhāng Míng bú shòu.

8. 張明不笨。
张明不笨。
Zhāng Míng bú bèn.

9. 張明不懶。
张明不懒。
Zhāng Míng bù lǎn.

10. 張明不可靠。
张明不可靠。
Zhāng Míng bù kěkào.

2. 1. 她不是學生。
她不是学生。
tā bù shì xuéshēng.

2. 我不喜歡做飯。
我不喜欢做饭。
wǒ bù xǐhuān zuò fàn.

3. 公共汽車票不貴。
公共汽车票不贵。
gōnggòng qìchē piào bú guì.

4. 我不要買那本書。
我不要买那本书。
wǒ bú yào mǎi nà běn shū.

5. 那個人不好看。
那个人不好看。
nà ge rén bù hǎo kàn.

6. 我不想跟你說話。
我不想跟你说话。
wǒ bù xiǎng gēn nǐ shuō huà.

7. 這不是一個很大的問題。
这不是一个很大的问题。
zhè bú shì yī ge hěn dà de wèntí.

8. 你在這兒不可以抽煙。
你在这儿不可以抽烟。
nǐ zài zhèr bù kéyǐ chōu yān.

9. 我不會說日語。
我不会说日语。
wǒ bú huì shuō rì yǔ.

10. 那張畫兒不（很）漂亮。
那张画儿不（很）漂亮。
nà zhāng huàr bù (hěn) piàoliang.

3. 1. 他沒有一個弟弟。
他没有一个弟弟。
tā méi yǒu yī ge dìdi.

2. 桌子上沒有書。
桌子上没有书。
zhuōzi shàng méi yǒu shū.

3. 他們沒有問題。
他们没有问题。
tāmen méi yǒu wèntí.

4. 屋子裏沒有人。
屋子里没有人。
wūzi lǐ méi yǒu rén.

5. 他沒有錢。
他没有钱。
tā méi yǒu qián.

4. 1. 挺 tǐng or 很 hěn
2. 很 hěn
3. 非常 fēicháng
4. 最 zuì
5. 非常 fēicháng
6. 尤其 yóuqí or 特別 tèbié
7. 太 tài，有一點/有一点 yǒu yìdiǎn
8. 比較/比较 bǐjiào
9. 很 hěn
10. 真 zhēn

5. 1. 他的朋友越來越多。
他的朋友越来越多。
tā de péngyou yuè lái yuè duō.

2. 他的問題越來越少。
他的问题越来越少。
tā de wèntí yuè lái yuè shǎo.

3. 你的故事越來越複雜。
你的故事越来越复杂。
nǐ de gùshì yuè lái yuè fùzá.

4. 書越來越貴。
书越来越贵。
shū yuè lái yuè guì.

5. 汽車越來越快。
汽车越来越快。
qìchē yuè lái yuè kuài.

6. 1. 越做越好。yuè zuò yuè hǎo.
2. 越念越快。yuè niàn yuè kuài.
3. 越睡越累。yuè shuì yuè lèi.
4. 越吃越胖。yuè chī yuè pàng.
5. 越練習越準。/越练习越准。
yuè liànxí yuè zhǔn.

7. 1. He runs faster and faster.
2. I am more and more tired.
3. You are (you look) younger and younger!
4. His pronunciation is more and more accurate.
5. He's growing taller and taller.
6. Chinese green tea gets more and more expensive.
7. Math gets harder and harder.
8. This situation gets more and more complex.
9. She has more and more friends.
10. This kind of music gets more and more popular.

8. 1. d:
It was so hot today that we couldn't sleep.
2. a
He is so poor that he doesn't even have an overcoat.
3. f
I was so tired that I was unable to do my homework.
4. j
I was so busy that I forgot to eat.
5. g
French wine is so expensive that no one can afford to buy it.
6. c
His feet are so big that he can't put on shoes.
7. e
This test was so long that we couldn't finish.
8. h
I was so frightened that I began to cry.
9. i
He is so lazy that he doesn't even cook.
10. b
She is so nice that everyone likes her.

9. 1. 姓 xìng
2. 姓 xìng
3. 有 yǒu
4. 是 shì
5. 是 shì
6. 有 yǒu
7. 是 shì
8. 是 shì

10. 1. 能 néng
2. 能 néng
3. 會/会 huì

4. 會/会 huì

5. 可以 kéyǐ

6. 會/会 huì

7. 會/会 huì

8. 能 néng or 可以 kéyǐ

9. 能 néng

10. 可以 kéyǐ

11.1. 你能在圖書館借那本書。
你能在图书馆借那本书。
nǐ néng zài túshūguǎn jiè nà běn shū.

2. 你當然可以借我的車。
你当然可以借我的车。
nǐ dāngrán kéyǐ jiè wǒ de chē.

3. 開車的時候可以用手機嗎？
开车的时候可以用手机吗？
kāi chē de shíhou kéyǐ yòng shǒujī ma?

4. 我可以不可以跟你談話？
我可以不可以跟你谈话？
wǒ kéyǐ bù kéyǐ gēn nǐ tán huà?

5. 美國人都會開車嗎？
美国人都会开车吗？
Měiguó rén dōu huì kāi chē ma?

6. 我今天晚上能不能跟你念書？
我今天晚上能不能跟你念书？
wǒ jīntiān wǎnshang néng bù néng gēn nǐ niàn shū?

7. 這個門你能開得開嗎？
这个门你能开得开吗？
zhè ge mén nǐ néng kāidekāi ma?

8. 我只會做早飯。
我只会做早饭。
wǒ zhǐ huì zuò zǎofàn.

9. 貓都會抓老鼠。
猫都会抓老鼠。
māo dōu huì zhuā lǎoshǔ.

10. 你會不會說外語？
你会不会说外语？
nǐ huì bú huì shuō wàiyǔ?

12.1. 我聽音樂聽了一個小時。

我听音乐听了一个小时。
wǒ tīng yīnyuè tīng le yī ge xiǎoshí.

2. 我每天看一個半鐘頭的電視。
我每天看一个半钟头的电视。
wǒ měitiān kàn yī ge bàn zhōngtóu de diànshì.

3. 我去年坐了三次飛機。
我去年坐了三次飞机。
wǒ qùnián zuò le sān cì fēijī.

4. 我去過四次法國。
我去过四次法国。
wǒ qùguo sì cì Fǎguó.

5. 我每天晚上學中文學三個
小時。
我每天晚上学中文学三个
小时。
wǒ měitiān wǎnshang xué Zhōngwén xué sān ge xiǎoshí.

6. 我看那個電影看了兩次。
（我那個電影看了兩次。）
我看那个电影看了两次。
（我那个电影看了两次。）
wǒ kàn nà ge diànyǐng kàn le liǎng cì.
（wǒ nà ge diànyǐng kàn le liǎng cì.）

7. 我睡了七個鐘頭的覺。
我睡了七个钟头的觉。
wǒ shuì le qī ge zhōngtóu de jiào.

8. 我吃過幾次中國飯。
我吃过几次中国饭。
wǒ chīguo jǐ cì Zhōngguó fàn.

9. 我用過一次筷子。
我用过一次筷子。
wǒ yòngguo yī cì kuàizi.

10. 我每天寫一個小時的中國字。
我每天写一个小时的中国字。
wǒ měitiān xiě yī ge xiǎoshí de Zhōngguó zì.

13.1. 妹妹寫英文寫得很慢。
妹妹写英文写得很慢。
mèi mèi xiě Yīngwén xiě de hěn màn.

2. 中學生吃飯吃得很多。
中学生吃饭吃得很多。
zhōngxuéshēng chī fàn chī de hěn duō.

3. 姐姐說話說得很快。
姐姐说话说得很快。
jiějie shuō huà shuō de hěn kuài.

4. 弟弟吃飯吃得很慢。
弟弟吃饭吃得很慢。
dìdi chī fàn chī de hěn màn.

5. 爸爸看書看得很多。
爸爸看书看得很多。
bàba kàn shū kàn de hěn duō.

6. 我寫字寫得不好。
我写字写得不好。
wǒ xiě zì xiě de bù hǎo.

7. 媽媽開車開得很好。
妈妈开车开得很好。
māma kāi chē kāi de hěn hǎo.

8. 哥哥喝咖啡喝得少。
哥哥喝咖啡喝得少。
gēge hē kāfēi hē de shǎo.

9. 姐姐寫字寫得很漂亮。
姐姐写字写得很漂亮。
jiějie xiě zì xiě de hěn piàoliang.

10. 弟弟看電視看得很多。
弟弟看电视看得很多。
dìdi kàn diànshì kàn de hěn duō.

14.1. 他偷偷地把蛋糕吃完了。
tā tōutou de bǎ dàngāo chīwán le.

2. 你得好好兒地做。
你得好好儿地做。
nǐ děi hǎohāor de zuò.

3. 慢慢走。
mànmān zǒu.

4. 快快寫吧！
快快写吧！
kuàikuāi xiě ba!

5. 她慢慢地把門開開了。
她慢慢地把门开开了。
tā mànmān de bǎ mén kāikai le.

6. 她靜靜地躺在床上看書。
她静静地躺在床上看书。
tā jìngjìng de tǎng zài chuángshàng kàn shū.

7. 風從南方輕輕地吹來。
风从南方轻轻地吹来。
fēng cóng nánfāng qīngqīng de chuī lái.

8. 他不知不覺地哭起來了。
他不知不觉地哭起来了。
tā bù zhī bù juéde kūqilai le.

9. 他們高高興興地跑回家了。
他们高高兴兴地跑回家了。
tāmen gāogāo xìngxìng de pǎo huí jiā le.

10. 請你慢慢兒地把事情再說一邊。
请你慢慢儿地把事情再说一边。
qǐng nǐ mànmār de bǎ shìqing zài shuō yībiān.

15.1. 我沒看那個電影。
我没看那个电影。
wǒ méi kàn nà ge diànyǐng.

2. 他沒坐公共汽車。
他没坐公共汽车。
tā méi zuò gōnggòngqìchē.

3. 我們星期六不上課。
我们星期六不上课。
wǒmen xīngqīliù bú shàng kè.

4. 我昨天沒上中文課。
我昨天没上中文课。
wǒ zuótiān méi shàng Zhōngwén kè.

5. 她今天沒吃冰淇淋。
wǒ jīntiān méi chī bīngqílín.

6. 我今天沒戴手錶。
我今天没戴手表。
wǒ jīntiān méi dài shóubiǎo.

7. 他沒穿大衣。
tā méi chuān dàyī.

8. 他沒送禮物。

他没送礼物。

tā méi sòng lǐwù.

9. 我今天沒吃早飯。

我今天没吃早饭。

wǒ jīntiān méi chī zǎofàn.

10. 我們明天不考中文。

我们明天不考中文。

wǒmen míngtiān bù kǎo Zhōngwén.

Chapter 4

1. 1. 並/并 bìng

2. 一向 yīxiàng

3. 暫時/暂时 zànshí

4. 老 lǎo

5. 從來/从来 cónglái

6. 仍然 réngrán

7. 一向 yīxiàng

8. 常 cháng

9. 又 yòu

10. 應該/应该 yīnggāi; 多 duō

11. 應該/应该 yīnggāi; 少 shǎo

12. 應該/应该 yīnggāi; 多 duō

13. 不應該/不应该 bù yīnggāi

14. 仍然 réngrán

15. 老 lǎo

16. 必須 bìxū

17. 的確/的确 díquè

18. 差不多 chàbuduō

19. 也許/也许 yěxǔ

20. 果然 guǒrán

21. 一定 yīdìng

22. 的確/的确 díquè

23. 甭 béng

24. 忽然 hūrán

25. 一向 yīxiàng

2. 1. 都 dōu

2. 就 jiù

3. 就 jiù

4. 還/还 hái

5. 才 cái

6. 再 zài

7. 才 cái

Chapter 5

1. 1. 跟 gēn

2. 對/对 duì

3. 對/对 duì

4. 跟 gēn, 跟 gēn

5. 給/给 gěi

6. 對/对 duì

7. 往 wǎng, 向 xiàng or 朝 cháo

8. 給/给 gěi

9. 在 zài

10. 從/从 cóng, 從/从 cóng

11. 替 tì

12. 對/对 duì

13. 到 dào

14. 往 wǎng, 向 xiàng or 朝 cháo

15. 由 yóu

16. 為/为 wéi

Chapter 6

1. 1. Your child has become taller.

2. I took the bus today (for a change.)

3. I don't eat breakfast anymore.

4. Younger sister says she doesn't like you anymore.

5. Younger brother writes characters fast now.

6. I've become really busy this week.

7. I don't ride planes anymore.

8. I don't want to take tests anymore.

9. Today it suddenly became cold.

10. We've already walked very far. I've become tired. I can't walk anymore.

2. 1. 我看了一個電影。

我看了一个电影。

wǒ kàn le yī ge diànyǐng.

2. 我吃了晚飯。

我吃了晚饭。

wǒ chī le wǎnfàn.

3. 哥哥畢業了。

哥哥毕业了。

gēge bì yè le.

4. 我今天早上考試了。
   我今天早上考试了。
   wǒ jīntiān zǎoshang kǎo shì le.

5. 我這個星期考了中文。
   我这个星期考了中文。
   wǒ zhè ge xīngqī kǎo le Zhōngwén.

6. 我今天早上買了兩枝鉛筆。
   我今天早上买了两枝铅笔。
   wǒ jīntiān zǎoshang mǎi le liǎngzhī
   qiānbǐ.

7. 我們昨天晚上吃了意大利菜。
   我们昨天晚上吃了意大利菜。
   wǒmen zuótiān wǎnshang chīle Yìdàlì
   cài.

8. 他們在海邊玩了一天。
   他们在海边玩了一天。
   tāmen zài hǎibiān wán le yītiān.

9. 我在香港住了幾個月。
   我在香港住了几个月。
   wǒ zài Xiānggǎng zhù le jǐ ge yuè.

10. 我昨天晚上看電視看了半個
    小時。
    我昨天晚上看电视看了半个
    小时。
    wǒ zuótiān wǎnshang kàn diànshì
    kànle bàn ge xiǎoshí.

11. 昨天晚上宿舍很冷。
    zuótiān wǎnshang sùshè hěn lěng.
    (Note: 冷 lěng is a stative verb)

12. 我在北京看了幾次京劇。
    我在北京看了几次京剧。
    wǒ zài Běijīng kàn le jǐ cì jīngjù.

3. 1. 我昨天没在公園裏跑步。
      我昨天没在公园里跑步。
      wǒ zuótiān méi zài gōngyuán lǐ pǎo bù.
      I didn't run in the park yesterday.

   2. 我妹妹没買毛衣。
      我妹妹没买毛衣。
      wǒ mèimei méi mǎi máoyī.
      My younger sister didn't buy a sweater.

3. 我姐姐没買鞋子。
   我姐姐没买鞋子。
   wǒ jiějie méi mǎi xiézi.
   My older sister didn't buy shoes.

4. 妹妹今天没穿她的毛衣。
   mèimei jīntiān méi chuān tā de máoyī.
   *Younger sister didn't wear her sweater
   today.*

5. 弟弟昨天没給他的女朋友寫信。
   弟弟昨天没给他的女朋友写信。
   dìdi zuótiān méi gěi tā de nǚ péngyǒu
   xiě xìn.
   *Yesterday younger brother didn't write a
   letter to his girlfriend.*

6. 我哥哥昨天没跟朋友打球。
   wǒ gēge zuótiān méi gēn péngyou dǎ
   qiú.
   *My older brother didn't play ball with his
   friends yesterday.*

7. 我昨天晚上没看電視。
   我昨天晚上没看电视。
   wǒ zuótiān wǎnshang méi kàn diànshì.
   I didn't watch television last night.

8. 我昨天没給媽媽寫電子郵件。
   我昨天没给妈妈写电子邮件。
   wǒ zuótiān méi gěi māma xiě diànzi
   yóujiàn.
   Yesterday I didn't write an email to mom.

9. 我昨天晚上没洗頭。
   我昨天晚上没洗头。
   wǒ zuótiān wǎnshang méi xǐ tóu .
   Last night I didn't wash my hair.

10. 我今天早上没上中文課。
    我今天早上没上中文课。
    wǒ jīntiān zǎoshang méi shàng
    Zhōngwén kè.
    *This morning I did not attend Chinese
    class.*

4. 1. After younger brother sees a movie he
      goes home.
   2. After I bought a car I drove to New York.
   3. After we eat we go to class.
   4. After the guests come we say 'welcome.'
   5. After that child saw the dog he cried.
   6. Last night after I ate dinner I went to sleep.

7. After they returned home they watched television.
8. After my older sister buys something she brings it home to show it to me.
9. What are you going to do after you graduate?
10. Every day after she gets out of bed she drinks a cup of tea.

5. 1. 我考了試以後就看電影。
我考了试以后就看电影。
wǒ kǎo le shì yǐhòu jiù kàn diànyǐng.

2. 我畢了業(以後)就到中國去。
我毕了业(以后)就到中国去。
wǒ bì le yè (yǐhòu)jiù dào Zhōngguó qù.

3. 我昨天下了課以後就到公園去了。
我昨天下了课以后就到公园去了。
wǒ zuótiān xià le kè yǐhòu jiù dào gōngyuán qù le.

4. 我復習了中文(以後)就看了电視。
我复习了中文(以后)就看了电视。
wǒ fùxí le Zhōngwén yǐhòu jiù kàn le diànshì.

5. 我們下了課以後去公園吧！
我们下了课以后去公园吧！
wǒmen xià le kè yǐhòu qù gōngyuán ba!

6. 1. I'm eating now.
2. He's singing.
3. He's playing ball.
4. Xiaoming is doing school work right now.
5. Quiet! The teacher is speaking.
6. The teacher is seated talking to the students.
7. Dad eats breakfast while reading.
8. Mrs. Qian walked to the library holding a book.
9. Students often do school work while listening to music.
10. Mom is drinking coffee while reading the paper.

7. 1. I've already read that book. I don't want to read it again.
2. Mom studied Japanese but she's never been to Japan.
3. I've never eaten French food before.

4. Have you driven a car before?
5. When we were in China we rode on a public bus.
6. I've never been to the teacher's house. Have you?
7. I've never seen a Chinese movie before.
8. I've used a writing brush before to write characters.

8. 1. 我 (去過/沒去過) 中國。
我 (去过/没去过) 中国。
wǒ (qùguo/méi qùguo) Zhōngguó.

2. 我 (吃過/沒吃過) 北京烤鴨。
我 (吃过/没吃过) 北京烤鸭。
wǒ (chīguo/méi chīguo) Běijīng kǎoyā.

3. 我 (玩過/沒玩過) 飛盤。
我 (玩过/没玩过) 飞盘。
wǒ (wánguo/méi wánguo) fēipán.

4. 我 (看過/沒看過)萬里長城。
我 (看过/没看过)万里长城。
wǒ (kànguo/méi kànguo) Wànlǐ Chángchéng.

5. 我 (唱過/沒唱過) 卡拉 OK。
我 (唱过/没唱过) 卡拉 OK。
wǒ (chàngguo/méi chàngguo) kǎlāOK.

6. 我 (做過/沒做過) 中國飯。
我 (做过/没做过) 中国饭。
wǒ (zuòguo/méi zuòguo) Zhōngguó fàn.

7. 我 (看過/沒看過) 中文報紙。
我 (看过/没看过) 中文报纸。
wǒ (kànguo/méi kànguo) Zhōngwén bàozhǐ.

8. 我 (開過/沒開過) 跑車。
我 (开过/没开过) 跑车。
wǒ (kāiguo/méi kāiguo) pǎochē.

9. 我 (喝過/沒喝過) 綠茶。
我 (喝过/没喝过) 绿茶。
wǒ (hēguo/méi hēguo) lǜchá.

10. 我 (看過/沒看過) 京劇。
我 (看过/没看过) 京剧。
wǒ (kànguo/méi kànguo) jīngjù.

Chapter 7

1. 1. 看懂 kàndǒng

2. 買到/买到 mǎidào

3. 寫錯/写错 xiěcuò

4. 看完 kànwán

5. 看到/看到 kàndào or
   看見/看见 kànjian

6. 看懂 kàndǒng

7. 用完 yòngwán

8. 找到 zhǎodào or
   找着 zhǎozháo

9. 看懂 kàndǒng

10. 打開/打开 dǎkāi

2. 1. 我沒找到我的手錶。
   我没找到我的手表。
   wǒ méi zhǎodào wǒde shóubiǎo.

   2. 我聽懂了老師的話。
   我听懂了老师的话。
   wǒ tīngdǒng le lǎoshī de huà.

   3. 我把那個字寫錯了。
   我把那个字写错了。
   wǒ bǎ nà ge zì xiěcuò le.

   4. 我寫完了那封信。
   我写完了那封信。
   wǒ xiěwán le nà fēng xìn.

   5. 我沒做完作業。
   我没做完作业。
   wǒ méi zuòwán zuòyè.

   6. 我買到了新的大衣。
   我买到了新的大衣。
   wǒ mǎidào le xīn de dàyī.

   7. 我沒吃飽。
   我没吃饱。
   wǒ méi chībǎo.

   8. 我把我的行李收拾完了。
   我把我的行李收拾完了。
   wǒ bǎ wǒ de xíngli shōushí wán le.

   9. 我沒找到那個新的中國飯館。
   我没找到那个新的中国饭馆。
   wǒ méi zhǎodào nà ge xīn de Zhōngguó
   fànguǎn.

   10. 我記住了那首詩。
   我记住了那首诗。
   wǒ jìzhule nà shǒu shī.

3. 1. 聽不懂/听不懂 tīngbudǒng

   2. 買不到/买不到 mǎibudào

   3. 借得到 jièdedào

   4. 坐不下 zuòbuxià

   5. 看不見/看不见 kànbujiàn

   6. 找不到 zhǎobudào

   7. 吃不下 chībuxià or 吃不完
   chī buwán

   8. 買不起/买不起 mǎibuqǐ

   9. 記不住/记不住 jìbuzhù

   10. 看得見/看得见 kàndejiàn

4. 1. 走不回去 zǒubuhuíqu or
   走不回來. zǒubuhuílai

   2. 進不去/进不去 jìnbuqu

   3. 拿不起來/拿不起来 nábuqilai

   4. 爬不上去 pábushàngqu

   5. 開不進去/开不进去 kāibujìnqu

5. 1. I don't have money. I cannot buy things.
   2. There are no chopsticks. We can't eat
      (rice).
   3. That door is very heavy. Children certainly
      cannot open it.
   4. We cannot eat this many dumplings.
   5. She is unable to help you.
   6. He doesn't have experience. He can't do
      this work.
   7. You can't carry this many things.
   8. You've bought another raincoat. Can you
      wear this many (raincoats)?

Chapter 8

1. 1. 你喜歡吃中國飯嗎？
   你喜欢吃中国饭吗？
   nǐ xǐhuan chī Zhōngguó fàn ma?

   2. 你是不是學生？
   你是不是学生？
   nǐ shì bú shì xuésheng?

   3. 你家在加州嗎？
   你家在加州吗？
   nǐ jiā zài Jiāzhōu ma?

4. 你會不會用筷子吃飯？
你会不会用筷子吃饭？
nǐ huì bú huì yòng kuàizi chī fàn?

5. 你累嗎？
你累吗？
nǐ lèi ma?

6. 你會不會說漢語？
你会不会说汉语？
nǐ huì bú huì shuō Hànyǔ?

7. 她有沒有男朋友？
tā yǒu méi yǒu nán péngyou?

8. 你去過中國沒有？
你去过中国没有？
nǐ qùguo Zhōngguó méi yǒu?

9. 你看過那個電影沒有？
你看过那个电影没有？
nǐ kànguo nà ge diànyǐng méi yǒu?

10. 那本書有沒有意思？
那本书有没有意思？
nà běn shū yǒu méi yǒu yìsi?

11. 你是否對中國歷史有興趣？
你是否對中國歷史有興趣？
nǐ shìfǒu duì Zhōngguó lìshǐ yǒu xìngqù?

12. 你吃飽了沒有？
你吃饱了没有？
nǐ chībǎo le méi yǒu?

2. 1. 是。我是美國人。
是。我是美国人。
shì. wǒ shì Měiguó rén.

2. 會。我會開車。
会。我会开车。
huì. wǒ huì kāi chē.

3. 去過。我去過中國。
去过。我去过中国。
qùguo. wǒ qùguo Zhōngguó.

4. 可以。你可以借我的車。
可以。你可以借我的车。
kéyǐ. nǐ kéyǐ jiè wǒde chē.

5. 要。我要買那件毛衣。
要。我要买那件毛衣。
yào. wǒ yào mǎi nà jiàn máoyī.

6. 有。我有錢。
有。我有钱。
yǒu. wǒ yǒu qián.

7. 願意。我願意跟你去
(買東西)。
愿意。我愿意跟你去
(买东西)。
yuànyi. wǒ yuànyi gēn nǐ qù (mǎi dōngxi).

8. 會。我會說漢語。
会。我会说汉语。
huì. wǒ huì shuō Hànyǔ.

9. 喜歡。我喜歡吃冰淇淋。
喜欢。我喜欢吃冰淇淋。
xǐhuan. wǒ xǐhuan chī bīngqilín.

10. 看過。我看過那個電影。
看过。我看过那个电影。
kànguo. wǒ kànguo nà ge diànyǐng.

3. 1. 你是誰？
你是谁？
nǐ shì shéi?
Who are you?

2. 你每天（幾點(鐘)/什麼時候）
吃早飯？
你每天（几点(钟)/什么时候）
吃早饭？
nǐ měitiān(jǐ diǎn zhōng/shénme shíhòu) chī zǎofàn?
What time do you eat breakfast every day?

3. 你昨天買了幾本書？
你昨天买了几本书？
nǐ zuótiān mǎi le jǐ běn shū?
How many books did you buy yesterday?

4. 你明天跟誰去看電影？
你明天跟谁去看电影？
nǐ míngtiān gēn shéi qù kàn diànyǐng?
Who are you going with tomorrow to see a movie?

5. (我們/你們) 怎麼去？
   (我们/你们) 怎么去？
   (wǒmen/nǐmen) zěnme qù?
   How are (we/you) going?

6. 電影票多少錢？
   电影票多少钱？
   diànyǐng piào duōshǎo qián?
   How much money is a movie ticket?

7. 你喜歡看哪國電影？
   你喜欢看哪国电影？
   nǐ xǐhuan kàn nǎ guó diànyǐng?
   What country's movies do you like to see?

8. 我們晚上（什麼時候/幾點鐘）
   回家？
   我们晚上（什么时候/几点钟）
   回家？
   wǒmen wǎnshang (shénme shíhòu/ jǐ
   diǎn zhōng) huí jiā?
   What time are we returning home at night?

9. 誰跟我們去？
   谁跟我们去？
   shéi gēn wǒmen qù?
   Who is going with us?

10. 你每天晚上吃幾碗飯？
    你每天晚上吃几碗饭？
    nǐ měitiān wǎnshang chī jǐ wǎn fàn?
    *How many bowls of rice do you eat every
    night?*

11. 你姐姐什麼時候買了新的大衣？
    你姐姐什么时候买了新的大衣？
    nǐ jiějie shénme shíhòu mǎi le xīn de
    dàyī?
    *When did your older sister buy a new
    coat?*

12. 你最喜歡哪件毛衣？
    你最喜欢哪件毛衣？
    nǐ zuì xǐhuan nǎ jiàn máoyī?
    Which sweater do you like best?

13. 這雙鞋子是在哪兒買的？
    这双鞋子是在哪儿买的？
    zhè shuāng xiézi shì zài nǎr mǎi de?
    Where were those shoes bought?

14. 你是幾月幾號生的？
    你是几月几号生的？
    nǐ shì jǐ yuè jǐ hào shēng de?
    What month and date were you born?

15. 這個學校一共有多少學生？
    这个学校一共有多少学生？
    zhè ge xuéxiào yīgòng yǒu duōshǎo
    xuésheng?
    *How many students does this school
    have altogether?*

4. 1. 怎麼樣/怎么样 zěnmeyàng
   2. 難道/难道 nándào
   3. 可不是嗎/可不是吗 kěbushìma
   4. 怎麼/怎么 zěnme
   5. 可不是嗎/可不是吗 kěbushìma
   6. 怎麼一回事/怎么一回事
      zěnme yī huí shì.

5. 1. 什麼地方都好。
      什么地方都好。
      shénme dìfāng dōu hǎo.

   2. 我什麼時候都有空。
      我什么时候都有空。
      wǒ shénme shíhòu dōu yǒu kòng.

   3. 誰都喜歡喝咖啡。
      谁都喜欢喝咖啡。
      shéi dōu xǐhuan hē kāfēi.

   4. 什麼電影都可以。
      什么电影都可以。
      shénme diànyǐng dōu kéyǐ.

   5. 什麼時候都行。
      什么时候都行。
      shénme shíhòu dōu xíng.

   6. 我什麼時候也沒有空。
      我什么时候也没有空。
      wǒ shénme shíhòu yě méi yǒu kòng.

   7. 誰都認識他。
      谁都认识他。
      shéi dōu rènshi tā.

   8. 什麼時候都好。
      什么时候都好。
      shénme shíhòu dōu hǎo.

9. 什麼安靜的地方都行。
什么安静的地方都行。
shénme ānjìng de dìfang dōu xíng.

10. 誰都爬不上那座山。
谁都爬不上那座山。
shéi dōu pábushàng nà zuò shān.

6. 1. Q: How should we do this?
A: Do it how ever you want.
2 Q: Whom should we invite to eat?
A: Invite whomever you want.
3 Q: What should we buy mom?
A: Buy whatever you want.
4 Q: Where are we going?
A: We'll go wherever you want.
5 Q: How much tip do we give?
A: Give as much as you want.
6 Q: How do you write this character?
A: Write it however you want.
7 Q: Where is your younger brother?
A: Probably with my older brother.
Wherever older brother goes, younger
brother goes.
8 Q: Who will you dance with tonight?
A: I will dance with whomever I want.

Chapter 9

1. 1. 房子的上頭/房子上
房子的上头/房子上
fángzi de shàngtou/fángzi shàng

2. 房子的裏頭/房子裏
房子的里头/房子里
fángzi de lǐtou/fángzi lǐ

3. 房子的左邊/房子的西邊
房子的左边/房子的西边
fángzi de zuǒbian/fángzi de xībian

4. 房子的右邊/房子的東邊
房子的右边/房子的东边
fángzi de yòubian/fángzi de dōngbian

5. 房子的下頭/房子下
房子的下头/房子下
fángzi de xiàtou/fángzi xià

6. 房子的東邊
房子的东边
fángzi de dōngbian

7. 湖的北邊/湖的東北邊
湖的北边/湖的东北边
hú de běibiān/hú de dōngběibian

8. 房子的南邊/房子的東南邊
房子的南边/房子的东南边
fángzi de nánbian/fángzi de
dōngnánbian

9. 山的南邊/山的西南邊
山的南边/山的西南边
shān de nánbian/ shān de xīnánbian

10. 山的中間
山的中间
shān de zhōngjiān

2. 1. the person on the right
2. behind the house
3. the house in the middle
4. between the houses
OR in the middle of the house.
5. the lake to the west
6. to the north of the park
7. the park in the north
8. that girl in the front
9. in front of that girl
10. to the east of the school

3. 1. 湖在公園裏。
湖在公园里。
hú zài gōngyuán lǐ.

2. 湖在公園的西邊。
湖在公园的西边。
hú zài gōngyuán de xībian.

3. 湖在公園的東北邊。
湖在公园的东北边。
hú zài gōngyuán de dōngběibian.

4. 湖在公園的南邊。
湖在公园的南边。
hú zài gōngyuán de nánbian.

5. 湖在公園的南邊。
湖在公园的南边。
hú zài gōngyuán de nánbian

6. 湖在公園的中間。
湖在公园的中间。
hú zài gōngyuán de zhōngjiān

4. 1. at my side
2. to the left of the teacher
3. outside of the country
4. to the right of that person
5. in front of you
6. There is a book on the table.
   (On the table there is a book.)
7. There is a person behind the house.
   (Behind the house there is a person.)
8. Inside of the house there are no people.
9. My younger brother is between those two girls.
10. The library is in front of you.

5. 1. She climbed up the mountain.
2. He ran out of (from) that gate.
3. Everyday he runs up from there.
4. He took all of my money.
5. Younger sister brought over a lot of things.
6. Please bring this book back to the library.
7. Every afternoon he walks to the post office to mail letters.
8. Please bring your Chinese textbook.
9. He walked home.
10. He doesn't want to walk into the room.

6. 1. 她把孩子背回家了。
   tā bǎ háizi bēi huíjiā le.

2. 我們把桌子搬進屋子裏去了。
   我们把桌子搬进屋子里去了。
   wǒmen bǎ zhuōzi bān jìn wūzi lǐ qù le.

3. 爸爸把報紙放在桌子上。
   爸爸把报纸放在桌子上。
   bàba bǎ bàozhǐ fàng zài zhuōzi shàng.

4. 誰把杯子掉在地上了？
   谁把杯子掉在地上了？
   shéi bǎ bēizi diào zài dì shàng le?

5. 我們不能把車開進公園去。
   我们不能把车开进公园去。
   wǒmen bù néng bǎ chē kāi jìn gōngyuán qù.

6. 我明天要把車開到王先生那兒去。
   我明天要把车开到王先生那儿去。
   wǒ míngtiān yào bǎ chē kāi dào Wáng xiānshēng nàr qù.

7. 我把弟弟從水裏拉出來了。
   我把弟弟从水里拉出来了。
   wǒ bǎ dìdi cóng shuǐ lǐ lā chū lái le.

8. 你什麼時候把車開到我家來？
   你什么时候把车开到我家来？
   nǐ shénme shíhòu bǎ chē kāi dào wǒ jiā lái?

9. 我明天要把我弟弟帶到學校去。
   我明天要把我弟弟带到学校去。
   wǒ míngtiān yào bǎ wǒ dìdi dài dào xuéxiào qù.

10. 車壞了！我們只好把它推回家了。
    车坏了！我们只好把它推回家了。
    chē huài le! wǒmen zhǐhǎo bǎ tā tuī huí jiā le.

7. 1. 圖書館離書店二十英里路。
   图书馆离书店二十英里路。
   túshūguǎn lí shūdiàn èrshí yīng lǐ lù.

2. 圖書館離書店兩英里路。
   图书馆离书店两英里路。
   túshūguǎn lí shūdiàn liǎng yīng lǐ lù.

3. 圖書館離書店十八英里路。
   图书馆离书店十八英里路。
   túshūguǎn lí shūdiàn shíbā yīng lǐ lù.

4. 圖書館離書店一百英里路。
   图书馆离书店一百英里路。
   túshūguǎn lí shūdiàn yī bǎi yīng lǐ lù.

5. 圖書館離書店六英里半路。
   图书馆离书店六英里半路。
   túshūguǎn lí shūdiàn liù yīng lǐ bàn lù.

6. 公園離我家不遠。
   公园离我家不远。
   gōngyuán lí wǒ jiā bù yuǎn.

7. 公園離我家很遠。
   公园离我家很远。
   gōngyuán lí wǒ jiā hěn yuǎn.

8. 公園離我家非常遠。
公园离我家非常远。
gōngyuán lí wǒ jiā fēicháng yuǎn.

9. 公園離我家不太遠。
公园离我家不太远。
gōngyuán lí wǒ jiā bú tài yuǎn.

10. 公園離我家很近。
公园离我家很近。
gōngyuán lí wǒ jiā hěn jìn.

8. 1. 法國離意大利不遠。
法国离意大利不远。
Fǎguó lí Yìdàlì bù yuǎn.

2. 美國離中國很遠。
美国离中国很远。
Měiguó lí Zhōngguó hěn yuǎn.

3. 紐約離波士頓差不多兩百英里
路。
纽约离波士顿差不多两百英里
路。
Niǔyuē lí Bōshìdùn chàbuduō liǎng bǎi
yīng lǐ lù.

4. 澳大利亞離英國多遠？
澳大利亚离英国多远？
Aòdàlìyà lí Yīngguó duō yuǎn?

5. 加州離佛羅里達州遠嗎？
加州离佛罗里达州远吗？
Jiāzhōu lí Fúluólǐdá zhōu yuǎn ma?

6. 加拿大離美國很近。
加拿大离美国很近。
Jiānádà lí Měiguó hěn jìn.

7. 墨西哥離得州不太遠。
墨西哥离得州不太远。
Mòxīgē lí Dézhōu bú tài yuǎn.

8. 芝加哥離密西根不到一百英里
路。
芝加哥离密西根不到一百英里
路。
Zhījiāgē lí Mìxīgēn bú dào yī bǎi yīng lǐ
lù.

9. 日本離韓國很近。
日本离韩国很近。
Rìběn lí Hánguó hěn jìn.

10. 喀麥隆離巴西相當遠。
喀麦隆离巴西相当远。
Kāmàilóng lí Bāxī xiāngdāng yuǎn.

Chapter 10

1. 1. He loaned the camera to me to use.
2. Wang Ming sent the chocolates to his girlfriend.
3. Mom hung that picture on the wall.
4. Don't put the cup on the television.
5. My dog ate my homework.
6. I wiped the bike clean.
7. My younger brother crashed his car.
8. I enlarged the photo.
9. Please pull open the door.
10. In less than an hour they finished packing the suitcases.
11. Can you wash this piece of clothing clean?

2. 1. He drove the car into the park.
2. I carried the child home on my back.
3. The students carried all of the things to Professor Gao's house.
4. I have to return the books to the library.
5. Younger brother drove my car to school.
6 Where are you shipping the things to?
7. Please move the bookcase to the study.
8. Please bring your books here.
9. Please take (pull) the dog outside.
10. Please bring my dictionary here.
11. She pushed her boyfriend out the door.

3. 1. 我把書拿回家了。
我把书拿回家了。
wǒ bǎ shū ná huí jiā le.

2. 我把書看了一半。
我把书看了一半。
wǒ bǎ shū kàn le yībàn.

3. 我把書看完了。
我把书看完了。
wǒ bǎ shū kàn wán le.

4. 我把書借給我弟弟。
我把书借给我弟弟。
wǒ bǎ shū jiè gěi wǒ dìdi.

5. 我把書丟了。
我把书丢了。
wǒ bǎ shū diū le.

Chapter 11

1. 1. 中文比英文難。
中文比英文难。
Zhōngwén bǐ Yīngwén nán.

2. 餃子比比薩好吃。
饺子比比萨好吃。
jiǎozi bǐ bǐsà hàochī.

3. 文學比數學有意思。
文学比数学有意思。
wénxué bǐ shùxué yǒu yìsi.

4. 妹妹比弟弟用功。
mèimei bǐ dìdi yònggōng.

5. 孩子比大人多。
háizi bǐ dàren duō.

2. 1. 貓比狗小。老鼠更小。
猫比狗小。老鼠更小。
māo bǐ gǒu xiǎo. lǎoshǔ gèng xiǎo.

2. 摩托車比自行車貴。車子更貴。
摩托车比自行车贵。车子更贵。
mótuōchē bǐ zìxíngchē guì. chēzi gèng guì.

3. 餅乾比水果甜。巧克力更甜。
饼干比水果甜。巧克力更甜。
bǐnggān bǐ shuíguǒ tián. qiǎokèlì gèng tián.

4. 姐姐比妹妹高。哥哥更高。爸爸最高。
姐姐比妹妹高。哥哥更高。爸爸最高。
jiějie bǐ mèimei gāo. gēge gèng gāo. bàba zuì gāo.

5. 她是我校最聰明的學生。
她是我校最聪明的学生。
tā shì wǒxiào zuì cōngming de xuésheng.

6. 她是我最好的朋友。
tā shì wǒ zuì hǎo de péngyou.

3. 1. 弟弟沒有姐姐那麼高。
弟弟没有姐姐那么高。
dìdi méi yǒu jiějie nàme gāo.

2. 我下午沒有上午那麼忙。
我下午没有上午那么忙。
wǒ xiàwǔ méi yǒu shàngwǔ nàme máng.

3. 南瓜沒有西瓜那麼甜。
南瓜没有西瓜那么甜。
nánguā méi yǒu xīguā nàme tián.

4. 德國沒有俄國那麼冷。
德国没有俄国那么冷。
Déguó méi yǒu Èguó nàme lěng.

5. 大西洋沒有太平洋那麼大。
大西洋没有太平洋那么大。
Dàxīyáng méi yǒu Tàipíngyáng nàme dà.

6. 我的狗沒有我的貓那麼懶。
我的狗没有我的猫那么懒。
wǒde gǒu méi yǒu wǒ de māo name lǎn.

4. 1. 這件毛衣跟那件毛衣一樣貴。
这件毛衣跟那件毛衣一样贵。
zhè jiàn máoyī gēn nà jiàn máoyī yīyàng guì.

2. 男孩子跟女孩子一樣聰明。
男孩子跟女孩子一样聪明。
nánháizi gēn nǚháizi yīyàng cōngming.

3. 小狗和小貓一樣可愛。
小狗和小猫一样可爱。
xiáogǒu hé xiǎomāo yīyàng kěʼài.

4. 電腦和計算機不一樣有用。
电脑和计算机不一样有用。
diànnǎo hé jìsuànjī bù yīyàng yǒu yòng.

5. 朋友跟家裏人不一樣。
朋友跟家里人不一样。
péngyou gēn jiālǐ rén bù yīyàng.

6. 叉子跟筷子一樣方便。
叉子跟筷子一样方便。
chāzi gēn kuàizi yīyàng fāngbiàn.

7. 高跟鞋和球鞋不一樣舒服。
高跟鞋和球鞋不一样舒服。
gāogēnxié hé qiúxié bù yīyàng shūfu.

8. 飛盤和足球一樣好玩。
飞盘和足球一样好玩。
fēipán hé zúqiú yīyàng hǎowán.

9. 萬里長城跟埃及的金字塔一樣有
名。
万里长城跟埃及的金字塔一样有
名。
Wànlǐ Chángchéng gēn Āijí de jīnzìtǎ
yīyàng yǒumíng.

10. 法語跟漢語不一樣難。
法语跟汉语不一样难。
Fáyǔ gēn Hànyǔ bù yīyàng nán.

5. 1. 弟弟比妹妹聰明。
弟弟比妹妹聪明。
dìdi bǐ mèimei cōngming.

2. 妹妹沒有弟弟快。
mèimei méi yǒu dìdi kuài.

3. 弟弟比妹妹高。
dìdi bǐ mèimei gāo.

4. 弟弟比妹妹吃得快。
dìdi bǐ mèimei chī de kuài.

5. 弟弟沒有妹妹説得快。
弟弟没有妹妹说得快。
dìdi méi yǒu mèimei shuō de kuài.

6. 弟弟跟妹妹學得一樣多。
弟弟跟妹妹学得一样多。
dìdi gēn mèimei xué de yīyàng duō.

7. 弟弟比妹妹吃得多。
dìdi bǐ mèimei chī de duō.

8. 弟弟跟妹妹看書看得一樣快。
弟弟跟妹妹看书看得一样快。
dìdi gēn mèimei kàn shū kàn de yīyàng
kuài.

9. 哥哥更聰明。
哥哥更聪明。
gēge gèng cōngming.

10. 哥哥更高。
gēge gèng gāo.

11. 哥哥吃得更快。
gēge chī dé gèng kuài.

12. 哥哥吃得更多。
gēge chī dé gèng duō.

6. 1. 巧克力沒有紅豆那麼好吃。
巧克力没有红豆那么好吃。
qiǎokèlì méi yǒu hóngdòu nàme hǎo
chī.
Chocolate is not as tasty as red beans.

2. 老師沒有學生那麼忙。
老师没有学生那么忙。
lǎoshī méi yǒu xuésheng nàme máng.
Teachers are not as busy as students.

3. 自行車沒有摩托車那麼快。
自行车没有摩托车那么快。
zìxíngchē méi yǒu mótuō chē nàme
kuài.
Bicycles are not as fast as motorcycles.

4. 太極拳沒有空手道那麼難。
太极拳没有空手道那么难。
tàijíquán méi yǒu kōngshǒudào nàme
nán.
Taijiquan is not as difficult as karate.

5. 金子沒有銀子漂亮。
金子没有银子漂亮。
jīnzi méi yǒu yínzi piàoliang.
Gold is not as pretty as silver.

6. 手機沒有電腦那麼有用。
手机没有电脑那么有用。
shǒujī méi yǒu diànnǎo nàme yǒuyòng.
Cell phones are not as useful as computers.

7. 狗沒有馬那麼快。
狗没有马那么快。
gǒu méi yǒu mǎ nàme kuài.
Dogs are not as fast as horses.

8. 廣東菜沒有四川菜那麼辣。
广东菜没有四川菜那么辣。
Guǎngdōng cài méi yǒu Sìchuān cài
nàme là.
Cantonese food is not as spicy as Sichuan food.

9. 日本沒有中國那麼大。
日本没有中国那么大。
Rìběn méi yǒu Zhōngguó nàme dà.
Japan is not as big as China.

10. 冬天没有春天那麼美。
冬天没有春天那么美。
dōngtiān méi yǒu chūntiān nàme měi.
Winter is not as pretty as spring..

7. 1. 中國人比美國人喝茶喝得多。
中国人比美国人喝茶喝得多。
Zhōngguó rén bǐ Měiguó rén hē chá
hē de duō.

2. 我姐姐寫字寫得比我漂亮。
我姐姐写字写得比我漂亮。
wǒ jiějie xiě zì xiě de bǐ wǒ piàoliang.

3. 我没有我哥哥玩飛盤玩得多。
我没有我哥哥玩飞盘玩得多。
wǒ méi yǒu wǒ gēge wán fēipán wán de
duō.

4. 媽媽做菜做得比爸爸好。
妈妈做菜做得比爸爸好。
māma zuò cài zuò de bǐ bàba hǎo.

5. 哥哥跟爸爸唱歌唱得一樣好。
哥哥跟爸爸唱歌唱得一样好。
gēge gēn bàba chàng gē chàng de
yīyàng hǎo.

6. 我的馬跑得比別的馬快。
我的马跑得比别的马快。
wǒ de mǎ pǎo de bǐ bié de mǎ kuài.

Chapter 12

1. 1. 又 yòu, 又 yòu
2. 還／还 hái or 也 yě; ∅
3. 跟 gēn or 和 hé; 還／还 hái, 也 yě,
or ∅
4. 也 yě or ∅; 跟 gēn or 和 hé
5. ∅, 還／还 hái or 也 yě; ∅ or 也 yě;
跟 gēn or 和 hé
6. 還／还 hái, 也 yě, or 另外 lìngwài
7. ∅; 還／还 hái or 也 yě; 跟 gēn or
和 hé
8. ∅, 又 yòu, or 就 jiù
9. ∅; 還是／还是 háishi
10. 跟 gēn or 和 hé or 還是／还是 háishi;
∅; 還／还 hái or 也 yě
11. 跟 gēn or 和 hé

12. ∅ 又 yòu, or 也 yě
13. ∅
14. ∅
15. ∅; 還/还 hái or ∅; 跟 gēn or 和 hé

2. 1. 我們看了電影以後就回學校去。
我们看了电影以后就回学校去。
wǒmen kàn le diànyǐng yǐhòu jiù huí
xuéxiào qù.

2. 我們寫了字以後就念了一本中
文書。
我们写了字以后就念了一本中
文书。
wǒmen xiě le zì yǐhòu jiù niàn le yī běn
Zhōngwén shū.

3. 學生吃了早飯以後就到公園去。
学生吃了早饭以后就到公园去。
xuéshēng chī le zǎofàn yǐhòu jiù dào
gōngyuán qù.

4. 他們買了票以後就上車了。
他们买了票以后就上车了。
tāmen mǎi le piào yǐ hòu jiù shàng chē
le.

5. 我跑了步就回家。
wǒ pǎo le bú jiù huí jiā.

3. 1. 我畢業了以後就到中國去。
我毕业了以后就到中国去。
wǒ bìyè le yǐhòu jiù dào Zhōngguó qù.
OR
我畢了業以後就到中國去。
我毕了业以后就到中国去。
wǒ bì le yè yǐhòu jiù dào Zhōngguó qù.

2. 我哥哥畢業了以後就到中國
去了。
我哥哥毕业了以后就到中国
去了。
wǒ gēge bìyè le yǐhòu jiù dào Zhōngguó
qù le.   **OR**
我哥哥畢了業以後就到中國
去了。
我哥哥毕了业以后就到中国
去了。
wǒ gēge bì le yè yǐhòu jiù dào
Zhōngguó qù le.

3. 我吃了晚飯以後就去看電影。
   我吃了晚饭以后就去看电影。
   wǒ chī le wǎnfàn yǐhòu jiù qù kàn
   diànyǐng.

4. 我吃了晚飯以後就看了電影。
   我吃了晚饭以后就看了电影。
   wǒ chī le wǎnfàn yǐhòu jiù kàn le
   diànyǐng.

5. 我考了試以後就想吃冰淇淋。
   我考了试以后就想吃冰淇淋。
   wǒ kǎo le shì yǐhòu jiù xiǎng chī
   bīngqilín.

4. 1. 我每天吃早飯以前都洗澡。
   我每天吃早饭以前都洗澡。
   wǒ měitiān chī zǎofàn yǐqián dōu xǐ
   zǎo.

2. 看電影以前先把功課做完。
   看电影以前先把功课做完。
   kàn diànyǐng yǐqián xiān bǎ gōngkè
   zuòwán.

3. 我來中國以前已經學了兩年的
   中文。
   我来中国以前已经学了两年的
   中文。
   wǒ lái Zhōngguó yǐqián yǐjing xué le
   liǎng nián de Zhōngwén.

4. 去公園以前先看天氣好不好。
   去公园以前先看天气好不好。
   qù gōngyuán yǐqián xiān kàn tiānqì hǎo
   bù hǎo.

5. 回家以前請到郵局去寄信。
   回家以前请到邮局去寄信。
   huí jiā yǐqián qǐng dào yóujú qù jì xìn.

5. 1. 我去中國以前不會説中文。
   我去中国以前不会说中文。
   wǒ qù Zhōngguó yǐqián bú huì shuō
   Zhōngwén.

2. 我們學漢字以前先學拼音。
   我们学汉字以前先学拼音。
   wǒmen xué hànzì yǐqián xiān xué
   pīnyīn.

3. 電影開始以前可以説話。
   电影开始以前可以说话。
   diànyǐng kāishǐ yǐqián kéyǐ shuō huà.

4. 我上大學以前在銀行工作了
   一年。
   我上大学以前在银行工作了
   一年。
   wǒ shàng dàxué yǐqián zài yínháng
   gōngzuò le yīnián.

5. 你回家以前我們先喝茶吧。
   你回家以前我们先喝茶吧。
   nǐ huí jiā yǐqián wǒmen xiān hē chá ba.

6. 1. When the weather is hot you should drink
   more water.
   2. When you are studying it is best not to
   listen to music.
   3. When younger brother is busy he doesn't
   eat lunch.
   4. When the weather is good the children
   all play outside.
   5. When I ride the bus I always review
   Chinese characters.

7. 1. 我小的時候老騎自行車。
   我小的时候老骑自行车。
   wǒ xiǎo de shíhou lǎo qí zìxíngchē.

2. 爸爸吃早飯的時候都看報紙。
   爸爸吃早饭的时候都看报纸。
   bàba chī zǎofàn de shíhou dōu kàn
   bàozhǐ.

3. 我累的時候考得不好。
   我累的时候考得不好。
   wǒ lèi de shíhou kǎode bù hǎo.

4. 你吃中國飯的時候應該用筷子。
   你吃中国饭的时候应该用筷子。
   nǐ chī Zhōngguó fàn de shíhou yīnggāi
   yòng kuàizi.

5. 我姐姐開車的時候都唱歌。
   我姐姐开车的时候都唱歌。
   wǒ jiějie kāi chē de shíhou dōu chàng
   gē.

8. 1. 不過/不过 búguò, 可是 kěshì,
   但是 dànshì

2. 然而 rán'ér, 不過/不过 búguò,
   可是 kěshì, 但是 dànshì

3. 不過/不过 búguò, 可是 kěshì,
   但是 dànshì

4. 反過來/反过来 fǎnguolái

5. 要不然 yàoburán or 否則/否则 fǒuzé

6. 可是 kěshì, 但是 dànshì

7. 要不然 yàoburán or 否則/否则 fǒuzé

8. 不但 búdàn … 而且 érqiě or
   不但 búdàn … 反而 fǎn'ér

9. 不過/不过 búguò, 可是 kěshì,
   但是 dànshì

10. 不過/不过 búguò, 可是 kěshì,
    但是 dànshì

9. 1. 如果 rúguǒ (or other conditional in same
   category)

2. 雖然/虽然 suīrán … 可是 kěshì,
   但是 dànshì

3. 不過/不过 búguò, 可是 kěshì,
   但是 dànshì

4. 雖然/虽然 suīrán … 可是 kěshì,
   但是 dànshì

5. 不過/不过 búguò, 可是 kěshì, 但是
   dànshì

6. 雖然/虽然 suīrán … 可是 kěshì,
   但是 dànshì

7. 因爲/因为 yīnwei … 所以 suóyǐ

8. 因爲/因为 yīnwei … 所以 suóyǐ

9. 除非 chúfēi … 否則/否则 fǒuzé

10. 因此 yīncǐ or 所以 suóyǐ

11. 要不然 yàoburán or 否則/否则 fǒuzé

12. 要不然 yàoburán or 否則/否则 fǒuzé

13. 既然 jìrán or 因爲/因为 yīnwei

14. 就是 jiùshì

15. 如果 rúguǒ (or other conditional in
    same category)

Chapter 13

1. 1. 我是今天買的書。
   我是今天买的书。
   wǒ shì jīntiān mǎi de shū.
   OR

我是今天買書的。
我是今天买书的。
wǒ shì jīntiān mǎi shū de.
It was today that I bought the book.

2. 我是在公園裏看到王老師的。
   我是在公园里看到王老师的。
   wǒ shì zài gōngyuán lǐ kàndào Wáng
   lǎoshī de.
   *It was in the park where I saw teacher
   Wang.*

3. 我是去年認識陳麗麗的。
   我是去年认识陈丽丽的。
   wǒ shì qùnián rènshi Chén Lìlì de.
   It was last year that I met Lili Chen.

4. 我是在車上買的票。
   我是在车上买的票。
   wǒ shì zài chē shàng mǎi de piào.
   It was on the car that I bought the ticket.

5. 我是跟張老師借書的。
   我是跟张老师借书的。
   wǒ shì gēn Zhāng lǎoshī jiè shū de.
   I borrowed the book from teacher Zhang.

6. 我是在南京吃豆沙包的。
   wǒ shì zài Nánjīng chī dòushā bāo de.
   *It was in Nanjing where I ate red bean
   paste buns.*

7. 我是二零零一年去的中國。
   我是二零零一年去的中国。
   wǒ shì èr líng líng yī nián qù de
   Zhōngguó.
   It was in 2001 that I went to China.

8. 我是昨天晚上看的那個電影。
   我是昨天晚上看的那个电影。
   wǒ shì zuótiān wǎnshang kàn de nà ge
   diànyǐng.
   It was last night that I saw that movie.

9. 我哥哥是在中國練太极拳的。
   我哥哥是在中国练太极拳的。
   wǒ gēge shì zài Zhōngguó liàn tàijíquán
   de.
   *It was in China where my older brother
   practiced taiji quan.*

10. 你是幾月幾號生的？

你是几月几号生的？

nǐ shì jǐ yuè jǐ hào shēng de?

What month and day were you born?

2. 1. 我是在美國長大的。

我是在美国长大的。

wǒ shì zài Měiguó zhǎng dà de.

2. 我是一九八五年畢業的。

我是一九八五年毕业的。

wǒ shì yī jiǔ bā wǔ nián bì yè de.

3. 我是從中國來的。

我是从中国来的。

wǒ shì cóng Zhōngguó lái de.

4. 我是在美國學中文的。

我是在美国学中文的。

wǒ shì zài Měiguó xué Zhōngwén de.

5. 他們是一九九二年結婚的。

他们是一九九二年结婚的。

tāmen shì yī jiǔ jiǔ èr nián jiéhūn de.

3. 1. 八月的天氣也很熱。

八月的天气也很热。

bāyuè de tiānqì yě hěn rè.

In addition to July, August's weather is also very hot.

2. 我也喜歡喝茶。

我也喜欢喝茶。

wǒ yě xǐhuan hē chá.

Besides coffee, I also like to drink tea.

3. 媽媽也會做中國飯。

妈妈也会做中国饭。

māma yě huì zuò Zhōngguó fàn.

Besides American food, mom can also cook Chinese food.

4. 除了我弟弟以外

chúle wǒ dìdi yǐwài

In addition to my younger brother, my younger sister is also married.

5. 我們去年都到中國去了。

我们去年都到中国去了。

wǒmen qùnián dōu dào Zhōngguó qù le.

Except for older sister, we all went to China last year.

6. 除了我名字以外

chúle wǒ míngzi yǐwài

Except for my name, I wrote all of the characters wrong.

7. 我們都吃飽了。

我们都吃饱了。

wǒmen dōu chībǎo le.

Except for younger brother, we all ate until we were full.

8. 我其他的(別的)字都認識。

我其他的(别的)字都认识。

wǒ qítā de (biéde) zì dōu rènshi.

Except for this character, I know all of the other characters.

9. 除了我以外

chúle wǒ yǐwài

In addition to me, my younger brother also studies Chinese.

10. 除了趙明以外

除了赵明以外

chúle Zhào Míng yǐwài

Except for Zhao Ming, we've all seen that movie.

4. 1. 我連一個字都不認識。

我连一个字都不认识。

wǒ lián yī ge zì dōu bú rènshi.

2. 他連日語也聽得懂。

他连日语也听得懂。

tā lián Rìyǔ yě tīng dé dǒng.

3. 弟弟連紐約也沒去過。

弟弟连纽约也没去过。

dìdi lián Niǔyuē yě méi qùguo.

4. 連哥哥也喜歡她。

连哥哥也喜欢她。

lián gēge yě xǐhuan tā.

5. 我連一塊錢也沒有。

我连一块钱也没有。

wǒ lián yī kuài qián yě méi yǒu.

6. 連你的名字也寫錯了。

连你的名字也写错了。

lián nǐ de míngzi yě xiěcuò le.

7. 他連一句話也没説。
他连一句话也没说。
tā lián yī jù huà yě méi shuō.

8. 連弟弟也去過。
连弟弟也去过。
lián dìdi yě qùguo.

9. 連冰淇淋也不會吃。
连冰淇淋也不会吃。
lián bīngqilín yě bú huì chī.

10. 他連苦瓜也吃。
他连苦瓜也吃。
tā lián kǔguā yě chī.

5. 1. 蛋糕讓妹妹吃完了。
蛋糕让妹妹吃完了。
dàngāo ràng mèimei chī wánle.

2. 我的行李讓人家拿走了。
我的行李让人家拿走了。
wǒ de xíngli ràng rénjiā názǒu le.

3. 房子讓火燒了。
房子让火烧了。
fángzi ràng huǒ shāo le.

4. 我的車被人家碰壞了。
我的车被人家碰坏了。
wǒ de chē bèi rénjiā pèng huài le.

5. 我妹妹叫別的孩子嘲笑了。
wǒ mèimei jiào bié de háizi cháoxiào le.

6. 1. The wife was hit by the husband.
2. The teacher's pen was taken away by the students.
3. His shoe was chewed up by the dog.
4. The window was broken by younger brother.
5. My little bird was released (set free) by my younger brother.
6. My package was lost by the post office.

Chapter 14

1. 1. 實際上/实际上 shíjìshang or
其實/其实 qíshí

2. 好像 hǎoxiàng or 顯得/显得 xiǎndé

3. 白 bái or 徒然 túrán

4. 竟然 jìngrán or 居然 jūrán

5. 據我所知/据我所知 jù wǒ suǒ zhī

6. 好像 hǎoxiàng or 顯得/显得 xiǎndé

7. 看上去 kàn shàng qù

8. 徒然 túrán or 白 bái

9. 居然 jūrán or 竟然 jìngrán

10. 簡直/简直 jiǎnzhí

11. 没想到 méi xiǎng dào

12. 依我看 yī wǒ kàn

2. 1. 吧 ba or 嘛 ma
2. 啊 a or 哦 o
3. 啊 a or 喔 wo
4. 吧 ba or 啦 la
5. 吧 ba or 嘛 ma, 啦 la
6. 吧 ba or 嘛 ma
7. 呀 ya or 呢 ne or 哦 o
8 呢 ne
9. 吧 ba
10. 呢 ne or 呀 ya

3. 1. 呀 ya or 啊 a or 呢 ne
2. 吧 ba or 啦 la
3. 啦 la
4. 啦 la or 啊 a
5. 啦 la

Index